Talking for Success

Jonathan Clifton

Talking for Success

The Secret Codes of Conversation and How to Master Them

Jonathan Clifton

Haythorp Books

First published by Haythorp Books, a divison of Canbury Press 2024

This edition published 2024

Kingston upon Thames, Surrey, United Kingdom

haythorp.co.uk

Typeset in Athelas (body), Futura PT (heading)

This is a work of non-fiction

CONTENTS

Contents

To Anne, with love

WHY READ THIS BOOK?

Language surrounds us. It is essential to us as social animals, yet like the air we breathe we are often unaware of it, and how it works. Not in an abstract way, but as something that determines how we fare in our interconnected world. Of course we all know skilled talkers, who seem to have an instinctive flair for choosing the right words and *saying them in the right way*. Then there are the career talkers: lawyers, politicians and salespeople *must* be good with words to thrive at work. Yet it is wrong to think that skilled talking must be the preserve of the professionally trained or the innately talented. *You can learn to be a better talker and improve your life* – by understanding the hidden codes that run conversations.

How do I know this? I study talk for a living. I am a conversation analyst. I have been teaching business communication at various European universities for the past 20 years, and during this time I have published many scientific papers about how language works. As I get older, however, I am becoming increasingly aware that academics are publishing quite obscure work that is for, and really only understandable by, other academics. I want to change that with this book. Working from the knowledge that I've gained over the past 20 years of teaching and researching, my aim is to let you into the secrets of conversation.

Although we all have an intuitive grasp of language, imagine how much more effective we could be if we paused conversations and looked at what was happening. What makes people effective and persuasive talkers? What goes wrong when people say something stupid?

Language is not an innate skill. It's not a case of being silver-tongued, or not. Rather, being a 'good' speaker is something we can learn. And we can learn best by looking at actual language use: this is what makes this book unique. It does not tell you what to do. It is not based on made-up dialogues and anecdotes of language use. It does not ask you to apply some kind of theory to your language use. Rather, I will show you how real people in the real world use language, and help you develop your awareness of language so that you can adopt your own strategies to your own circumstances. As we open up the black box of real-time language use, I aim to be the guide by the side, not the sage on the stage telling you what to do.

We will focus on spoken language, rather than written, because spoken language is often overlooked. At school when we study language, we often focus on literature to the detriment of the everyday language surrounding us. Yet, this everyday mundane language is the medium through which we live our lives. In the first section of the book, we will analyse 23 examples of language use ranging from high-profile conversations with Prince Harry and his wife Meghan, or politicians such as Donald Trump, Rishi Sunak, and Boris Johnson, to more mundane conversations that we come across every day such as sales pitches, small talk between strangers, and business meetings. I have grouped these chapters so that they follow on from each other, but each 'stands alone' and may be read independently of the others: feel free to dip in and out. In the second part of the book, I draw together all the language codes identified and set out 100 strategies that will help you improve your language skills and allow you to speak more effectively. For life, for work, for love, and for fun.

1. INTRODUCTION

The Importance of Language

Imagine a day without language. Language surrounds us. We wake up in the morning and we might exchange a few words with our partner, we go down for breakfast and we chat, we switch on the TV and listen to the news, we scroll through our messages. All this is achieved through language. It is essential to our existence as social beings. Without it we would have no society, no relationships, no common understanding of the world as it is, as it was, or as we hope it will be. Only the hermit in the hills has no need of language, and even then he may be praying, or speaking to himself.

Yet, our relationship with language is paradoxical. We are supremely aware of its importance: problems are often cast as problems of 'communication'. Good relationships are said to be founded on good communication, and communication skills are essential to anybody's workplace toolkit. But language is sometimes treated as superfluous or inferior to actions. As the 'common sense' sayings go: talk is cheap; actions speak louder than words. Is this actually true? Exploring extracts of real-world language use, this book sets out to decode how language is used and what strategies we can deploy to improve our speech. Because when we can spot the underlying hidden patterns of our conversations, we can use them to protect ourselves from skilled practitioners who want to gain an advantage and also use them ourselves to achieve our goals. Mastering the 'secret codes' of language improves life in many fields, for instance in your social life and career.

Language Codes and Doing Things with Words

Before looking at examples of language use, we need to pause for a minute and reflect on the nature of language. Simply defined by Merriam-Webster's online dictionary, language is: 'the words, their pronunciation, and the methods of combining them used and understood by a community'. However, language is more than this. It does things. It is action and it causes action. In the words of the language philosopher, John Austin (1911-1960), 'words do things'. Let's look at an everyday example of how language codes work. Imagine that it's a hot stuffy summer's day and you're working in your office. You may ask your colleague, who is sitting near the window, to open the window and let some air in. You may say something like: 'It's stuffy in here, could you open the window?' And he might reply: 'Sure, no problem.' Your words have therefore acted on your colleague and he has done something that he may not have otherwise done. You have done something with words: you have made a request. But, you have also crafted this request so that it comes across as polite and respectful, and so is more likely to be successful. So, getting things done through language not only depends on what is said, but also how it is said. As the adage would have it: 'It's not what you say, it's the way that you say it.'

However, there is no predefined script that we must follow. Rather, we have to adapt and to choose language that is appropriate for the situation depending on what we want to achieve. We can do this by knowing how the codes of language work and deploying them, according to the situation. Just like life, these scenarios are very varied. Maybe some will be familiar and more recurrent, such as buying a train ticket, ordering a round of drinks, and so on. So, perhaps we can rely on past experience to get us through without thinking too much about what language to use. Perhaps other situations will leave us literally 'lost for words' as we stumble around trying to deal with them. Most situations probably fall somewhere in between these extremes and we can draw on our social experience and knowledge of what we should, and shouldn't say; and how we should, or shouldn't, say it.

Returning to the example of asking a colleague to open a window, if you were to say 'Oi mush, open window will ya,' your colleague may feel that you were not addressing him with enough respect and he would refuse your request. Or maybe, if you know each other well, he would understand your request as light-hearted humour and agree anyway. You might even consider such an informal style to be a display of friendship: you are so close with your colleague that you can do away with normal politeness conventions. This 'asking to open the window scenario' is just a simple example, but it underlines the fact that whatever situation you are in, you are designing your talk, crafting it, and using it so that it is effective and gets you the result that you want.

In some instances, especially fast-flowing conversations, this crafting is often sub-conscious and we rarely slow down the process to examine exactly how we are using words. Making a simple request, such as asking a colleague to open a window, involves little conscious effort and the stakes are quite low. Asking your boss for a pay rise, defending yourself in court, or arguing for a particular project during a business meeting may have dire consequences if you get the language wrong. These situations may require hours of preparation and rehearsal. But generally speaking, unless you're a copywriter, spokesperson, marketer, poet, writer, journalist, or otherwise in the 'communications business', we rarely think about how language works, and in particular the techniques, or codes, that provide its structure. Like the air that we breathe, conversation is essential to our existence but it passes by, unnoticed. Unexamined.

'Good' and 'Bad' Language Use

What is 'good' or 'bad' language use? Obviously, this depends on the context and what you want to achieve. We follow rules, or codes, of what can, and cannot, be said. We adopt strategies, consciously or unconsciously, so that we achieve our ends. Careers advisors might tell us how to deal with certain questions in a job interview, a solicitor might advise us how to deal with certain questions in the witness box, sales representatives are taught what to say to a reluctant client, and so on. So, we may have an overall plan for some situations. But even if we have a plan, we have to adapt as the conversation progresses, utterance by utterance. If the situation is adversarial – an argument, a debate, a difference of opinion – you may seek to build up your case, and undermine the other's position. But, not all situations are adversarial: language use is also cooperative and supportive as we align and affiliate with our interlocutors' moves to work as a team, to be sympathetic, to display understanding, and so on. Even arguments are to some extent co-operative ventures. They require a minimum of two parties. They don't happen if one side walks away.

We may all appreciate a good football match, but it takes an aficionado to spot the strategies and to appreciate the skills of the players as they move the ball around the field. Professional pundits discuss the game on TV, giving predictions, commenting on what is happening as the match unfolds, and, after the match, dissecting what happened. Rarely, however, do TV pundits or journalists dissect a speech, an interview, or a conversation to analyse the language used. Rarely are schoolchildren taught to look in detail at everyday conversation. It is precisely this skill and awareness that this book wants to bring to you. To slow down language, so that we can analyse what rules, or codes, are being used, and how, and to judge whether they are skilful or inept, effective or ineffective. Developing such skills may allow you to analyse the language of your interlocutors, to better see what strategies they are using and in adversarial situations to better counter their arguments. Improving your language awareness will allow you to strengthen your arguments, to be more persuasive, to be able to say the right thing at the right moment, and to lessen the risk of 'putting your foot in it' by saying the wrong thing at the wrong time. As the American 19th Century novelist, Nathaniel Hawthorne, once said: 'Words – so innocent and powerless as they are, as standing in a dictionary, how potent for good and evil they become in the hands of one who knows how to combine them.' It is such an awareness of the power of language, for good or for evil, that I hope to bring to you.

What is Language?

We should also remember that language is more than just 'words', whether written or spoken (see figure one, below). Language includes other vocal phenomena, which we call paralinguistic features, such as stress, laughter, tone, volume, exclamations, groans, sighs, and so on. It also includes non-verbal phenomena, commonly called body language, such as gestures, eye gaze, touch, the use of space, body position, and so on. We could add 'things' to this list, such as symbols, places, buildings, statues, clothes, and so on. While it would be going too far to say that these 'things' literally speak to us, nevertheless they always communicate something to us, and so they also have a part in the codes of language. So, in this book, where appropriate, we'll move beyond words to also look at body language, paralinguistic features of talk, and the use of artefacts, and we'll also consider how they can be deployed to make your message more effective.

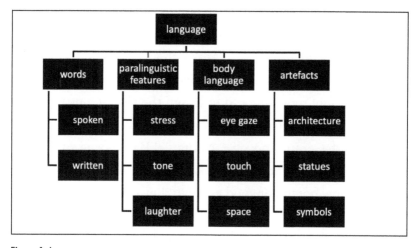

Figure 1: Language

The Structure of this Book

Each chapter in this book takes a short extract of spoken language use. The extracts are transcribed and then analysed so that the underlying codes of language are revealed. Consequently, rather than prescribing language use, what you should, and shouldn't, say in a particular situation, we'll look at real-world language use: the actual strategies and tactics that people use in their speech. What works, and what doesn't. Surprisingly, actually looking at language use in real-world situations is rare. Much advice that people are given comes from theories, such as neurolinguistic programming, or transactional analysis. Such theories are not based on actual observation of what happens 'on the ground'. They're like football commentators talking about a football match that never happened and speculating on how best to put the ball into the net. Similarly, other advice on how to communicate, or use language, comes from intuition. For example, Dale Carnegie's best-selling book *How to Win Friends and Influence People*, first published in 1937, tells you how to communicate to influence people. However, it is not based on actual observation of real-world people playing real-world language games. It is based on intuition and anecdote. This is not to say that it doesn't contain useful advice, but it is telling you how to play a game, with reference to the rules of the game, but with little, or no, commentary on how the game is actually 'pulled off' in real life.

Finally, and this may be of comfort. As a professor of linguistics, I don't believe that 'good' language use is an innate skill, 'the gift of the gab', something you either have, or don't have. Rather, I believe, that your language skills, your ability to identify and deploy language techniques, is something that can be worked on. You can master the codes of conversation.

The language use we'll look at comes from various sources. It includes the analysis of some fairly high-profile people and well-known exchanges. For example, we look at recordings of: Donald Trump's attempt to persuade a Georgian politician to 'find' new votes; the infamous interview with Prince Andrew concerning his relationship with Jeffrey Epstein; and Martin Luther King's

'I have a dream' speech. We also look at more mundane language use that we come across every day, such as: (hard sell) sales pitches, small talk, and business meetings. The language games that we highlight may be played with varying degrees of skill. Prince Andrew's press interview was widely seen as a car crash and therefore exemplifies what can go wrong. Other examples, such as the interview that Prince Harry and Meghan Markle did with the BBC just after their engagement, illustrate how language can be used to great effect.

In each chapter, I have marked key words and concepts with an asterisk*. In the second section of the book, I've elaborated on these strategies marked by an asterisk* and I have provided 100 tips that will help you make your language use more effective.

A Word on Transcription

The language that we analyse in this book are all either transcripts of talk that are publicly available or videos of people talking, which are available on YouTube. If I have used extracts of publicly available transcripts, I have acknowledged the source. If I have used extracts of video clips on YouTube, I have transcribed them myself. You'll notice that sometimes there is limited punctuation and that sometimes there are 'ers' and 'ums', repetitions, grammatical inaccuracies, false starts, and so on. This is because I have tried to give you something that is as readable as possible, but which is also as close as possible to the actual delivery of the words used. In some cases, I have taken talk from French sources; I have translated these recordings myself.

I have numbered each line of talk for easy reference. If multiple speakers are present, I use the initials of the speaker, or similar, to indicate who is speaking. In order to capture the spoken quality of the interaction, I've used some symbols (figure two, below).

A: straight to set.[Just coming back into it B: [yeah	square brackets	indicate that people are speaking at the same time.
(laughs)	brackets	provide details of non-verbal behaviours
you CAN'T	capitals	indicate shouting
Will you **please**	bold	indicates words spoken louder than surrounding talk
right↓	↓	indicates falling intonation
correct↑	↑	indicates rising intonation

Figure 2. Transcription symbols

PART ONE

ANALYSES OF REAL-LIFE TALK

2. COURTROOM TALK

'You're mischaracterising what occurred'

Courtroom drama allows us to observe sometimes high stakes language games in action. Underpinning the judicial system is the idea that, by a process of investigating the events in question, judge and jury will be able to pick out truth from untruth and pronounce somebody as guilty or innocent. So, we have notions of justice, and the idea behind the legal system is that the 'truth will out'. Well, that's the theory and it's all very nice, but let's look at it from a different perspective. Parties to a legal dispute, whether criminal or civil, have access to lawyers – at least in Western democracies. These lawyers are paid to argue the case in favour of their clients, to present their side of the story. Lawyers marshal arguments* foregrounding certain aspects of the events and backgrounding, or omitting, others. Lawyers attack unfavourable witnesses and gently coax the 'right' response from favourable witnesses. In short, lawyers are experienced players in the language games. Such games are their bread and butter. One would hope that the truthful stories win the day. However, what gets the accused, rightly or wrongly, off the hook and what gets the accused, rightly or wrongly, condemned, is to a large extent dependent on how the codes of language are deployed.

So, let's look at some courtroom drama and consider how top flight lawyers use these codes. The purpose here is not to look at what is true and what is false. Rather, our purpose here is to look at how lawyers and expert witnesses 'do' things with words during cross examination in a courtroom.

The extract we're going to look at comes from the defamation case brought by Johnny Depp against his ex-wife Amber Heard. Depp and Heard met whilst filming in 2009. They married in 2015, and in 2016 Heard filed for divorce on the grounds that Depp had physically abused her. In 2018, Heard published an article about domestic violence in the *Washington Post*. Depp alleged that Heard's claims in this article were false, and he sued Heard claiming that she, rather than he, had been the perpetrator of the domestic violence.

The court case took place in Fairfax, Virginia, between April and June 2022. It was live streamed. The particular extract we're going look at concerns an exchange between Heard's lawyer, Elaine Bredehoft, and an expert witness for Johnny Depp, Sharon Curry[1]. Curry is a clinical and forensic psychologist specialising in conjugal violence. She gave testimony in court to the effect that in her opinion Heard had borderline personality disorder and histrionic personality disorder.

---

[1] Available at: https://www.youtube.com/watch?v=wuH2sUPcKNg

The Opening Move – Attacking Professional Competence

1. EB: Dr Curry I just want to make sure that uh we all remember, you're not
2.   Board Certified. Correct↑
3. SC: No, I'm not.

The first move concerns professional competence. Is the expert witness credible* enough to be believed? Bredehoft points out that Curry is not board certified. Board certification is awarded to medical and other professionals to show that they have advanced knowledge or skills in their field. Despite the fact that it's not a legal requirement, not being board certified may hint at a lack of advanced competence and therefore could threaten the credibility of a Curry-as-expert.

Curry replies that she is not board certified. Bredehoft accepts this reply and then asks 'You've been licensed for how long?' Curry replies that she has been licensed for ten years. We can't know how the judge and jury, as the primary audience, understood these opening moves. But, I have difficulty seeing them as effective. On the one hand, not being board certified appears to attack the credibility of the expert, but this move is not followed up immediately. The second question*, to which I assume Bredehoft knew the answer, hands an opportunity for Curry to display her experience. Ten years practice is not bad, so maybe she has expertise.

We could also note that using the honorific* 'Doctor' accords a certain amount of professional knowledge and expertise to Curry. Now, this could be a politeness* strategy; courtrooms are not the legal equivalent of bare knuckle fighting where anything goes, they have a veneer of civility to them. However, Bredehoft could have just said 'Ms Curry', therefore avoiding reference to professional competence.

So, in my opinion, this is a somewhat half-hearted attempt to attack the credibility of Curry. Yes, she's not board certified, but she is a doctor, and she has experience. If you attack the credibility of the other in an argument, drive the argument home, or forget it. Don't pull your punches.

Impartiality

4. EB   Okay and you've been licensed for how long?
5. SC: I have been licensed for 10 years.
6. EB: Okay, and you are being paid by Mr Depp's legal team to be here. Correct↑
7. SC: Yes.
8. EB: How much have you charged so far?
9. SC: I actually don't know.
10. EB   Over a 100,000?
11. SC: I truly don't know. I don't do my own books.
12. EB: Over 200,000?
13. SC: I don't know.
14. EB: Over 300,000?
15. SC: That would be way too much but I **do** not know.

In line six, Bredehoft moves on to a new topic: is Curry being paid by Mr Depp's legal team? On the face of it, this is a strange question. Obviously she's being paid, as no doubt Bredehoft was being paid by Heard. Bredehoft then builds up her line of argument: how much has Curry been paid? The reply is 'I actually don't know.' As we see in Chapter II, memory* can be part of language games: what can you reasonably be expected to remember? Here, in my opinion at least, the 'I don't know' reply seems reasonable. However, Bredehoft considers it insufficient and probes for more.

In a series of questions*, she asks if it was over 100,000 , 200,000 , or 300,000 . Each time the reply is 'I don't know' and an explanation is provided (line 11: 'I don't do my own books'), which accounts* for this lack of knowledge.

So, what does asking about payment achieve, or attempt to achieve? Whilst we can never be sure what Bredehoft intended, asking about payment implies that the expert witness is not impartial. She has been 'bought' by Depp's legal team and therefore she has a stake* in providing biased expert testimony.

In an argument*, suggesting that your opponent has a stake* or a vested interest is one way of attacking their credibility. It's a kind of 'You would say that wouldn't you' argument. In this case, implicitly, you would give favourable testimony to Depp because you're being paid to give favourable testimony. However, this line of attack doesn't really work because Curry displays that she has no knowledge of, or interest in, the sums involved. Bredehoft drops her line of argument and shifts to another topic: having dinner with Depp.

Dinner or an Interview?

16. EB: Okay, now just so that we all remember you had **dinner** at Mr Depp's **house**

17.   for 3 to 4 hours with Mr Depp, Mr Waldman, Mr Chew and Ms

18.   Vasquez. Correct↑

19. SC: I was interviewed. I asked if there was anything I could eat because at about

20.   3 hours I started to get hungry. Mr Depp then offered to order take-out for

21.   the entire team.

22. EB: So you had dinner with ... at Mr Depp's home with Mr Waldman, Mr Chew

23.   Ms Vasquez, and Mr Depp. Correct↑

24. SC: Yes.

Bredehoft opens her next line of attack by making the statement that Curry 'had dinner at Mr Depp's house for three to four hours with Mr Depp, Mr Waldman, Mr Chew and Ms Vasquez' (i.e. Depp and his legal team). She then seeks confirmation of this ('Correct↑'). Dinner suggests a cosy, non-professional, relationship. It is therefore an implied attack on Curry's impartiality. This attack is bolstered by the addition of a duration (line 17: 'three to four hours') which adds to the impression of cosiness.

Curry defends herself by reframing* the event as 'an interview'. An interview is professional and by implication non-partisan. Curry then accounts* for the fact that they had a take-out. Legal battles are often to do with how an event is framed, in this case was it dinner or an interview? It makes a difference to the judge and jury's perception of events. An interview implies that everything was above-board. The witness is credible. Dinner implies a non-professional relationship. The witness may not be credible. Framing* events can be key to winning arguments – in court or elsewhere.

However, Bredehoft ignores Curry's framing of the event as dinner and she continues (line 22: 'So you had dinner with ... at Mr Depp's home with Mr Waldman, Mr Chew, Ms Vasquez, and Mr Depp'). So, even though Curry never said she had dinner, Bredehoft projects this classification of events onto her. She does this by using, what in technical terms is called a 'formulation'. A formulation* sums up the gist of prior talk. This can be an effective tool in adversarial context. You can sum up the talk so far, but in doing so you can put your spin on it, as Bredehoft does here. So, sum up to your advantage, and listen attentively when others sum up, maybe they're spinning the understanding of the talk to their advantage.

30

Bredehoft then follows up:

25. EB: And you had drinks as well. Correct↑
26. SC: I actually don't know. I **do** remember that there were drinks.
27. EB: Do you recall testifying earlier that you did have a drink, a mule something
28. SC: No, I remember testifying that there might have been a mule (pause) a Moscow
29.   Mule (slight laugh)
30. EB: Okay, thanks we … we didn't have animals there as well right↓
31. SC: No animals.

In line 25, she adds 'and you had drinks as well'. In this way, she builds on the dinner to make the event seem even cosier and in doing so she bolsters the implication that Curry is far from independent. Curry uses the 'I don't remember defence.' She is not sure, but she does remember that 'there were drinks'. Consequently, she reframes the event from 'I had a drink' to the somewhat vague 'there were drinks', and more specifically there might have been a mule. There is then a pause, and Curry adds 'Moscow Mule' (a vodka based cocktail) with a slight laugh* which orients her comments as slightly humorous*. Bredehoft responds with sarcasm* which in this case takes the form of a 'thanks' and the obvious observation that there were no animals there. Of course, the sarcasm works because Bredehoft means the opposite of what she says i.e. what she means is that I am not thanking you for pointing out the obvious. It's a put down that slightly belittles Curry and so makes her look less like an expert. Bredehoft wins one point. So, use humour* with care, especially in formal contexts*.

The Questioning Technique
The particular questioning technique that Bredehoft uses is interesting and is quite emblematic of courtroom talk.

32. EB: Okay, that's good to know and … and you talked about transparency. I just
33.   wanted to make sure, you have served several designations, expert designations,
34.   and reports in this case.
35. SC: Yes.
36. EB: And in **not** one of them did you disclose that you had dinner and drinks **at** Mr
37.   Depp's house for 3 to 4 hours with Mr Waldman, Mr Chew, Ms
38.   Vasquez. Is that correct↑
39. SC: Ms Bredehoft you're mischaracterising what occurred.
40. EB: I … Dr Curry, please answer the question. Not once did you disclose this in any
41.   of your [reports
42. SC: [I did not disclose I was interviewed as that's standard procedure

Bredehoft picks up after Heard's failed joke and continues her questioning. It is interesting to note that she uses a 'statement + correct ↑' format for most of her question. The tag 'correct', with rising intonation, seeks confirmation. It turns a statement into a closed question, designed to elicit either 'yes' or 'no' as a response. By eliciting a series of 'yeses' Bredehoft can move the talk forward, so building up incremental agreement on small 'things' until flaws in the witness's argumentation are revealed. In this case, having got agreement that Curry had dinner with Depp and his legal team and that there were drinks, she can now move in for the kill and make her point. The blow comes in line 36: Curry didn't disclose any dinners. The implication for the jury and judge to infer is that Curry is hiding something. She is not credible. She is not impartial.

Curry defends herself by saying that what occurred is being 'mischaracterised'. In other words, she realises what Bredehoft is trying to do and resists the characterisation, or framing, of events as dinner and drinks. She thus also contests the implication that she is not impartial. Bredehoft is not happy with such resistance and repeats her question. Curry still resists saying: 'I did not disclose I was interviewed as that's standard procedure.' In doing so, she returns to her characterisation of events as an interview, not dinner and drinks, and she brings in the new information that non-disclosure of being interviewed is standard.

The technique that Bredehoft is using is one of getting little agreement, elicited by the use of the tag 'correct?'. Once enough agreement has been reached, she then attempts to prove a point. In this case: Curry has already agreed it was a dinner with drinks, so why didn't she disclose it. This kind of aggressive questioning is common in courtroom talk, but you may see it, or similar, being used in other instances. For example, as a sales technique, the seller might try to manoeuvre you into agreement on several minor points and then hit you with the big one, to buy or not to buy. It's more difficult to say 'no' if you've been agreeing with the sales argument. Conversely, if you want to be aggressive: get agreement on minor points first, and then hit your interlocutor with the big one. In negotiating, this is sometimes called a minor points close* whereby at the close of a deal the seller gets the buyer to agree to a series of minor propositions before hitting them with the logical conclusion of a series of small agreements which is that the client has good reason to purchase the product.

Sentence Stress*

There are two kinds of stress* in English. In words with more than one syllable, one of the syllables will be stressed. So, for example, in the word 'ordinary' the stress falls on the first syllable: or·din·ar·y. The second kind of stress is sentence stress, whereby certain words in a sentence are stressed to give them prominence. Compare for example: 'I went to the bakers to buy some **bread**' and 'I went to the **bakers** to buy some bread.' In sentence one we stress bread rather than croissant or whatever and in sentence two we stress the bakers rather than, say, the supermarket. So, playing with the stress pattern can serve to emphasise your message. Bredehoft uses this with skill. For example: 'Okay now just so that we all remember you had **dinner** at Mr Depp's **house**.' The word stress here falls on the key words dinner and house, and the action of remembering is backgrounded.

But it is not only the stressed words that are important, sometimes a particular grammatical form* is used to emphasise certain meanings. For example, Curry says 'That would be way too much but I **do** not know.' The grammatical form 'do not' when spoken serves to emphasise. 'Don't know', with the contraction, doesn't have the same effect. Similarly, Curry says 'I **do** remember that there were drinks.' This is more forceful than 'I remember'. In technical terms, this is called the 'emphatic do'. Similarly, putting the adverb (e.g. never, rarely, not only, etc.) at the beginning of the utterance makes it stronger and gives it a theatrical twist. Compare, 'I have never lied' to 'never have I lied.' In technical terms, this is an anastrophe, whereby the normal word order is changed, often for emphasis.

To Sum Up

In sum, courtroom talk has within it the very essence of adversarial language games. The game here is about destroying the credibility of a witness. This is basically attempted via a series of questions forcing yes/no answers and then an attempt to reveal flaws that show the witness to be unreliable. If you lack credibility, your words will have less effect. You won't be believed.

You can defend against such attacks by reframing the projected categorisation of the event. It was not a dinner, it was an interview.

This is interesting because it shows that the kind of activities that you take part in can play up, or play down, your credibility. A credible expert witness is interviewed by a client. An expert witness lacking credibility is wined and dined by her client.

So, while you may never end up in court, building up your credibility, your ethos*, is key to understanding the code and making your talk more effective. So, hide any vested interest, real or projected, that you may have in the argument*. Build up your credibility by stressing your experience, qualifications, and knowledge*. Conversely, if you want to be aggressive, attack your adversary's lack of credibility, lack of qualifications, lack of experience, and his or her vested interests.

3. APOLOGISING

'To them and to this House I offer my heartfelt apologies'

Apologies are defined in the Merriam-Webster's online dictionary as expressing 'regret for something done or said'. They may have several components, such as a confession of wrongdoing, an acknowledgement of harm to others, an explanation of the breach of some (supposed) moral order or perhaps an (extenuating) account* of why the breach happened, and a promise of change for the better. Further, apologies may take the form of some kind of public spectacle that allows the contrite wrongdoer back into society. In the Middle Ages this might have taken the form of penance. For example, Henry II, who was forced to acknowledge his part in the murder of Thomas Becket, was made to walk to Canterbury Cathedral barefoot, dressed in sackcloth, covered in ashes. At the cathedral, he was whipped by monks. After this very public spectacle, he was reconciled with the church and allowed to continue his reign. Whilst things have obviously moved on since the Middle Ages, the spectacle of the public apology, confession of sins, and the promise to make amends before reconciliation and forgiveness is still very present.

In order to analyse this contemporary spectacle, we'll take a look at two public apologies. The first is the opening of the apology by Tiger Woods, the famous golfer, who in February 2010 was forced to apologise for his infidelity and behaviour towards his wife[1]. The second public apology we'll look at is that of Boris Johnson, the former British prime minister. In January 2022, he was forced to apologise[2] for his role in the so-called Partygate scandal in which it was alleged that he had attended parties in Downing Street (the prime minister's official residence in London) which broke the Covid restrictions that were then in place. His alleged partying activities could therefore not only constitute a breach of the moral order, but could also constitute a criminal offence. At the time of his 'apology', both a criminal investigation by the Metropolitan Police and an investigation by Sue Gray, a senior civil servant, were ongoing. However, later, the Metropolitan Police fined a number of people including Johnson for breaking Covid restrictions and when the Gray report was published in May 2022 it was highly critical of Johnson's involvement in the parties. And, in June 2023, Johnson resigned as an MP just before publication of a report by the parliamentary privileges committee, which ruled that Johnson had deliberately misled parliament by claiming that Covid rules had been followed at all times in Downing Street.

Of course, the sincerity of any apology can never be known for sure. We can never be sure of the extent to which the speakers are

---

[1] Available at: http://edition.cnn.com/2010/US/02/19/tiger.woods.transcript/index.html

[2] Available at: https://www.youtube.com/watch?v=Z-LPbvvVnM4

'just going through the motions' of an accepted part of sporting/ political rehabilitation. However, we can look at how apologisers craft their talk so that it comes off as a true apology, or not. In this case, Wood crafts his apology so that he is publicly seen to be eating humble pie, with relish. On the other hand, Johnson not only refuses to eat the humble pie that he has been offered, but he manages to make out that the people (the electorate) offering the sandwich are faulty in their judgement. It's not for nothing that Johnson has been given the sobriquet the 'greased piglet' for his ability to talk himself out of tricky situations. How does he do it! Let's see by comparing his and Woods's apologies.

Apology One – Tiger Woods

1. Good morning. And thank you for joining me.
2. Many of you in the room are my friends. Many of you in this room know me. Many of
3. you have cheered for me, or worked with me, or supported me, and now, every one of you
4. has good reason to be critical of me. I want to say to each of you, simply, and directly, I
5. am deeply sorry for my irresponsible and selfish behaviour I engaged in. I know people
6. want to find out how I could be so selfish and so foolish. People want to know how I
7. could have done these things to my wife, Elin, and to my children. And while I have
8. always tried to be a private person, there are some things I want to say. Elin and I have
9. started the process of discussing the damage caused by my behaviour. As she pointed out
10. to me, my real apology to her will not come in the form of words. It will come from my
11. behaviour over time. We have a lot to discuss. However, what we say to each other will
12. remain between the two of us. I am also aware of the pain my behaviour has caused to
13. those of you in this room. I have let you down. I have let down my fans. For many of you,
14. especially my friends, my behaviour has been a personal disappointment. To those of you
15. who work for me, I have let you down, personally and professionally. My behaviour has
16. caused considerable worry to my business partners.

Defining the Audience*

After the short greeting, Woods acknowledges the audience, and draws attention to the public he is addressing. To do this, Woods uses the rhetorical technique of repeating* 'many of you' three times in close succession which gives the talk emphasis and rhythm. The 'many of you' are then defined as the people who have: (i) cheered for me, (ii) worked with me, or (iii) supported me. This is presented using the rule of three*. One or two examples of the people he is addressing is not exhaustive, but three examples stand for a multitude and so encompasses everybody who might consider themselves connected in some way with Woods. In this way, the whole audience who have 'good reason to be critical', including those watching on the TV, the overhearing audience, are addressed. They are the targets of this apology. This is important since if Woods wants to be rehabilitated and not treated as a sporting pariah, the 'public' have to forgive him. Therefore, his talk is recipient designed* for 'the public' and as a public apology.

Pronoun* Use

After discerning the audience, he apologises (*I am* deeply sorry) for his faults which are set out as '*my* irresponsible and selfish behaviour *I* engaged in'. As the use of the first person pronouns ('I' and 'my') indicate, he takes personal responsibility for these actions. He thus, publicly, recognises his fault and displays his remorse. He, further, acknowledges that the audience 'want to find out how I could be so selfish and so foolish' and 'how I could have done these things to my wife, Elin, and to my children'. Through the use of the first person pronoun ('I') the focus remains on Woods-the-wrongdoer, but he shifts from the issue of his behaviour to the need to change over time. The details of this are under discussion with his wife, Elin, and are not revealed. However, despite not revealing any details, Woods does at least tick the box of saying that he will change his offending behaviour.

He then shifts tack to focus on the pain he has caused to the present and non-present audience who he has let down, worried, and disappointed. These are: those of you in this room; the fans; his friends; those who work with him; and his business partners. This, as previously, identifies the recipients of his apology and is designed to be inclusive. Again, it is significant that Woods uses the first person pronouns, 'I' and 'my', which stress his responsibility for his bad behaviour.

So in the opening we see four elements of an apology: its public nature; admission of wrongdoing; the promise of a remedy; and recognition of harm. While the sincerity of Woods is not our concern, from a linguistic point of view, the opening of his apology begins to tick the boxes paving the way for rehabilitation. However, other apologisers do not offer a public admission of fault, promise of a remedy and admission of doing harm to others with such humility, as we see below.

Apology Two – Boris Johnson

1. I want to apologise. I know that millions of people across this country have made
2. extraordinary sacrifices over the last 18 months. I know the anguish they have been
3. through - unable to mourn their relatives, unable to live their lives as they want or to do
4. the things they love. I know the rage they feel with me and with the government I lead
5. when they think in Downing Street itself the rules are not being properly followed by the
6. people who make the rules. And though I cannot anticipate the conclusions of the current
7. inquiry, I have learned enough to know there were things we simply did not get right and
8. I must take responsibility. Number 10 is a big department with a garden as an extension of
9. the office which has been in constant use because of the role of fresh air in stopping the
10. virus. When I went into that garden just after six on 20th May 2020, to thank groups of
11. staff before going back into my office 25 minutes later to continue working, I believed
12. implicitly that this was a work event. With hindsight I should have sent everyone back
13. inside. I should have found some other way to thank them. I should have recognised that
14. even if it could be said technically to fall within the guidance, there are millions and
15. millions of people who simply would not see it that way, people who have suffered
16. terribly, people who were forbidden from meeting loved ones at all inside or outside, and
17. to them and to this House I offer my heartfelt apologies. All I ask is that Sue Gray be
18. allowed to complete her inquiry into that day and several others so that the full facts can
19. be established. I will of course come back to this House and make a statement.

Side-stepping Responsibility – 'It's Not Me, Guv'

In the opening lines of his speech, Johnson frames* his upcoming talk as an apology ('I want to apologise'). So far so good, but having framed his talk as an apology, what follows is not especially apologetic. First, just as Woods, he addresses the public – 'millions of people'. He acknowledges their hurt, rage, and sacrifices, but, unlike Woods, he does not take responsibility for this. We can also note that Johnson employs certain rhetorical techniques that are similar to the ones deployed by Woods. For example, he uses repetition* ('I know' three times) and uses the rule of three* to suggest the extensive nature of the people's sacrifice, i.e., they were (i) unable to mourn their relatives, (ii) unable to live their lives as they want, (iii) or to do the things they love. However, the key observation is that, unlike Woods, Johnson does not admit fault. The people feel rage 'with me and with the government I lead when they think in Downing Street itself the rules are not being properly followed by the people who make the rules'. So the rage is directed at the government, which he happened to lead, not with him per se. The morally, and in this case criminally, reprehensible behaviour is in Downing Street. However, this admission of breaching the moral code and law is significantly watered down through word choice*: the rules are not broken, they 'are not being properly followed'. Further, the wrongdoers, who are not properly following the rules, are introduced as the 'people who make the rules'. This is vague*, and does not explicitly include Johnson. Unlike Woods who specifically uses first person pronouns to accept blame for wrongdoing, Johnson sidesteps attributing fault to himself.

Vagueness*

Like Woods, having defined his target audience, Johnson then moves on to his behaviour. First he makes reference to the Gray Inquiry, the conclusions of which he cannot anticipate. He therefore again sidesteps taking responsibility for any potential breach of moral codes. It is up to the inquiry to establish this. However, he has 'learned enough to know there were things we simply did not get right and I must take responsibility'. Interestingly here, what was not right is concealed by the vagueness* of the word choice*: 'things' (line 7). Further, the people doing these 'things' are also very vague. To obscure the wrongdoers, Johnson employs the very slippery 'we' pronoun*. At a minimum, 'we' is me and you. But, in this case, who are the mysterious we? And what is Johnson's relationship with this 'we'? Responsibility for the 'things' that 'we' got wrong is therefore extremely diluted. And, Johnson's role in this is vague* – perhaps almost non-existent. However, shifting to the 'I', it is Johnson who 'must take responsibility'. But, accepting responsibility for 'things we did not get right' does not admit direct involvement in the wrongdoing.

(Re)Defining the Event

Johnson then goes on to account* for the events. First, he says Number 10 is a big department, so therefore can he reasonably be expected to oversee all of it, all the time? Moreover, the garden, where the alleged parties took place, was not a potential venue for frivolity and spreading of Covid. Quite the reverse, in Johnson's account it is vital in providing fresh air and so stopping the virus. According to Johnson's description of events, he went into the garden, which implicitly was in use to prevent the spread of the virus, to thank staff – a very honourable intention – and he went back into his office 25 minutes later to continue working. This not only minimises the time spent at the event but it is also designed to display his work ethic. Moreover, Johnson in the here-and-now of the 'apology', citing Johnson in the there-and-then of the event, describes his assessment of the event as a work event at which he was scarcely present. In sum, Johnson turns talk which is framed* as an apology into a narrative* of a past work event in which he is displayed in a good light. So far, there is no admission of a breach of any moral code or legal responsibility.

Whose Fault is it?

The fault, presented in a list of three, is that (i) 'I should have sent everyone back inside', (ii) 'I should have found some other way to thank them' and (iii) 'I should have recognised that there are millions and millions of people who simply would not see it that way'. The wrongdoing for which he is accountable* is now not that he attended a party during lockdown. Rather, it is that he should have sent everyone inside and thanked them differently. Moreover, according to Johnson, the event 'could be said technically to fall within the guidance'. Therefore, he doesn't even admit to a breach of a moral code or legal requirement: 'technically' the event was neither of these. Consequently, the 'problem' is not with Johnson. Rather, the problem lies with the 'millions and millions of people who simply would not see it that way'.

The people who would not see it this way are the people 'who have suffered terribly' and 'who were forbidden from meeting loved ones at all inside or outside'. One could add here, not only have they suffered, but they are also so stupid that they are incapable of seeing Johnson's behaviour for what it is: entirely honourable and morally correct, though, in hindsight, open to improvement in how he should have dealt with some events. Johnson offers his 'heartfelt apologies' to these (ignorant) people and the House (i.e., fellow MPs in the House of Commons). He adds to this that all he asks 'is that Sue Gray be allowed to complete her inquiry into that day and several others so that the full facts can be established'. This implies that those who have so far failed to understand the events will see that Johnson is right once the full facts are established. The hope is that once the full facts are established, the heat will be off and the political world will have moved on to other issues. He is in fact playing for time.

Is it an Apology?

By ending his speech with 'heartfelt apologies', Johnson closes his talk as he started i.e., by framing* it as an apology. But is it an apology? Woods's apology contained an admission of wrong-doing, recognition of having done harm, and a promise to change. Johnson does none of these. He does not admit any wrongdoing. Indeed, in his narrative* of the events he is totally blameless in his behaviour. The fault lies with the people who don't realise that it was a work event; Johnson did not breach any moral code or legal requirement. If he has done nothing wrong, there is no need to change. So, this element of the apology is entirely absent. Harm has been done to the public, but Johnson sidesteps taking responsibility for this. Rules were not being properly followed by the people who make the rules, but the people who make the rules remain vague and, unlike Woods, there is no clear use of the first person personal pronoun to accept wrongdoing.

In short, rather than eating the humble pie of public humili-ty offered to him by the people affected by Covid restrictions, Johnson turns this round and offers them humble pie. The fault lies not with him, but with their ignorance of the true situation. The greased piglet not only wriggles free again, but he also bites his detractors on the way out. However, as we all know, following numerous scandals, Johnson was forced to resign a few months after this (non)apology. Woods on the other hand continued his career. To apologise or not to apologise, that is the question. Is it better to eat the humble pie of public humility and be rehabilitat-ed, or is it better to refuse to submit to such moral exigencies? This is a question that I suspect will be answered when, and if, Johnson ever resumes his political career.

To Sum Up

Public apologies are, in my opinion, very much like public re-pentance and penance in the Middle Ages. Sporting celebrities, politicians, and others in the public eye who have committed in-discretions or criminal acts are forced to publicly apologise, admit their faults, express a desire to change their ways, and recognise that they were the cause of hurt to others. Once this ritual has been completed, maybe they will no longer be pariahs and maybe they will be allowed to continue their careers. Though, as we see in the case of Johnson, he apologises but he doesn't do so humbly. He manages to pull this off by framing his talk as an apology, without ever actually admitting fault. This is the power of framing*.

4. THE SALES PITCH

'£282 is what each and every one of you have just saved'

We live in a consumer society whereby buying and owning goods, even those that we don't really need, is considered to be a 'normal' activity. As we saw to some extent during the Covid crisis and lockdown, if we fail to consume, the economic machinery that drives our society will also grind to a halt. Moreover, the conspicuous consumption of goods is often related to displays of status and identity*, rather than any concern for the functionality or usefulness of the product. Being able to sell, to convince the potential buyer that 'your' product is the product that matches the needs and wants of the buyer, is thus the bread and butter of any salesperson. On the one hand, part of selling is related to the potential buyer's (the prospect's) disposable income and his or her needs and wants. Before any face-to-face sales interaction, the product has been shaped by marketers so that, for example, the product has the 'right' price, packing, promotion, and point of sale. On the other hand, selling is also related to how good the salesperson is at convincing the prospect, face-to-face, that this or that product is the right product for them.

But how do salespeople use the codes of language when selling products? In this chapter we look at a sales pitch taken from daytime television in which a salesperson sells jewellery – notably a tanzanite ring - to the TV viewers[1].

1. This, now, this is beautiful. Are you a tanzanite lover? Are you a tanzanite lover? This is
2. coming on white gold. (figure 3: close-up of ring) We have ask ... been asked for
3. tanzaniteon white gold with blue diamonds. Look at the amount of tanzanite you are
4. getting. Minimum total gem weight of 0.7 carats. That's 13 tanzanites (figure 4: technical
5. spec).13 tanzanite .611 and 12 round cut blue diamonds at .084, giving you a total gem
6. weight of .695 and a total gram weight of 3.13 white gold. That is impressive. If you are
7. interested in tanzanite, this has got to be in your collection. Now tanzanite is December's
8. first stone (figure 5: ring on finger). Let's see how many we've got in this game. Look
9. at the array of colours that you're getting from lilac to purple to instant green and blue as
10. well, sometimes. This is incredible (figure 6: snatch logo). People are already on the
11. phone lines. 084561XXXX is what they phoned. They pressed number one. They've just
12. got theirs. Congratulations. We've only got 12, a very, very low quantity. If you're
13. interested, do it now because we promise you, we'll crash to silly prices. Press one to stay
14. on the line. Two have just gone. We've only got 10 left, 8 left. We've had a crash. We've
15. had a crash. Otherwise, it's going to go. Get on the phone now. Do it right now. The
16. colour, it's bouncing and reflecting off those wonderful, captivating, sparkling, tanzanite
17. gem stones. Tanzanite. 8 chances. At £84. [figure 7] You know that if you're not on the
18. phone right now somebody is going to take that away from you. 8 chances. You've got to
19. be on it. Tanzanite for £84. 084561XXXX and it's yours. You've got to be on the
20. line. So, if you want tanzanite, this is incredible. Not surprised. I'm not surprised. 12
21. opportunities in this game. £282 is what each and every one of you have just
22. saved. You're going to be delighted, delighted.

---

[1] https://www.youtube.com/watch?v=Z3qkXs9GHos

Word Choice: Strong Adjectives

The seller introduces the sales pitch by stating that 'This, now, this is beautiful.' The repetition* of 'this' (i.e., the ring for sale) draws attention to the product and she uses a strong adjective ('beautiful') to describe the product. Word choice* and descriptions are never neutral, they are designed to 'do' things and in this case the description is designed to show off the product and convince the prospect to buy. The use of strong adjectives to describe the product can be seen elsewhere in the pitch as well. For example, in line 16, the stones are described as: wonderful, captivating, sparkling, tanzanite gem stones. Not only are these adjectives strong, but they also appear as a list of three*. One is just a number, two could be a coincidence, but three in a list suggests that there is a general pattern. So, by using three adjectives, the salesperson suggests that this is a general trend.

Props*

The product then appears on the screen in a close-up (see figure 3) and a technical description is given. To take a term from the theatre, the ring acts as a prop*. In other words artefacts such as rings, clothes, badges, and other symbols, can be used to support the speaker. In this case, obviously, showing the prospect the product is a key prop. In other cases, the prospect might be invited to touch the product or even try it on, or taste it, but in this case the TV images are the closest that the prospect is going to get to the product. As the close-up of the ring appears on screen (figure 3), the salesperson gives a technical specification of the product. This is then recapitulated in a table on the screen (see figure 4). This technical specification is prefaced by the words 'Look at the amount of tanzanite you are getting.' This not only draws attention to the quantity, but it also addresses the prospect directly (you) and so builds a bond between seller and prospect. Further, it assumes the sale – 'you are getting' this amount, not 'should you buy this ring you might get this amount'. The idea of a successful sale is therefore being subtly introduced to the prospect. The giving of the technical spec is summed up as being 'impressive' (line 6). This again is a strong adjective which adds to the overall persuasive nature of the pitch.

9 K White Gold Tanzanite and				
Blue Diamond HTCW 0.7 ct. RING				
Item No:	12700			
Setting:	WHITE GOLD 9K			
Gram Weight:	3.133			
Gem Stone	Shape	Size	Pcs	Ct. Wt.
TANZANITE	ROUND	2.5 mm	13	0.611
BLUE DIAMOND	ROUND	1.3mm	12	0.084
		Total Gem Weight (Cc.): 0.695		

Figure 3: Close-up of the ring   Figure 4: The technical spec

Expert Identity*

Having given the technical specifications and having described the product as 'impressive', the seller then evaluates the product by arguing that 'If you are interested in tanzanite this has got to be in your collection.' The client is thus once again addressed directly, and the seller uses a strong form of advice giving ('this *has got to be* in your collection'). The seller, who knows your wants and needs, is telling you what to do in a very direct way. Giving the technical specifications also displays that the seller is knowledgeable about the product. It therefore helps create an expert, and thus more convincing, identity. Speakers, playing language games, shift between different roles and identities*. For strategic reasons, we may, chameleon-like, choose to play different roles such as friend, boss, colleague, and so on. Each identity that we may claim, or project onto others, may have particular characteristics, states of knowledge, rights and responsibilities attached to it. It is these characteristics that we use to play our games: to convince; to show sympathy; to attribute blame; and so on. Expert identities can be a key element of persuasion in sales-talk. This can be seen in classic genres of advertising: actors playing the role of dentists are used to sell toothpaste; sports stars endorse sports equipment; and, staying with clichéd stereotypes, housewives are (or were) used to sell cleaning products.

Ideologies-in-action: Framing* Shopping as a Game

After the technical specifications, the screen shifts to a second close-up of the ring on the seller's finger (figure 5), and the seller describes the sales pitch as a 'game'. Talk never exist in a vacuum, it draws on wider ideologies*. In this case, framing* the shopping experience as a game enacts a wider ideology* of shopping/consumerism as a leisure activity. Shopping is fun, and the darker sides of consumerism such as consumer debt, over-consumption of the world's resources, and inequalities in trade between the so-called developed and developing worlds are obscured. The game is later revealed as 'snatch it' which appears on the screen with the image of a person with a net (figure 6). The logo 'let's play snatch it' not only sends the message that shopping is a game, but through the inclusive pronoun* 'us', it creates a team which consists of the prospect and the seller (let us play). The seller shifts roles from the knowledgeable expert to the likeable* gameshow host who has the prospect's interests at heart. The game consists of snatching the product before others do. The choice of the word 'snatch', defined by Merriam-Webster's online dictionary as 'to take or grasp *abruptly* or *hastily*', is interesting here. It projects a need to act quickly, so putting time* pressure on the prospect. Moreover, this time pressure is increased because the game is played against others. If the prospect doesn't act fast, the others will get the product. This therefore creates a (false) demand which the seller emphasises, through the repetition of 'they': 'People are already on the phone lines. 08456XXXX is what they phoned. They pressed number one. They've just got theirs.' Addressing the buyers directly, the seller adds 'congratulations'. Thus, she implies that those who have 'snatched' a ring are smart and have secured a good deal. They are good people because they have made a smart purchase and she is a good person, because she congratulates them. Who said flattery gets you nowhere? In this case, whilst not achieving the sale in itself, it nevertheless smooths the way for future sales.

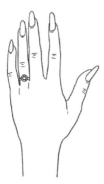

Figure 5: Ring on finger

Let's play snatch it!

Figure 6: Let's play snatch it

Scarcity*

The pressure to buy is also stepped up by creating scarcity-value and a buy 'now or never' moment. The seller informs the TV audience*/prospect that there are only 12 products available which, to up the ante, is described as 'a very, very low quantity'. The count-down of products sold and remaining products appears on the screen (figure 7), and the commentary of the seller (line 14: 'Two have just gone. We've only got 10 left, 8 left') adds to the visual display, which serves as a prop, of the (rapidly) diminishing number of products available. The seller then announces 'We've had a crash. We've had a crash.' This repeated phrase, using a strong noun (crash rather than 'fall' or 'reduction'), relates to a crash in the price. It is also visually represented on the screen with a flashing red light and audibly by a buzzer going off, as the counter giving the price begins to drop to an as yet unknown sale price (figure 7). If the prospect buys now, she is to some extent gambling on the price, which remains unknown. She is playing a game. Further, as the number of products available is going down, the seller assesses the situation: 'You know that if you're not on the phone right now somebody is going to take that away from you.' The use of 'you know'* projects common knowledge onto the audience, and therefore assumes agreement. The seller also adds to the pressure by using imperative* forms to create a sense of urgency as she exhorts the prospect to buy (line 13 'Do it now' and line 15 'Get on the phone now. Do it right now'). Finally, if you listen to the clip, you'll see that the need to act quickly is accentuated by the music which has a fast beat.

Item	1270
Guide	£366
Now at	£84
Remaining	8

Figure 7: Display of number of remaining rings and falling price

Social Pressure*

Moreover, not only does this now or never strategy create an impression of the need to buy now, but it also creates social pressure. If others are seizing the opportunity to buy the product, then why shouldn't I? Surely, the product must be a good product? We also note that on the screen (see figure 7 above), the sale price (£84) is revealed and it is juxtaposed with, and therefore compared to, a 'guide' price (£366). How these prices are worked out remains vague*. It is something that the salesperson does not draw attention to. Nevertheless, we note that having the guide makes the original price appear 'fair', 'standard', and 'normal'. It also makes the sale seem a bargain and therefore something not to be missed. The buyer saves money (line 21: '£282 is what each and every one of you have just saved'). The seller thus shifts focus away from what the buyer has paid, to what they have allegedly saved. The shift of focus from spending to saving thus makes the cost incurred more attractive.

To close the pitch and before moving on to the next product on sale, the host/seller reassures the buyer that they have made a good purchase, repeating the strong adjective twice, for emphasis: 'You're going to be delighted, delighted.'

To Sum Up

The language games that the seller engages in here are common techniques in any sales pitch. How many times have we been told that somebody else is interested in the product that we're looking at and that we'll have to move fast if we want to secure a sale? How many times do we see flash sales with a limited window in which to buy products? And how many times have we been told that this is a special offer 'while stocks last'? Having some knowledge of how sales language games are played may make you more alert to these little 'tricks of the trade' that are designed to pressure you into buying.

Moreover, these techniques are not limited to selling products as we see here. They are used in many other persuasive situations. At a job interview, you may have to sell yourself – convince a future employer that you are the best person for a job. If you're presenting a new project at work, you may have to convince your boss that the project is a goer. Or even mundane situations such as, let's say, convincing a group of friends that it is better to go to the Indian restaurant rather than the Chinese are all about persuasive language, selling your point of view.

5. DEBATING

All Questions, No Answers!

Let's debate what good language looks like. And there's no better place than Prime Minister's Questions (often abbreviated to PMQs) in the British Parliament. On Wednesdays at noon, the serving prime minister answers questions submitted by Members of Parliament. In general, the prime minister does not know what the questions will be, though they can expect several hostile questions about the topics of the day from the Leader of the Opposition. Whatever the political merits of such a system of public questioning, Prime Minster's Questions often takes the form of a show in which the party leaders battle it out, providing a spectacle of claim and counter-claim. While being neutral as to the truth, and untruth, of these claims and counter-claims, let's have a look at how the main characters of this show attempt to land a blow that will discredit the other and gain points in the eyes of the electorate, party faithful, journalists and fellow MPs. (The adversaries must abide by the rules* of the House of Commons, which adds a degree of orderliness, ritual, and a veneer of decorum to the spectacle.) What we are most interested in, however, is how the party leaders use language techniques – our secret codes – to aim their blows.

We focus on one particular exchange between Keir Starmer, the Leader of the Opposition and Rishi Sunak, the prime minister, which took place on 23rd November 2022.*

1.	KS	Britain faces the lowest growth of any OECD[1] nation over the next two years.
2.		Why?
3.	RS	Mr Speaker. Mr Speaker. Mr Speaker. (background shouts and jeers)
4.		But this country since 2010 has the third highest growth in the G7[2] and
5.		unemployment at a multi-decade low. We're getting on to deliver more growth
6.		Mr. Speaker, we're delivering free ports, we're investing in apprenticeships, we're
7.		protecting our R and D and if the Labour Party is serious about actually supporting
8.		growth maybe they should get on their phone with their union pay-masters and
9.		call off the strikes.
10.	S	Keir Starmer.
11.	KS	Mr. Speaker we're … we're … we're … (background shouts, cheers, and jeers)
12.	S	Order, order. We want to get through this Prime Minister's Questions and you've
13.		got to help me. Keir Starmer.
14.	KS	He's in total denial we're bottom of the 38 OECD countries. We are all in the
15.		same boat when it comes to Covid and the Ukraine, and he wants a pat on the
16.		back. It's like a football manager, bottom of the league at Christmas, celebrates an
17.		away draw three months ago. And it won't wash. So let's … they don't like their
18.		record. That's the problem. So let's try it another way. Why is Britain set to be the
19.		first country into recession and the last out?

*Available at: https://parliamentlive.tv/event/index/e248627d-a5af-4213-8adf-2e04b3a0c54d?in=12:00:40

[1] The Organization for Economic Co-operation and Development (OECD) which comprises of: Australia, Austria, Belgium, Canada, Chile, Colombia, Costa Rica, the Czech Republic, Denmark, Estonia, Finland, France, Germany, Greece, Hungary, Iceland, Ireland, Israel, Italy, Japan, Korea, Latvia, Lithuania, Luxembourg, Mexico, Netherlands, New Zealand, Norway, Poland, Portugal, the Slovak Republic, Slovenia, Spain, Sweden, Switzerland, Turkey, the United Kingdom, and the USA.

[2] The G7 is an informal grouping of seven of the world's most advanced economies, comprising of: Canada, France, Germany, Italy, Japan, the United Kingdom, and the United States.

Questions* and Making Comparison*

The Speaker of the House gives the floor to Keir Starmer. The first part of talk is a statement which has no hedging* or downgrading in any way (i.e., maybe, might, could, I think, etc.). It purports to present the world as it is. It is presented as fact*, rather than opinion. It is a world in which 'Britain faces the lowest growth of any OECD nation over the next two years.' The venom in the statement is that in comparison with other OECD countries, Britain is a loser, and that this is implicitly the fault of the prime minister and the Conservative Party. Comparison* can be a way of scoring points in a debate. In this case, it is the comparison between Britain and the other OECD countries that makes Britain look like a loser. But of course, the comparison has to be valid, you should compare like with like. But in debate you can look for selective comparisons that make your point appear more forceful even if the comparison is not particularly fair. So, use comparisons strategically and be wary of other's use of comparisons: are they valid?

Not Answering the Question*

In the continuation of the talk, Starmer transforms the statement into a question 'Why' (is this the case)? A question* requires an answer, and it is inherent in the structure of PMQs that the prime minister replies to this question.

Having asked the question, those present in the House know that it is for Sunak to answer. So nobody takes the floor to answer, but nevertheless the House erupts in a wave of jeers or cheers. The other MPs know their role: they are the immediately present audience* who are there to cheer on their side as the prime minister and Leader of the Opposition slog it out. The Speaker acts as a kind of chair* who has certain rights and privileges for directing and controlling talk. Without such order, the whole thing would collapse into a free for all: a pub brawl, rather than carefully cho-reographed 'sparring'. Sunak begins his answer by addressing the Speaker. This is a parliamentary convention which acknowledges the role of the Speaker in running the show by controlling who speaks to whom, about what, and when, and so imposes some form of order on an apparently chaotic shambles.

When the House has quietened down enough for Sunak to be heard, he uses 'But' to introduce a counterpoint and block the punch that Starmer is trying to deliver. The blocking move, as with Starmer's attack, takes the form of a bald comparison: 'this country has experienced since 2010 the third highest growth in the G7'. The source of this statement is not given, but it is presented as if it were fact, rather than as if it were opinion or conjecture (i.e., there are no hedges*: 'I think', 'I believe', 'it could be' and so on). However, whilst Sunak does fill the slot where an answer should be, he doesn't answer the question. He does not explain why Britain faces the lowest growth of any OECD nation over the next two years. Rather, he denies the premise of the question: Britain does not have low growth. Thus denying the premise on which a question is based is one way of not answering a question.

Keeping the floor, Sunak then introduces a new topic; one that will show him and the Conservatives in a better light and so win them points. Shifting topic when you have the floor is thus one way of countering aggressive questioning. In other words: acknowledge the question in some way, make a show of answering it, and the transit to another safer topic. In this case, Sunak, using the booster* 'multi-dec-ade', adds to his comparison with other members of the G7 and claims that unemployment is at a 'multi-decade low'. This has absolutely nothing to do with Starmer's question, but since he has the floor, Sunak can deftly shift topic by slight transitions that are barely ob-servable unless the talk is slowed down and transcribed for analysis.

Sunak then builds on this Conservative Party success by introducing new topics. Going beyond the rule of three*, Sunak provides a list of four positive things that his party is doing: 'We're getting on to deliver more growth'; 'we're delivering free ports'; 'we're investing in apprenticeships'; and 'we're protecting our R and D'. As before, no evidence is provided to support these claims but nevertheless they are presented without any hedges and so they are made to appear as 'fact'.

Counter-attacking

Having effectively blocked Starmer's attack, by refuting the premise of the question and by providing a list of Conservative successes, Sunak now counter-attacks: 'if the Labour Party is serious about actually supporting growth maybe they should get on their phone with their union pay-masters and call off the strikes'. Since he has the floor, he uses it to shift topic to the strikes, which is a subject that is damaging to Keir Starmer and the Labour Party who have been accused of being too sympathetic to the strikers. Sunak also suggests that Labour is not serious about growth and that they are in the pockets of the unions. He is thus able to direct a punch at Labour's credibility*. Attacking the credibility of your adversary can be a way of winning a debate. If you can show that your opponent is in some way flawed, not a good person, acting out of selfish interest, or whatever, then you weaken the strength of their augment – even if that argument* hangs together well. However, this technique is to be used with moderation. If over-used, the technique will come back to bite you as you'll be regarded as a bully and your good character and goodwill will be called in to question. PMQs and parliamentary debates in general are highly ritualised partisan slagging matches in which parties are thick-skinned and aware of these theatrics. Generally speaking, though, you should use scorn, sarcasm*, insults and ridicule sparingly.

This fairly robust counter-attack elicits cheers from supporters of the blue corner, and jeers from supporters of the red corner. The rules of the game* are that Starmer should now move on to the next question. The Speaker, in his role of chairman/referee, hands the floor to Starmer. Starmer, respecting the rules of the game, begins his next turn by addressing the Speaker, but he can't be heard over the crowd. The Speaker has to intervene, calling for order, and he hands the floor again to Starmer.

Evaluating the (Non)Answer with a Strawman* Argument

Before asking a second question, Starmer uses his turn as an opportunity to evaluate, and to attack, Sunak's (non)answer. Again presenting his claim in a straightforward way with no hedges, he asserts that, using the booster* 'total', Sunak is 'in total denial [of the fact that] we're bottom of the 38 OECD countries'. He then points out that 'We are all in the same boat when it comes to Covid and the Ukraine, and he [Sunak] wants a pat on the back.' Now, Sunak hasn't mentioned Covid or the war in Ukraine. These 'excuses' for the UK's poor economic performance are attributed to him by Starmer. Starmer thus puts words, an argument, into Sunak's mouth, and then dismisses them. This move in the language game is sometimes called a strawman argument: you set up a simplified caricature of your opponent's argument that is weak, and then you knock it down as easily as you'd knock down a strawman.

Metaphor*

Starmer then uses a metaphor. Metaphors in debate make the argument clearer by taking an already known situation (in this case, what we all know about football), and comparing it to the current issue (Sunak's handling of the economy). The metaphor, which may or may not be valid, is that Sunak is 'like a football manager, bottom of the league at Christmas, celebrates an away draw three months ago'. Just as the football manager tries to put a positive spin on things, so does Sunak. But Starmer knows 'it won't wash'. The problem is that they, the Tory Party and the failing football manager, don't like their record. So, metaphor is a useful tool in language games. It can make your argument more accessible, and perhaps harder hitting. Is Sunak really like a second-rate football manager, maybe, maybe not, but the image is strong and clear, and Starmer's punch clearly lands on target.

Then, revealing that he is not satisfied with Sunak's response, which has not answered his question, Starmer uses his access to the floor to reframe the question: 'Why is Britain set to be the first country into recession and the last out?' And so the boxers move into another round, neither of them having sustained any real damage, nor gained significant points from these exchanges.

To Sum Up

While you may never be prime minister, nor have the opportunity to grill a prime minister on the country's economic performance, nevertheless the techniques that Sunak and Starmer use could be useful for you. Though be careful because pouring scorn on the opposition is part of the game in parliament, but this is related to its particularly theatrical, dare one say pantomimic, aspect. What works in one context* does not work in another.

The most important observation here is the power of questions*. People talk in turns. As in a game of cards, players go one after the other. If a question is asked, it requires a response in the next turn, or to put it another way, if someone asks you a question you must reply. Once you have replied the game moves on and in a dialogue the turn passes back to the person who asked the first question. He/she may then ask another question and/or evaluate the response of the second speaker. So we see the possible moves in the game being:

Speaker one	Move one	question
Speaker two	Move two	answer
Speaker one	Move three	evaluation of the answer or ask another question

Figure 8: Question and answer sequences in talk

Starmer's question requires a reply. But, the trick here is to reply, but not to answer. Sunak uses his turn to talk about what he claims the Tories are doing. He replies, but he does not answer. So, if you're on the ropes and facing difficult questions: reply but don't answer. Use your turn at talk to change the topic. If on the other hand, you're the questioner and somebody is trying to get off the ropes by replying but not answering, you can use the next turn to ask a further question. Asking questions rather than responding puts you in a stronger position.

What is also interesting here is that each politician presents totally different pictures of the UK's economy. One sees the UK as bottom of the league, the other as top of the league. Which is true, which is false doesn't interest us here, what is interesting is that they present their opinion as if it were fact. Neither of them hedges their talk in any way with phrases such as: 'in my opinion', 'I think', 'it may be', and so on. No, they use bold statements to present their opinion as if it were fact. They also use comparisons, to bolster their arguments. But comparisons and metaphors are only valid if you compare like with like. Whether Sunak is really like a failed football manager is beside the point; Starmer makes this comparison and so the idea, the image is 'out there' regardless of its 'truth'.

6. DOING TEACHER-TALK IN DEBATE

'Now here's my question. I am a history teacher'

E ven if you're not a teacher, the ways in which teachers talk extends beyond the classroom to both argumentative settings and other, non-classroom, learning situations. In this chapter, we look at a televised debate on gun control that took place in February 2018, one week after a shooting at a school in Florida in which 17 students and staff were killed and 17 injured[1]. Many of the survivors and those directly impacted by the killings were in the audience. The panel of discussants consisted of politicians, Sheriff Scott Israel, the local police chief at the time of the shooting, and Dana Loesch, the then spokeswoman for the National Rifle Association (NRA), the pro-gun lobby group.

In this analysis we focus on one exchange between Dana Loesch and Diane Wolk Rogers, a teacher who survived the shooting. Whilst Rogers is not in the classroom, her debating style bears all the hallmarks of teacher-talk and therefore serves to showcase

---

[1] Available at: https://www.youtube.com/watch?v=4AtOUodDXv8

how teacher-talk is structured and how it can be effective in argumentative situations.

In order to understand what is going on, some background is needed. The teacher-talk we're going to look at centres around two different interpretations of the second amendment to the US constitution which states: 'A well-regulated militia, being necessary to the security of a free state, the right of the people to keep and bear arms, shall not be infringed.' In simple terms: on the one hand, pro-gun lobbyists cite the amendment as legal justification for carrying arms in more or less any circumstances. On the other hand, the anti-gun lobby argues that the second amendment was intended to protect citizens of the fledgling United States and so allowed them to carry arms only as part of a militia that could be called upon in case of need. So, now we have some background, let's look at how pro and anti-gun lobbyists play the game.

Initiation of Topic (question one)

In this move, Rogers sets up her question very much as a teacher would. Indeed, in the preamble to the question she explicitly makes her identity* as a teacher relevant so referencing her talk as 'teacher-talk' even though it is out of the classroom.

1. DWR: Now here's my question. I am a history teacher. I ask my students to define
2. terms for me. So, I'd like you to define something for me because I've
3. wondered about it and I want to know what is your definition of a well-regulated
4. militia as stated in second amendment and, using supporting detail, explain how
5. (audience applause cheers) and let me finish let me finish and using supporting
6. detail explain how an 18-year-old with a military rifle is well-regulated. And
7. the world, our country, our nation is going to grade your answer (cheers from
8. audience).

The question* comes in two parts: 'what is your definition of a well-regulated militia as stated in second amendment' and 'explain how an 18- year-old with a military rifle is well-regulated'. She also requests, as a teacher would, that Loesch use 'supporting detail' and she notes that 'the world, our country, [and] our nation is going to grade your answer'. The question is loaded to attack the gun-lobby's interpretation of the second amendment – a pillar on which their support for carrying arms rests. The question probes Loesch's understanding of the second amendment. If she takes the line that the second amendment was intended to allow citizens to carry arms only as part of a militia then, logically, it follows that the amendment cannot be invoked to justify the gunman's right to carry arms, and so one of the main arguments* of the pro-gun lobby collapses.

Questions are often understood and used as a way of getting information. Here that is not the case. The question is used as an argumentative device to glean, and critically scrutinise, the logic* underlying an opponent's argument in a debate.

Response (answer one)

As with any question, Loesch is obliged to provide some kind of response.

9. DL: Well, by all means, and I want to say as well as a parent I see my kids in these
10. students. I see my kids in these students that are here today. What you went
11. through is horrid. I am not going to pretend to understand what you went through.
12. There are no words for it. It is monstrous and no nobody should have to endure
13. that. I want to answer your question. George Mason was one of the founders and
14. he said the militia is the whole of the people. It's every man. It's every woman.
15. That's the militia. In the context of the time, a well-regulated militia meant an
16. American man and woman a citizen of the United States of America who could
17. operate and service their firearm.

First, Loesch prefaces her answer to the question with a classic piece of ethos*, building her own credentials as a 'good' person. She points out that she is a parent and so empathises with the audience (many of whom were parents of those killed or wounded), and she shows compassion for what the local community went through. Being a good and likeable* person can soften opposition to your argument. Having worked to present a likeable personality, she then answers the question by referring to George Mason, an 18th Century American politician who had a pivotal role in drafting the second amendment. In this way she uses Mason to answer the question much as a ventriloquist puts words into the mouth of his/her dummy. In technical terms, Loesch is simply the animator (the person speaking the words), but Mason is the author (the person responsible for the actual words) and the principal (the person with the ultimate responsibility for the words). In this way she not only provides authority* for her claim, but she also sidesteps personal responsibility, which allows her to maintain her 'likeability'. It is not her, personally, arguing for the right to carry arms. She is 'simply' giving voice* to one of the founding fathers of the United States of America.

Initiation (question two)

After asking a question, and getting a reply, the right to make the next move returns to the teacher (the questioner). This turn can either be used to ask another question, or evaluate the 'student's' reply. In this case, rather than evaluating the reply, Rogers shows that the answer is insufficient or at least insufficient for what she intended, and she asks a second question. Since she also asks for supporting details, the question has all the hallmarks of a teacher-student exchange.

18. DWR: How is an 18-year-old that is not that was in the context of the time …

19. DL: Yes.

20. DWR: How now is an 18-year-old with a military assault rifle well-regulated? Use

21.   supporting detail.

This second question, as with the first, also seeks to probe for 'logical' weaknesses in Loesch's reply. This is because according to the second amendment, well-ordered militia can carry arms, but an 18-year-old lone gunman with an assault rifle, logically, cannot be part of a *well-ordered* militia. Thus the question is designed to chip away at the foundations of Loesch's supposed argument. Rogers also shifts the timeframe* to better attack Loesch's argument. She states that the argument of the well-ordered militia was 'in the context of the time', i.e., 1791 when the second amendment was ratified. So, by shifting timeframe an argument can be played up, or played down. This gives us a 'that was true in the past, but is not true today' argument that can be deployed in many situations.

Response (answer two)

As before, a question obliges Loesch to provide a reply.

22. DL: Right, well, he's not … he shouldn't have been able to get a firearm (heckling).

23.   He should have been barred from getting a firearm. He should not have been able

24.   to … he should not have been able to purchase a firearm (heckling).

Loesch, to the accompaniment of heckling, answers the question in a way that aligns with the implication behind the question, i.e., that the gunman was not part of a well-organised militia, and therefore he shouldn't have had a firearm. Here, to make her point more forcefully she repeats* the modal verb 'shouldn't' three times with three slightly different clauses. Aligning with the questioner is thus one way in which an aggressive question can be calmed – 'we both agree on this point, so why argue?' The catch is: they agree, but on different terms. Here, implicitly, Rogers is trying to undercut Loesch's argument by saying that an 18-year-old with an assault rifle cannot be part of a *well-ordered* militia. Loesch agrees, but as we see later she agrees on the grounds that he is mentally unstable. So, seeking ground for agreement with an aggressive questioner can be a way of taking the sting out of an 'attack'.

Initiation (question three)

At this point a heckler from the audience shouts out a question which Rogers picks up.

1. Heckler: He bought it legally, so why have you done nothing about it?
2. DWR: So what are you going to do about it?

As mentioned earlier, the particular context* of the debate makes the audience largely pro-gun control and therefore hostile to Loesch. Normally, in teacher-talk the questions are asked by the teacher. In this case, a member of the audience takes the teacher role by asking a question. This could be seen as a breach of rules, a usurpation of the teacher's right to ask the questions. However, Rogers, unperturbed, takes ownership of the heckler's question and repeats it. Sharing* the questioner roles shows that that the audience, or certain vociferous members of the audience, are acting as a team with Rogers. So, if you want to show solidarity, that you are a team with similar aims rather than a collection of individuals, sharing talk is one way of doing this (see Chapter 22 for more on this).

Response (reply three)

As before, the same mechanism is in play: a question requires a response. In this case Loesch reiterates her argument*.

3. DL: What the NRA (heckling) ... let me answer if we're here to have a discussion
4.   that's why I am here. I want you to ask every question if you want to have a
5.   discussion answer every question.
6. Host: Let's have some respect. She's here to answer the question, let her answer the
7.   questions.

As she begins her answer the heckling continues. To her credit Loesch keeps her cool, and even seizes the opportunity to continue her projection of the 'good and reasonable' person. She's at the debate to answer the audience's question, to have a (civilised) discussion. A cool and reasonable person is more convincing than a hot head spouting off. Lose your cool, and you'll lose the debate. Though, depending on the situation, at other times it may be a useful strategy to play the role of the angry, aggrieved person, behind which you are in fact in complete control. Using emotions* can give your argument more force. But, the key is: never lose your cool. Remember, language games are, to some extent, theatre. So, play the role, don't let your unbridled emotions* drive your language use. I'm not saying this as some kind of Machiavellian tactic where emotions* can be switched on and off at will so that you can achieve your ends. Rather, to draw an analogy with a boxing match, in amateur boxing a fighter may get annoyed and start punching out wildly. This not only tires the fighter, but they also start making mistakes, dropping their guard, and it is at this point that a fighter who has kept their cool can place a knockout blow. Keep your cool when playing language games and don't let your emotions* take over.

After calmly dealing with the heckler, Loesch answers.

8. DL   He should A) never have been able to get a firearm B) people who are crazy
9.   should not be able to get a firearm C) people who are dangerous to themselves and
10.   other individuals should not be able to get … to obtain a firearm. We … and there
11.   isn't a loophole, it's a criminal act.

Using the rule of three*, here explicitly enumerated (A, B, C) and therefore easily recognised by the audience, Loesch provides three arguments explaining why the perpetrator should never have been allowed to carry a firearm. She closes this part of the argument by summing up that there isn't a 'loophole [in the law] it's a criminal act'. The massacre is nothing to do with the second amendment right to bear arms. It is the act of a crazy criminal. In this way, she moves the argument away from support for the second amendment to a criminal act. Having reframed* the argument in terms of criminality rather than constitutional rights, she drives the point home.

12. DL   And that's what we have to start calling it. Number one following up on red-flags.
13.   39 times in the past year it was law enforcement (looks at police officer) or it was
14.   social services that went to this individual's home. Now there are two Florida
15.   statutes one of them … I don't know if the comments he put on YouTube would
16.   have qualified for you to Baker Act him, but sending messages telling other
17.   students that he was going to murder them and he was going to kill them. I would
18.   think that certainly would qualify under a Florida state statute for you to have
19.   Baker Acted him.
20. PO   Let me respond to that.

To drive her point home, Loesch develops her argument that it was a criminal act and she deftly shifts blame away from support of the second amendment to failure in the police and social services to 'Baker Act' the gunman (i.e., to commit him to a mental health treatment centre). Thus, to stay with a boxing metaphor, Loesch manoeuvres herself off the ropes. She no longer submits to the questioning of Rogers. She has been able to shift blame away from pro-gun lobby support of the second amendment to failures in the criminal justice system. Not only does she do this, but by using eye gaze* to select the Police Chief as the immediate recipient of her talk, she takes the advantage by passing an implicit question on to him (why didn't you Baker Act him?). So, one way of taking the upper hand in an argument is to take control of the questioning, as Loesch does here. She answers Rogers's question, but then uses her right to respond to sneak in her own question and so she takes control of the talk, reversing the role of the (attacking) questioner and (defending) responder.

To Sum Up

Teacher-talk consists of asking a series of questions, or more specifically questions to which we know the answer, asked in a series. A question obliges the other to set out their argument. This argument can then be probed and scrutinised. Does it add up? The third turn in the sequence can be used to assess your interlocutor's response as adequate or not. So, teacher-talk, whilst obviously being a standard way in which teachers go about doing their job and push students to challenge their reasoning, can also be used in debate, to make others think and to probe their argument. Such questioning is sometimes called a Socratic dialogue*, since it is used to force somebody to (re)consider the premises of their argument.

In an adversarial situation, manoeuvre yourself into the role of the questioner; this is the attacking role. The responder is on the back foot and the defensive. The way to get yourself off the ropes if you are subject to aggressive questioning is, as Loesch does, to use your turn to return a question. This puts the boot on the other foot: you are now the questioner and the other is obliged to answer and submit their responses to your inspection.

However, teacher-talk is not only adversarial. In the classroom, the teacher works with the student, helping them to refine their argument. This would be the same in some types of facilitation or counselling in which a series of questions helps the 'subject' to come to new, more positive, understandings of a situation. Perhaps we can never really teach anybody anything, or make them change their minds in debate, but we can probe their arguments to make them think and one way of doing this is to get them to reflect on their proposals through a Socratic dialogue – a series of questions and evaluations.

7. ADVERTISING

'Pay it back early and it'll cost you less'

Advertising, of course, plays a central role in the consumer society in which we live. If only one type of washing powder were on sale, there would be no need to advertise. But since we are spoilt for choice, rival companies have to sell the merits (imagined or otherwise) of their particular product or service to us over and above the merits of other similar products or services that are on the market. Key to this is setting out their unique selling point. What is different about this product or service? What makes this product or service better than another in the eyes of the customer? Why does this product or service meet the needs and wants of the client better than a rival product or service? What makes this product or service unique? And, of course, central to this is the ability to persuade. Persuading is the language game that all advertisers are playing in one way or another.

The world of advertising and copywriters might be a long way from us, but nevertheless the techniques that they master are not their sole preserve. Persuasive techniques are also used in many other mundane everyday interactions – business meetings, pres-entations, and even casual conversations. So, having an idea of how copywriters 'do' persuasion might help you when you have to persuade. It will also help you notice the techniques that others, not necessarily advertisers, use to persuade you to do things. Having an understanding of how somebody is trying to talk you into doing something that you may not want to do will give you the edge in resisting.

So, in this chapter, we'll take a look at a TV advert from the now defunct payday loan company Wonga.com[1]. Since this is a TV ad-vertisement, it makes extensive use of visuals and music that add to its persuasive effect. However, we'll concentrate just on the talk.

1. There was a time when borrowing money went at a snail's pace. Page after page of form
2. -filling. Sign here and here and then wait. But now there's Wonga.com. Wonga.com is
3. there when you need a little extra cash in a flash. With Wonga.com you can borrow up to
4. £1,000 for up to 31 days and the cash will be in your bank within 15 minutes.
5. Decisions are instant and Wonga.com always shows you the total cost upfront so there'll
6. be no hidden costs. Pay it back early and it'll cost you less. This fresh approach to
7. lending saw Wonga.com voted as alternative lender of the year 2010. Wonga.com: little
8. loans, lots of control

Comparison*

The first thing to notice is that this advertisement functions through comparison between the past and present. In the past 'borrowing money went at a snail's pace'. This message is underlined through the use of a prop: the screen on which a snail appears. The text ('borrowing money went at a snail's pace') also appears on the

---

[1] Available at: https://www.youtube.com/watch?v=fUoxvSO3eMU

screen. So, we have the visual text, the spoken text, and the image of the snail all reinforcing each other. Reinforce your message using visual and auditory senses if you want to make it stronger.

Problem*

The 'old style' borrowing is presented as a problem: 'page after page of form-filling. Sign here and here and then wait'. This proposal is supported by an image of paperwork on the screen. Consequently, it multiplies the sensory channels* that are activated, visual and aural. Further, the copywriter uses repetition* of page (page after page) and here (sign here and here). This creates an image of excessive work. But, despite filling in page after page of paperwork and signing copiously the result is unsatisfactory: you wait. The repetition therefore serves to underline and reinforce the message and set out the problem.

Solution

The product or service that is being sold is then presented as *the* solution to this problem: 'But now there's Wonga.com. Wonga.com is there when you need a little extra cash in a flash.' The name, Wonga.com, is not innocent. Wonga is a slang expression for money. Its slanginess gives it a popular, familiar, and slightly humorous* connotation. The company and the act of lending money are therefore seen in these likeable terms. They are miles away from the image of the exploitative loan shark. So, just as people try to come across as good people, companies also try to come across as good companies. We're more likely to buy from a friendly 'good' company than a 'bad' one. Being likeable* is a key to persuading people.

Further, through setting out a solution to your problem, Wonga. com is there to help the client when they are in need. Wonga.com therefore adds to its image of a friendly and helpful company. Nobody wants to buy a product or a service from a miserable old git or a dodgy company, unless they have to. Moreover, the word 'Wonga.com' appears several times throughout the text, thus establishing the brand name. So, if you want to get your message across: repeat, repeat, and repeat.

The Advantages – what's in it for you!

Having set out the problem, to which Wonga.com bring the solution, the advert goes on to stress the advantages for the potential client. Obviously, when selling a service or product, it is important to stress what the product or service can do for the potential client, not what the potential client can do for Wonga.com. Indeed, for any kind of persuasion, you should concentrate on the advantages for the other, not what you get out of the deal. Think: what is it the audience* want to hear? The advantage here is that Wonga.com can provide 'cash in a flash'. This expression, to give it a technical name, is an example of assonance, i.e., words occurring in proximity that have the same, often rhyming, vowel sounds. Assonance is a technique that makes the proposition catchy and memorable, and thus more likely to persuade. The offer, the advantages to the clients, is that 'you can borrow up to £1,000 for up to 31 days and the cash will be in your bank within 15 minutes. Decisions are instant.' The main advantage, in comparison to the past, is one of speed. This is Wonga.com's unique selling point, what differentiates it from its competitors. Moreover, Wonga.com is such a good and fair company that it has your interests at heart. It 'always shows you the total cost upfront so there'll be no hidden costs'. This again adds to the image of goodwill that the company bears towards its clients. Somebody or something that has my interests at heart is more likely to encourage me to become a client – goodwill is persuasive.

Moreover, the advertisement goes on to say: 'Pay it back early and it'll cost you less.' This is a spin* that keeps up the image of goodwill. But let's change it around: 'Pay it back late and it'll cost you more.' This is the same proposition but presented negatively. So, to persuade, always spin positively, maximising the perceived benefits for the target audience*. We can also see this positive spin in the word choice*. The words used throughout the advert are: loan, lending, and borrowing. Words with negative connotations such as debt, indebtedness, repayment, and so on are noticeable by their absence.

The rate of interest is also spun. The annual percentage rate (APR), the cost you'd pay per year to borrow the money, appears at the bottom of the screen: 'Representative APR 4,214%. £400 max for 1st time customers.' Wonga.com was a short term lender, and the maximum length of a loan was limited to 31 days, but nevertheless 4,214% APR means that if you were able to borrow money for a year, without repaying, you'd owe just over 42 times the original amount. It is significant that the sums that the lender could be paying back are not mentioned. The foregrounding of the accessibility of the loan and the backgrounding of the possible downsides - such as the rate of interest and the cost of the loan - are thus further examples of spin.

Authority*

Another key aspect of advertising talk is the appeal to authority – people are more likely to be persuaded by an authority figure or an authoritative statement. In this case, the advert points out that: 'Wonga.com [was] voted as alternative lender of the year 2010.' This vote adds some kind of (pseudo) scientific validity, and therefore authority, to Wonga.com's claims to be a 'good' company. Who voted? What was the vote? What exactly is an 'alternative lender'? Regardless of the grounds for this claim, because Wonga.com achieved this accolade the target audience is led to believe that others (whoever the voters were) believe that Wonga.com is a good company.

Further, winning this vote is also an example of 'social proof'. Social proof* is one of the key methods of persuasion that works on the principle that people are more likely to follow the crowd. The reasoning goes that if enough people do something, then it's probable that they are right. There's a kind of safety in numbers appeal to this aspect of persuasion. And so showing that others voted Wonga.com as best 'alternative lender of the year' suggests that if others appreciate the service, then so should you.

Finally, Wonga.com end the advert with another key benefit for the client 'little loans, lots of control'. This slogan is notable both for its alliteration (i.e., the occurrence of the same letter or consonant sound at the beginning of the first three words) and for the juxtaposition of opposites 'little' and 'lots' which underlines and brings out the contrast. As these words are uttered a kind of simulator appears on the screen showing the various lengths of the loan related to various costs. Thus the words are reinforced by an image, so stressing the message and hitting both the target audience's auditory and visual senses.

To Sum Up

Any form of advertising is a form of persuasion. Wonga's advertisement exemplifies some of the techniques of persuasion, especially those set out by Robert Cialdini (see piece of advice 61, principles of persuasion*). Cialdini (b. 1945) is an American psychologist famous for his study of the principles* of persuasion, which he details in his book *Influence: The Psychology of Persuasion*. In this chapter for example, we see three of these principles: authority, likeability, and social proof. While you might never work in advertising these techniques are nevertheless used to persuade in many everyday situations we face. Some knowledge of how advertising works can therefore help us persuade and influence others, and it can help us defend against others who are trying to talk us into doing things. We can see their moves, and build up our defence against them.

8. THREATENING

'Well, you have to'

As we saw in the previous chapters, persuasion is, of course, part of our everyday experience, and as the saying goes we *talk* people into doing things, and we are talked into doing things that we are perhaps reluctant to do. But when does persuading become threatening? This is of course a moral, and perhaps at times a legal, matter. From a language games perspective, threatening could be seen as a 'no holds barred' kind of bare knuckle fight. Getting your way counts and any relational concerns are subordinated to achieving a winning outcome. So, I cannot advise threatening as strategy in the language game, but it is interesting to see how threatening works as an extreme case of persuasion

In this chapter, we look at a classic example of threatening behaviour drawn from a conference call between Donald Trump and his team and Brad Raffensperger, the Secretary of State of Georgia, and his team. The call was made on 2nd January 2021, and was recorded and subsequently made publicly available on numerous media outlets. The gist of the call is that Trump is asking Raffensperger to recount the votes of the 2020 presidential election. In the transcript, Trump is quoted as saying 'I just want to find 11,780 votes.' This is the minimum number of votes that he needed to overcome Biden's election victory in Georgia. In what follows, we'll take a look at just one extract of the hour-long call, and consider how Trump tries to talk Raffensperger into 'finding' 11,780 Trump votes, in an effort to overturn the election result. The transcript of the call and the full audio recording that I am working from is taken from CNN's website.[1]

We start the analysis as Ryan Germany, a lawyer for the Georgia Secretary of State's office, responds to a claim, made by one of Trump's team, that the 'data' shows that there has been electoral fraud and that despite several requests, the Secretary of State's office for Georgia has not seriously considered this data and 'so it stands to reason that if the information is not forthcoming, there's something to hide'. Germany defends against this accusation by saying: 'That's not the case sir. There are things that you guys are entitled to get. And there's things that under the law, we are not allowed to give out.' After addressing Germany's refusal to provide the 'missing information' (line one: 'Well, you have to [give the information]'), Trump then shifts tack to try to persuade Raffensperger and his team to 'find' the missing votes.

[1] Available at: https://edition.cnn.com/2021/01/03/politics/trump-brad-raffen-sperger-phone-call-transcript/index.html

1. **Trump:** Well, you have to. Well, under the law you're not allowed to give faulty election
2. results, Okay? You're not allowed to do that. And that's what you done. This is a faulty
3. election result. And honestly, this should go very fast. You should meet tomorrow
4. because you have a big election coming up and because of what you've done to the
5. president ... you know, the people of Georgia know that this was a scam. And because of
6. what you've done to the president, a lot of people aren't going out to vote and a lot of
7. Republicans are going to vote negative because they hate what you did to the president.
8. Okay? They hate it. And they're going to vote. And you would be respected. Really
9. respected, if this thing could be straightened out before the election. You have a big
10. election coming up on Tuesday. And therefore I think that it is really important that you
11. meet tomorrow and work out these numbers. Because I know Brad that if you think
12. we're right, I think you're going to say, and I'm not looking to blame anybody. I'm just
13. saying you know, and, you know, under new counts, and under uh, new views, of the
14. election results, we won the election. You know? It's very simple. We won the election.
15. As the governors of major states and the surrounding states said, there is no way you lost
16. Georgia, as the Georgia politicians say, there is no way, you lost Georgia. Nobody.
17. Everyone knows I won it by hundreds of thousands of votes. But I'll tell you it's going to
18. have a big impact on Tuesday if you guys don't get this thing straightened out fast.

Authority* and Emotional* Pressure

The first move in Trump's game is to cite the law. As far as our analyses are concerned the issue is not whether Raffensperger is acting outside the law or not. Though I can point out that Trump's allegation that Raffensperger acted in some way illegally has been criticised. And many people have claimed that it was Trump, rather than Raffensperger, who acted outside the law. What interests us is to show how invoking the law constitutes a persuasive move in the language game. The law, an external and independent entity disassociated with Trump, is invoked by Trump to arbitrate on what Raffensperger should, or should not, do. Of course, when the law is invoked and when you do something that 'you're not [legally] allowed to do', such as giving 'faulty election results' as Trump argues Raffensperger has done, you have committed a criminal offence. So, threatening occurs when one party puts unethical pressure on the other: in this case an implied recourse to the law. It is significant here that Trump cites the law – he is not telling Raffensperger that he has done something wrong, the law is. So, by invoking the law, Trump is giving his words some kind of legitimacy and authority and at the same time he is distancing himself from the pressure he is putting on Raffensperger.

Furthermore, one way of persuading people to do something is to play on their fears, and the threat of ending up in a US prison is certainly a fear that would put pressure on most people. As we see in many other places in this book, playing with fears, real or imagined, is a key way of doing persuasion. It is also a key element of rhetoric* – the art of persuasion. The ancient Greeks called the emotional element of persuasion *pathos*. Such a move could be seen as emotional* blackmail. Something, of course, that is not to be condoned, but which can nevertheless be a move in the language game. So, be aware of people playing with your fears and piling emotional pressure on you.

Victim and Perpetrator Identities*

After making this veiled threat, Trump then introduces a second line of attack in his language game, i.e., the fact that there is an election coming up and the people of Georgia will vote negatively. First, Trump states that the reason why Raffensperger will lose votes is because of what he has 'done to the president'. This sets up a classic victim and perpetrator scenario. Raffensperger is the perpetrator, the villain of the story who has hurt the victim. The victim is the president, not Trump. Consequently, in this subtle move, the emphasis is on the president as institution, not Trump as ex-president who might have a personal axe to grind and reason for criticising Raffensperger. Further, this projection of the president as victim is made twice, so emphasising the gravity of the perpetrator's acts. It therefore adds to the emotional* pressure that Trump is piling on Raffensperger. Raffensperger has done something wrong, and the way to right the wrong is to do as Trump wishes. So, beware of people projecting guilt on you – always challenge it and be aware of what they may be trying to achieve through such a manipulation.

Giving Others Voice*

As this attacking move develops, Trump now instrumentalises the people of Georgia on whose behalf he speaks. What 'the people' of Georgia think is no doubt difficult to know with any certainty, but here their thoughts are mobilised to put pressure on Raffensperger. Giving voice* to the people of Georgia allows Trump to distance himself from this attempt at persuasion and to depersonalise the pressure he is putting on Raffensperger. According to Trump, the people of Georgia know the presidential election results were a scam and they, returning to the victim and perpetrator scenario, hate what Raffensperger did to the president. Consequently, they will 'vote negative' in the forthcoming senate elections which were due to be held three days after the telephone call. So, be wary of somebody who puts words into the mouths of others when they are trying to persuade you to do something. It's as if they're hiding behind these people, making an attack on you but obscuring that they are the real source of the attack.

Moreover, as Trump makes these claims, he slips in a 'you know'*. A 'you-know' claims common ground and, unless refuted, it recruits the interlocutor into your argument. Similarly, we notice that Trump punctuates his talk with 'okay', which even though he doesn't wait for alignment, projects agreement.

Problem Solution*

The line of argument* that the people of Georgia think the election was a scam, that they hate Raffensperger for his actions, and that they won't vote Republican in the upcoming elections is presented as a problem. Whether this problem exists or not is beside the point, but a key tactic in some language games is presenting the image of there being a problem, whether there is one or not, and then presenting a solution (for another example of this, see Chapter 7).

The solution is, according to Trump, getting the respect of the people of Georgia and the way of earning this respect is getting 'this thing' straightened out before the election. According to many commentators, what Trump is asking Raffensperger to do is alter the election results – which would constitute a crime. Yet, here the issue of what some see as committing electoral fraud is presented euphemistically as 'this thing'. Avoiding putting a precise label on what Trump wants Raffensperger to do makes it more acceptable and morally loose. Similarly, the choice of verb 'straighten out' not only suggests correcting something that is not right, but it is also fairly informal, so minimising the magnitude of what Trump is in fact asking Raffensperger to do. We 'straighten out' minor problems, not major constitutional crises. Similarly, all Raffensperger needs to do is 'work out these numbers', not falsify an election result. Thus word choice* serves to distract from the magnitude of the 'ask'.

Imagined Argument*

In lines 11 following, Trump shifts his line of attack. He sets up an imagined argument in which Raffensperger is going to say that he's right and the vote counting was correct and he counters this. In other words, he predicts the other's argument and pre-emptively deals with it. First, this counter argument is set up so as not to blame Raffensperger (line 12: 'I'm not looking to blame anybody'). Through not blaming his interlocutor Trump shows that he is generous in his judgement and that Raffensperger is not a blame-worthy or 'bad' person; anybody can get it wrong. This plays, to some extent, to the emotional* side of persuasion: 'you're a good person, and I'm a good person, I'm not going to blame you, it's just that your understanding is faulty'. Being a 'good person' by not blaming is persuasive since if you can persuade your interlocutor that they are dealing with a good person, then maybe they should be more amenable to your requests. Likeable* people are more able to persuade.

Trump minimises the extent that Raffensperger is 'wrong' by prefacing this new move with 'I'm just saying*. This makes the upcoming talk appear as if it is something simple and obvious, and therefore true, presented without guile, honestly and openly (always beware of someone who is 'just saying'). Further, Trump adds a couple of 'you knows' to what he is 'just saying' which, as I argued before, is a technique used to assume agreement. What Trump is 'just saying' is that 'under new counts, and under uh, new views, of the election results, we won the election'. He then not only adds to this claim, 'you know'*, again projecting Raffensperger's agreement, but he also adds that 'It's very simple.' This presents the request (arguably to commit electoral fraud) as a no-brainer to which any reasonable person would agree (beware of people euphemistically describing complex issues as simple!).

Giving Voice* to Others

Trump then returns to the technique of recruiting other people to validate what he says (line 15: 'As the governors of major states and the surrounding states said, there is no way you lost Georgia, as the Georgia politicians say, there is no way, you lost Georgia.'). Creating a consensus* is one way of increasing the authority* of what you say and therefore of making your talk more persuasive - if others believe it, why shouldn't I? Further, it is noticeable that the people who believe the line of argument that Trump won the election are authoritative figures, who should be believed. They are state governors and Georgia politicians. Further, this consensus is presented in exaggerated terms: 'Everyone knows I won it by hundreds of thousands of votes.' Perhaps in the cold light of day these exaggerations* can be seen for what they are – exaggerations. However, when slipped into the cut and thrust of argument they often pass unseen, but nevertheless they leave an impression of magnitude and are therefore persuasive.

Trump then ends his talk by re-emphasising his argument: 'It's going to have a big impact on Tuesday if you guys don't get this thing straightened out fast.' In this particular case, the persuasion did not work and Raffensperger did not 'find' the extra votes. But despite this failure, we can nevertheless see the strategies that Trump uses to play the game of persuasion. In fact, one could even say that the veiled threats of prison could amount to threatening behaviour, defined by the *Oxford Pocket Dictionary of Current English* as making "a statement of an intention to inflict pain, injury, damage, or other hostile action on someone in retribution for something done or not done". Whether Trump's talk goes beyond the bounds of persuasion to become threatening is for you to decide, and depends where one places the moral boundaries of talk. I underline here that I am not condoning aggressive persuasive techniques that may amount to bullying or threatening behaviour, but it is useful to be able to recognise this when it occurs.

To Sum Up

The difference between a threat and persuasion may be a moral rather than a linguistic argument. In this analysis, Trump uses similar techniques to attempt to win the game to those we see elsewhere. The key difference is perhaps the hint at some kind of retribution. In this case, the threat of prison puts emotional* pressure on Raffensperger and this could be considered unethical. Further, it is noticeable that a degree of distance from what could be perceived as a threat is enacted. It is the people of Georgia and elected politicians who are recruited by Trump to put pressure on Raffensperger. He makes them speak as a ventriloquist makes a dummy speak, and he deploys their voices to put pressure on Raffensperger. This allows what could be regarded as a threat to be made, but it allows Trump to distance himself from the pressure that he is piling on. It is not he who wants to 'find the votes'; it is the people of Georgia and other politicians. The threat is veiled, and therefore deniable.

9. NEGOTIATING

'You can't pretend to be my ally. You are only my enemy you, see'

In their best-selling book on negotiating, *Getting to Yes*, Roger Fisher, William Ury and Bruce Patton of Harvard University define negotiating as a 'back-and-forth communication designed to reach an agreement when you and the other side have some interests that are shared and others that are opposed'. So how do we play language games to reach agreement? *Getting to Yes* is a classic and excellent book on negotiating, but it uses anecdotes of made-up scenarios. It does not show real-life negotiation as it unfolds moment by moment.

Conversely, in this chapter, we'll look at the real-time language games of negotiators during a high stakes negotiation. More specifically, we'll look at police negotiators trying to get a terrorist to surrender peacefully. The dialogue we'll look at in this chapter dates back to 2012 when French police laid siege to an Islamic terrorist, Mohammed Merah, who was traced to his flat in Toulouse. Mohammed Merah was a Franco-Algerian who converted to Islam while in prison and then sought to join the *mujahidin* in various countries such as Syria, Afghanistan, and Algeria. Upon his return to France, acting apparently alone, in three separate incidents he murdered three off-duty French soldiers, and three Jewish children and an adult at a Jewish school on the grounds that they were enemies of Islam. Merah was then traced to his flat in a suburb of Toulouse and there was then a standoff which ended in a shootout and the death of Merah. Some of the negotiation between police and Merah was recorded and a full transcript of this recording was published in the *Libération*, a French daily newspaper[1]. Here, we're going to work from a translation of parts of this transcript.

So, how do you negotiate with an armed Islamic terrorist, who has already killed seven people and is now cornered in his apartment? How do you convince him to surrender peacefully? Since the siege ended in a shootout which left Merah dead and several police officers injured, the police negotiators ultimately failed to negotiate a peaceful conclusion. Nevertheless, their approach is interesting. Amongst other things, it relied on playing with their and Merah's identity*. We often think of identity is 'something' that is in us 'somewhere' (a true self) that drives our actions and words. However, if we look at the language games people play it's perhaps more profitable to see identity as a role that we're playing: an actor on the stage. We are, of course, called on to play many different roles (parent, teacher, friend, taxpayer, football fan, etc.). In short: identity, rather than being something we have, is something that we do or perform.

---

[1] Available at: http://www.liberation.fr/societe/2012/07/17/transcription-des-conversations-entre-mohamed-merah-et-les-negociateurs_833784

So, from this way of looking at things, we have numerous identities that we can adopt according to the situation. Each of these identities has certain rights and obligations, and expected behaviours and ways of being attached to them. One interpretation of the *jihad* is that it involves a fight against non-Muslims which may end in martyrdom. If this *mujahidin*/jihadist identity is either claimed by, or ascribed to, Merah it's difficult to see how the siege could end in anything other than a shootout. However, since identities are like roles that we play, if a different and more peaceful identity can be foisted on Merah, then a more peaceful outcome may be achievable. Yet, since language games are rarely monologues, it is not only Merah's identity that is the target of the police negotiators, the negotiators also try to minimise their identities as 'servants of the French state at war (against Islam) in Afghanistan' and play up their 'just a regular guy' identity. So, the question here in this negotiation is how to try to align identities so that an acceptable outcome to the siege is achieved by both parties.

Mujahidin Identity

Given the situation, the *mujahidin* identity is perhaps the most relevant identity that is in play. It is certainly the identity that Merah claims for himself, as we see in the talk below.

1. MM: I'm not afraid you see. The *mujahidins alhamdulillah*
2. (Arabic: praise be to God) those … those who sincerely believe in Allah and his
3. messenger who … who … who are sincere they are not afraid of death because
4. they know that. So, the agony of a of a martyr is the equivalent … it's like a
5. mosquito who bites us, you see. So, in relation to that I'm not afraid. So, after
6. reflection, I can't allow myself to surrender and to go to prison for the rest of my
7. life.

This brief extract shows that Merah claims to be *mujahidin*. As a *mujahidin*, he believes in Allah and consequently he is not afraid of death any more than a mosquito bite. The consequence of having this identity is that he cannot surrender and go to prison. The fight with the French security forces is a fight to the death and from this position no negotiation is possible. It is a zero sum game: I get what I want, and you lose. No common ground or a possibility of negotiation is offered. In order to create conditions favourable for finding a mutually acceptable solution (i.e., to get to 'yes'), the police negotiators start playing identity games.

Changing Identities from Mujahidin Fighter to Civilised Me

1. MM: Listen you are my enemy you see. We fight on the same side, you see.
2. We fight head to head to head, you see … gun in hand. So, one can't … you
3. can't pretend to be my ally. You are only my enemy, you see.
4. Pol: But, I don't ask, I've no pretensions of either becoming your friend or your
5. ally, only that we can talk. That's all. Like civilised men. We are what in 2012.
6. We are no longer in the time when the prophet, that God *alahyhi wa salam*
7. (Arabic: May Allah honour him and grant him peace) who when he was a
8. warrior when there were the Koreishi, the Habaches when people, so it was, it
9. was the era of the warriors. We are in 2012. We can discuss without necessarily
10. having a go at each other; Do you understand that?
11. MM: But at the time of the prophet *wa salan,* they also talked. You, the RAID[2], the
12. police, the gendarmes, the soldiers, whether from France or America and allied
13. countries you fight to install your democracy. Why wouldn't we have
14. the right to an Islamic State?

In the first lines of this extract, Merah persists with his *mujahidin* identity which casts himself and the police negotiator as enemies

---

[2] RAID is the acronym given to an elite police unit that deals with hostage and terrorist situations.

destined to fight it out. The negotiator attempts to change these identities by projecting the identities of civilised men on both of them. If they are both civilised men, then they can talk and discuss without 'having a go at each other'. They are not in the warring times of the Prophet. However, identities, the roles we're playing in language games are always negotiable. They are never fixed. We can claim them, and they can be projected onto us, but they can also be rejected. In this case, Merah displays his understanding of this identity work by rejecting it and in his following talk he persists with his identification of the negotiator, the RAID, the police, the gendarmes, and the soldiers as being his enemies. With police and *mujahidin* identities in place, the outcome can only be bloody, and no agreement can be reached.

Muslim Identity

Another identity that the negotiator attempts to employ is that of 'good' Muslim.

1. Pol: Good, okay, so we'll say that the hajj ... the jihad for you is done. So
2.   you've already done an action. And what about the the hajj? Are you going to do it
3.   *insha'Allah* or not? I hope you do.
4. MM: I don't know, *insha'Allah*.
5. Pol: Yeah you've already done the first stage, so got to go on to the second stage,
6.   the hajj. When you get out.
7. MM: But when I get out, you think so? I will still fight

A Muslim identity, of course, doesn't necessarily equate to taking up arms to defend Islam. The *jihad* can also be interpreted as taking any action that makes personal and social life conform with God's guidance. An obligation for Muslims is the *hajj*, which is a peaceful pilgrimage to Mecca that demonstrates the solidarity of Muslims and their submission to the will of Allah. In this extract, the police negotiator suggests that Merah should do the *hajj*. By shifting talk to the fulfilment of the *hajj*, away from the *jihad*, the negotiator therefore projects a peaceful Muslim identity onto Merah. This could make a peaceful end to the siege possible. However, this peaceful Muslim identity is rejected.

The Negotiator as Muslim

1. Pol: No, I was speaking as a Muslim, you and me. You know, I have a mother
2. you also have a mother and mothers always care about their children and about
3. their actions, you must understand, it's like that I mean between I'm
4. speaking Muslim to Muslim okay.
5. MM: What, you say Muslim?
6. Pol: In your opinion, I'm what? I'm a Muslim. Because of you I've not done, well, I
7. I have not even had time to … and you, have you prayed or not?

In this part of the negotiation, the police negotiator tries to shift the identities in play to a Muslim-Muslim identity (line 1: 'I was speaking as a Muslim you and me'). Speaking as Muslim to Muslim, rather than as police officer to terrorist may put identities into play that will create common ground and a space for agreement. In the same exchange, the negotiator also brings into play the identities of son and mother which implies that Merah has a filial responsibility not to get himself killed in a firefight with police. This Muslim-Muslim identity and that of a mother-son identity are identities that, if accepted, could lead to a peaceful solution.

The Regular Non-political Guy

Essential to reaching an agreement is not only to change the *muja-hidin* identity, but also the 'police' identity which by extension is an identity that represents the French state which, in 2012, had troops in Afghanistan and could therefore be seen to be active in the fight against radical Islam.

1. Pol: Me, I don't ask that kind of question. Me, I'm from Toulouse. I live my life, I do
2.   my job, my graft, as well, as well as I can, but after, well the geo-strategic
3.   questions, what happens there ... I have other worries, family, professional, so
4.   me, I don't ask myself that kind of question, personally.
5. MM: So, why do you do this job?
6. Pol: I do this job because I like it, I like this job, I like this region. But well, I don't
7.   think about Afghanistan, I'm not, it's not my role. You understand what I
8.   want to say? I'm not involved, I'm not a soldier. I'm not involved there, so,
9.   I don't ask myself that kind of question. Everyone, everyone has their job. Me,
10.   my job is here. What they do there, well, listen ... me, I don't think about it
11.   personally.

In the prior talk, Merah has been talking about the war in Afghanistan. The negotiator replies that he's not interested in geo-politics. He's a local man from Toulouse who has his family and does his job – no more, no less. As such he is not the enemy, and with such a non-belligerent identity in place, there is a potential for finding room for agreement. Merah does not go along with this projected identity and he asks: 'So, why do you do this job?' The claim only partially works – is it reasonable for somebody who works for the counter-terrorism branch of the French security forces not to be interested in geo-politics? Thus even though identities are claimed, they still have to be negotiated and accepted; the parties to the negotiation have to be in agreement. So, in this case, the negotiator has to work harder to establish his credentials. He does so by repeating that he does the job just because he 'likes it' and he doesn't think about Afghanistan. Moreover, he directly distances himself from a military identity (line 8: 'I'm not a soldier'). Remember, Merah deliberately targeted soldiers, so a military identity would not be conducive to finding a peaceful solution.

To Sum Up

While we're probably never going to be police negotiators, and while there are no doubt other more common forms of negotiating in which we're thinking about price margins and so on, it's nevertheless interesting to see how professional negotiators try to play different roles in order to achieve their aims. Different identities have different rights and responsibilities and so playing with these identities can lead to different outcomes. In this case, police and terrorist identities led to a bloody end to the siege. But, we can also see that the negotiator was working hard to replace police/terrorist identities with more peaceful identities that may have opened the door to a peaceful solution. So, playing games with identities can be a negotiating tool.

10. BEING A GOOD PERSON

'Me, I am a normal citizen'

Whatever situation we find ourselves in, we always have a tendency to pass ourselves off as good people. In this chapter, we take a look at how people present themselves as being 'good' even in the most trying of circumstances. More specifically, we look at the speech of Christophe Dettinger, which I've translated from the original French. Dettinger, a former boxing champion, was arrested and imprisoned for assaulting police officers, allegedly kicking one who was on the ground, during the 'yellow vest' demonstrations in Paris, in 2019[1]. The incident was widely reported in the media and Dettinger was identified. Before handing himself in to the police, he made a video recording, posted on Facebook, in which he justified his acts and presented himself as 'a good person'[2]. To some extent coming across as a good person

---

[1] The yellow vest movement is the name given to the protesters who wore yellow high-visibility vests as a symbol of their anti-establishment protests which swept through France from late 2018 until late 2019.

[2] Available at: https://www.youtube.com/watch?v=I2VYIKersd4

is an element in many language games, but this particular extract is interesting because the *raison d'être* of the Facebook post is to justify his actions and cast himself as a good person.

As we saw in the previous chapter, we have multiple identities such as wife, father, colleague, friend, Brit, foreigner, old person, cyclist, dog-lover, teacher, and so on. These identities may be more or less relevant depending on the situation and they can be played up or played down. We may claim identities for ourselves, or they may be attributed to us. They can be politicised: one man's freedom fighter is another man's terrorist. Having an identity* when playing language games is more like an actor acting out a particular role, and less like a 'psychological' identity that we have inside us somewhere, our true self, coming out. These identities can be more, or less, consciously acted out. But regardless of the extent to which the speaker is intentionally manipulating the role that he/she is playing, identities are nevertheless an important part of the language games we play.

In this chapter, we'll see how Dettinger uses the victim-perpetrator identities* to justify his (violent) actions. These identities do not necessarily represent the facts* of the matter. No doubt, just as Dettinger presents himself as a victim, the police could equally depict themselves as victims of an aggressive, violent, and dangerous protester. So, without seeking to pass judgement on who's the victim and who's the perpetrator (I wasn't there, so how could I know?), let's see how Dettinger crafts his talk so as to cast himself as the victim and so justify his actions. In this version of events, despite attacking the police, he is still a good person.

1. Dear yellow vest friends, I'm Christophe Dettinger. It's me who confronted the
2. CRS[3] on Saturday 5th January. I wanted to set the record straight. I participated in the
3. eight acts[4]. The first act, I blocked the main road near to my place. I have attended all the
4. Saturday demonstrations in Paris. I **saw** the repression that happened. I **saw** the police use
5. gas. I **saw** the police hurting people with flash balls[5]. I **saw** injured people. I saw
6. pensioners being gassed[6]. I saw loads of things. Me, I am a normal citizen. I work and
7. get to the end of the month, but it's difficult. But I demonstrate for all the pensioners, the
8. future of my children, single women, everybody. I am a yellow vest … I am a yellow
9. vest. I have the anger of the people in me. I see all those presidents, I see all those
10. ministers, I see all the state getting fat and ripping us off. They are not even able to set an
11. example. They don't give us an example. They get fat on our backs. It's always us the
12. little people who pay. Me when I hear the poor, I feel concerned because I am French and
13. proud of it. I am not from the extreme left. I am not from the extreme right. I am a citizen
14. (unclear word). I am French. I love my country. I love my homeland. I love everything.
15. It's sure that because of being hit, being hit, being hit, but yes I was gassed these last
16. few days. Yes, I wanted to advance on the CRS. I was gassed with my friend, my wife. I
17. was gassed and after a while the rage increases and me, yes, I reacted badly. Yes, I
18. reacted badly, but I defended myself. I wanted to tell you that. I'll give myself up
19. tomorrow morning. I'll hand myself in if they haven't nabbed me before.

Who Am I, Who Am I Speaking to, and What Do I Want to Achieve?

First, Dettinger makes it clear who his audience* is and what he intends to achieve. His audience are fellow yellow vests, and the

[3] CRS is the abbreviation used for the Compagnies Républicaines de Sécurité – basically the French riot police.

[4] Acts were the name given to their weekly protest. These acts were numbered.

[5] Flash balls are a type of rubber bullet, widely used by the police. Their use was controversial on account of the number of injuries they caused.

[6] The CRS make extensive use of CS gas during the demonstrations.

purpose of the video is that he wants to set the record straight and give his version of events. To do this, he first establishes his credentials as a yellow vest who attended all the demonstrations. The claim that he is a yellow vest therefore protects him against any possible accusation that he was just there for the adrenaline, or that he is a violent anarchist who takes every opportunity to attack the police. He thus shows an awareness that his talk is not only about building up his good character (his ethos*), but it is also about predicting counter-arguments and building in a defence against these arguments* (defensive rhetoric*).

During these demonstrations he saw: repression; police using (tear) gas; the police hurting people with flash balls; injured people; and pensioners being (tear) gassed. The repetition emphasises the magnitude of the repression and the repeated word stress* on 'saw' emphasises his first-hand experience of events. He knows this for sure, because he was there as an eye-witness.

Depending on the situation, this can be a good way to start a 'speech'. Establish your credentials as somebody who is 'authorised' to speak and who is a 'good' person, define your audience* (what is it they want to hear), and give some kind of indication of what you want to achieve, what your message is. Interestingly, Dettinger's opening is very similar to that of the academic presentation discussed in chapter 15.

Victims and Perpetrators

Victims and perpetrator identities* are two key identities that are often used when trying to come across as a good person. In this case, the police are cast as perpetrators of violence, and as we'll see resistance against such violence is normalised. This is because he is a normal citizen, who is working but having difficulty to make ends meet. This mister-normal identity* is a caricature of one of the stereotypes of the 'yellow vest' identity, or indeed any protester identity, i.e., the normal, reasonable person who has been pushed too far.

Moreover, despite this situation, he is not demonstrating for personal gain. He is a 'good person' because, using the rule of three*, he's protesting for: pensioners, children, and single women. These are weak people who need protecting. Dettinger therefore almost becomes the modern-day knight in shining armour, protecting the weak (victims) against the overbearing and strong (perpetrators). However, this knight in shining armour is in the modern guise of a yellow vest who has the anger of the people in him. Dettinger, therefore, now gives voice* to the people who are angry.

Identity* of a French Citizen

This anger is directed against the perpetrators who are those presidents and ministers and the state who are 'getting fat and ripping us off' and getting fat 'on our backs it's always us the little people who pay'. Dettinger thus identifies with the 'us', the little people (victims) who are ripped off by the fat cats (perpetrators). When Dettinger hears the poor, he is concerned, and therefore acts against the perpetrators. This is because he is French, and therefore he taps into the historic revolutionary ideology* that inspired the French Revolution of the people against a corrupt and unfair state. He states that he is neither from the extreme left, nor from the extreme right and so pre-empts any accusation that he is politically motivated. Rather these actions are because he is a French citizen who loves his country, his homeland, and everything. To emphasise this, he uses the rule of three* and a repetition* of 'I love'. While the third element in the list is extremely vague* ('love everything') and, when analysed, a little nonsensical, it does perhaps draw attention to the power of the rule of three which is employed even if one of the elements is vague (line 14: 'I am French. I love my country. I love my homeland. I love everything').

Further, the word 'citizen' is not innocent. France is a republic and so while the citizen has certain rights and duties, so does the government. Amongst other things, the government is supposed to rule on behalf of the people, not against their will. Therefore, it is the government fat cats who are in the wrong, not the people whose anger is justified. Dettinger merely acts to rectify the situation.

Narrating the Events

Dettinger then shifts to narrating* the actual events. Is his description of events factual and 'true'? Who knows? I certainly don't. I wasn't there. If you're interested you can see video footage of the event[7] and judge for yourself. What interests us is not the truth or untruth, it is how he crafts his side of the story so that it achieves his objective and he comes across as a 'good' person and his violent actions are justified.

In Dettinger's version of events, he 'was being hit and gassed'. The passive* construction is used to project his passivity and the others' (the police's) agency in the events. He wanted to advance on the CRS. The choice of word is significant: to advance on is not the same as to attack, assault, hit etc. His choice of words therefore minimises the 'attack'. The fact that he was gassed led to an increase in his rage. Here it is significant that he used the expression 'after a while'. So, at first he controlled himself, it was only after repeated actions by the police that he reacted badly. This again stresses his

---

[7] Available at: https://www.youtube.com/watch?v=S9i-ErSMOQo

normality: any reasonable person may have acted in the same way 'after a while'. Further, the choice of the expression 'reacted badly' underplays the assault in which he is seen repeatedly punching the CRS. His actions are then described as defending himself, which again underplays the punches that were thrown and makes his actions look less aggressive and more reasonable than they may have been. In short, he is a reasonable and good person, defending the people and himself (the victims) from the CRS and the fat cats (the perpetrators of the violence). Any reasonable person may have done this. He ends the video by again aligning with the people and exhorting them to continue the combat peacefully. This, once again, underlies his good and non-violent character.

To Sum Up

In sum, Dettinger neatly positions himself as a good person. He is defending the victims, the weak, against the violent police and the state which consists of self-serving fat cats. Playing with victim and perpetrator identities* is a fairly simple, yet effective technique, in language games. In this case, making yourself appear to be the victim makes you appear to be the good guy, whereas the perpetrator is the bad guy. As I'm writing, the Harry and Meghan saga is raging back and forth. A key strategy in Harry's language games (his book, press interviews, use of social media etc.) is obviously the crafting of his victim identity. But, victim- perpetrator identities are not only limited to justifying your position in, albeit high profile, domestic rows. At a geopolitical level, Putin justifies his war/the special military operation (select whichever choice of words suits you) on the grounds that Russia is the victim of NATO threats. So, watch out for the victim and perpetrator identity, it's pervasive and can be played up and played down in order to 'win' the game.

11. REMEMBERING

'I have no recollection of ever meeting this lady, none whatsoever'

We often understand the way we deal with our memories by drawing on the metaphor of an archive. In other words, we stock memories of events in a kind of mental archive which is later available to us. Of course, over time, the documents in this archive fade away, especially if they are not that memorable. I can remember that I bought a particular brand of beer from the supermarket yesterday, but I'd be unable to tell you what brand of beer I bought from the supermarket on 8th September 2022 – the day Queen Elizabeth II died. Such unmemorable events are simply not retained in the archive. On the other hand, memorable events may indeed be retained for longer. You might remember where you were when you heard the news that John Lennon had been shot, the Twin Towers had been attacked, or Queen Elizabeth II had died.

But memories are not just stored and reproduced on demand. For various reasons, we may lie about what happened and build false accounts of past events, as no doubt many people in the witness box do. Similarly, we may wish to paint a slightly different story of events by playing up certain aspects of our memories and playing down others. We may rework our memories of events to make ourselves look more impressive than we actually were, or to come across as being more believable, or to gloss over weakness. Thus memories, what we can and cannot remember, can become an essential part of the language games we play. The rules of the game here are governed by what we are reasonably expected to remember. I may not be expected to know which brand of beer I bought on 8th September 2022, but I may be expected to know where I was when news of the death of Queen Elizabeth II was announced. And if I want my memories of a particular event to come off as truthful and accurate representations of those events, I may have to play the game by building up these memories so they appear accurate and truthful to others.

In order to investigate how memories are used in language games, let's consider the (infamous) interview between the journalist Emily Maitlis and Prince Andrew which was broadcast by the BBC in November 2019[1]. The interview focused on the prince's relationship with the convicted sex offender Jeffrey Epstein and his friend Ghislaine Maxwell, and allegations that the prince had had sex with Virginia Roberts, an alleged victim of sex trafficking. The interview was widely regarded as a disaster and portrayed an image of a 'guilty' man reaching for straws to try to stave off allegations of wrongdoing. The purpose of this analysis is not to comment on the truth or otherwise of Prince Andrew's account – only Prince Andrew and Roberts know what actually happened

---

[1] Available at : https://www.youtube.com/watch?v=AKQi3wzNFGQ

between them with any certitude. Rather, my purpose here is to slow the interview down, to analyse it utterance by utterance and to try to catch what we don't notice in the heat of the action in a somewhat confrontational news interview. I specifically focus on the way in which Andrew and the interviewer, Emily Maitlis, strategically deploy notions of what should, could, and is remembered as they play their language games. To do this, I'll present two extracts. Both extracts show, on the one hand, how Prince Andrew uses what should, and should not, be remembered to 'defend his corner' and, on the other hand, how Maitlis builds her, somewhat aggressive, questioning around the same theme.

Extract One

1.	PA:	I have no recollection of ever meeting this lady, none whatsoever.
2.	EM:	You don't remember meeting her?
3.	PA:	No.
4.	EM:	She says she met you in 2001, she dined with you, she danced with you, you
5.		bought her drinks, you were in Tramp Nightclub in London and she went on to
6.		have sex with you in a house in Belgravia belonging to Ghislaine Maxwell.
7.	PA:	It didn't happen.
8.	EM:	Do you remember her?
9.	PA:	No, I've no recollection of ever meeting her, I'm almost, in fact I'm convinced that
10.		I was never in Tramp with her. There are a number of things that are wrong with
11.		that story, one of which is that I don't know where the bar is in Tramp. I don't
12.		drink. I don't think I've ever bought a drink in Tramp whenever I was there.
13.	EM:	Do you remember dancing at Tramp?
14.	PA:	No, that couldn't have happened because the date that's being suggested I was at
15.		home with the children.
16.	EM:	You know that you were at home with the children, was it a memorable night?
17.	PA:	On that particular day that we now understand is the date which is the 10th of
18.		March, I was at home, I was with the children and I'd taken Beatrice to a Pizza
19.		Express in Woking for a party at I suppose sort of 4 or 5 in the afternoon.
20.		And then because the duchess was away, we have a simple rule in the family that
21.		when one is away the other one is there. I was on terminal leave at the time from
22.		the Royal Navy so therefore I was at home.
23.	EM:	Why would you remember that so specifically? Why would you remember a Pizza
24.		Express birthday and being at home?
25.	PA:	Because going to Pizza Express in Woking is an unusual thing for me to do, a very
26.		unusual thing for me to do. I've never been … I've only been to Woking a couple
27.		of times and I remember it weirdly distinctly. As soon as somebody reminded me
28.		of it, I went, 'Oh yes, I remember that.' But I have no recollection of ever meeting
29.		or being in the company or the presence.

Questions* and Answers

In the build-up to the question in line one, Maitlis has mentioned Virginia Roberts and her allegations, specifically in relation to a meeting with Prince Andrew in Tramp nightclub in 2001. In response to this Prince Andrew states 'I have no recollection of ever meeting this lady, none whatsoever.' Andrew thus deploys his memory* to fend off any allegations of wrongdoing. This is completed with the booster*, 'none whatsoever', which adds strength to the rebuttal.

Maitlis is obviously not going to let Andrew off the hook so easily and, by asking a second question*, she shows that she considers his answer to be insufficient. The second question (line 2: 'You don't remember meeting her?') serves to force Andrew into an either a 'yes' or a 'no' answer. Again, Andrew denies meeting Roberts (line 3: 'No'). It is at this point that Maitlis confronts him with Roberts's versions of events in which she says that she met Andrew in 2001 at Tramp. She dined and danced with Andrew, and he bought her drinks. They then went on to have sex in a house in Belgravia belonging to Ghislaine Maxwell. The meeting is presented in a simple narrative* form, as a chronology of events which ends in a sexual encounter. It is not downplayed in any way by verbs such as she remembers, she claims, she thinks, she alleges and so on. Rather the stark chronological presentation gives this version of events a veneer of fact. Presented like this, either Prince Andrew or Roberts is lying, or at least one of them has a faulty memory of events. This narrative of events is met by Andrew's flat denial: 'It didn't happen.'

A Further Question

Once more, Maitlis refuses to accept this as a sufficient account of events and asks 'Do you remember her?' This elicits a negative reply from Andrew ('No') who states that he has no recollection of meeting her. Moreover, he boosts this account by saying he is 'convinced' that he was never in Tramp with her. However, the fact that he is convinced comes after the adverb I'm 'almost'. Consequently, it can be understood as a correction from almost sure or whatever, to 'in fact convinced'. So, a tiny element displaying a lack of certainty creeps in. Is Andrew sure of his account? Sure, other issues, such as the fact that he had difficulty explaining a photo of him with Roberts, were perhaps more decisive, but nevertheless the accumulation of small, hardly perceptible, but significant 'errors' in the way he played the game may also have led to the impression that the interview was a disastrous public relations exercise. A convincing account of past events should be free of 'little' slips that may open it up to question.

After this denial, Andrew then adds that a number of details* in Robert's account are wrong: he doesn't know where the bar in Tramp is; he doesn't drink; and he's never bought a drink in Tramp. Here however, he says 'I don't think I've ever bought a drink'. Here, again through the use of 'I think', a lack of certainly is allowed to develop. This may be an honest account, or it may be designed to allow some wriggle room*: you can be mistaken in your recollection of an event and this lack of certainty can be exploited should you later be proved wrong. However, from another perspective, this production of wriggle room can also be seen as building in a defence should your account later be contested. Of course, the card then played is: 'I honestly' thought that was the case, but memories of events can be faulty. Wriggle room is thus a way of reducing the certainty of an account to allow for changing it at a later date should your version of events be challenged.

Maitlis, unsatisfied with this reply, attacks again. In line 13, she asks: 'Do you remember dancing at Tramp?' Andrew again denies dancing, but he also adds to his denial a reason that accounts* for the, in his opinion, falseness of Roberts' accounts. Andrew says that it 'couldn't have happened because the date that's being suggested I was at home with the children'. So a distinct memory of an event, 18 years prior to the interview, is used to dispel the accusations. However, the question that arises is: how does Andrew have such a specific memory of an event that occurred 18 years previously and which conveniently, if believed, would get him off the hook?

Making an Event Memorable

Maitlis picks up on this and asks if it was a memorable night? If it was memorable, then having a memory of it 18 years later could be believable. If the event was not memorable, Andrew's version of events could be undermined, making it appear to be a fabrication to provide a convenient alibi. Faced with this challenge, Andrew has to turn that date into a memorable event. To do this he adds detail* to his account, notably: the time, the location, and the name of the restaurant. The more detailed an account, the more believable it becomes (for more on this, see Chapter 13). The day was memorable because he took Beatrice to a Pizza Express in Woking for a party. Moreover, the fact that he was at home on that date is presented as following a rule that when one of the parents is away the other one is there. Invoking a 'rule' suggests that being at home was normal and uneventful and therefore his account of being at home is not designed to fend off a troublesome allegation. However, as before, there is a certain vagueness* surrounding some of the account, notably the timing which he 'supposes' was 'sort of' four or five in the afternoon. This, as before, could leave some wriggle room if he is later proved wrong, but nevertheless such vagueness also suggests a lack of certainty and so a lack of believability.

This reply is still inadequate for Maitlis, and she asks a further question: 'Why would you remember that so specifically?' She thus shows that, as far as she is concerned, going to Pizza Express is not a memorable enough event to justifying remembering exactly where he was on 10th March 2001. Who indeed would remember going to a pizza restaurant with their kids on an exact date 18 years prior to an interview? Andrew accounts for this because it is 'unusual': an unusual event is a memorable event. To make this assertion more convincing, he uses a reconstructed dialogue*: 'As soon as somebody reminded me of it, I went, 'Oh yes, I remember that.' The use of the exact words builds a theatrical element to his talk, acting out the event, thus making it more vivid and believable.

However, he says he remembers this event 'weirdly distinctly'. He recognises the unsualness of remembering such an event so distinctly. This again hints at a lack of credibility*. There is a further glitch in his account (line 26) when he begins a sentence 'I've never been'. Given the surrounding text, this projects 'I've never been to Woking', but this is corrected to 'I've only been to Woking a couple of times.' But despite the correction, the damage is done and this 'slip of the tongue' hints at the possible untruth of his account. Andrew then concludes his account by answering Maitlis's question: 'I have no recollection of ever meeting or being in the company or the presence [of Virginia Roberts]'.

Extract Two

Later in the interview, Maitlis says: 'for the record, is there any way you could have had sex with that young woman or any young woman trafficked by Jeffrey Epstein in any of his residences?' Andrew answers this by again denying having had sex with Roberts, but again he defends himself against this allegation in terms of memory and what one can be expected to remember.

1.	PA:	No and without putting too fine a point on it, if you're a man it is a positive act to
2.		have sex with somebody. You have to have to take some sort of positive action
3.		and so therefore if you try to forget … it's very difficult to try and forget a positive
4.		action and I do not remember anything. I can't, I've wracked my brain and thinking
5.		oh. When the first allegations, when the allegations came out originally I went
6.		well that's a bit strange, I don't remember this and then I've been through it and
7.		through it and through it over and over and over again and no, nothing. It just
8.		never happened.

Common Knowledge* and Memory*

The, somewhat sexist, reasoning behind Andrew's reply goes as follows: it's a 'positive' action for a man to have sex with a woman; it's difficult to forget positive actions; therefore he, as a man, doesn't remember anything because he didn't take any positive action, i.e., have sex with Roberts. If he had taken positive action (i.e., had sex with Roberts) he would have remembered it, and presumably would have admitted it to Maitlis. A strong argument has logic* to it. I'm not saying here that the 'logic' that Andrew uses is strong, but, in order to give his argument some kind of logical appeal, Andrew makes it appear common knowledge (if you're a man) and that because this is a man-thing, it is widespread and believable. This reasoning is not qualified or downgraded* in any way. There are no 'supposes', 'I thinks', or 'maybes'. This sets up his words as uncontested 'fact'* – what any person should know.

Internal Dialogue

Moreover, when the allegation came out, he wracked his brain and reports what he was thinking. These thoughts are presented as a kind of internal dialogue. This has the same effect as an episode of reported speech, or reconstructed dialogue*. It's a kind of staged presentation of what he said to himself which is designed to make this version of events more believable. Not unsurprisingly, Andrew, talking out loud to Andrew, downplays the allegation, which is presented as being 'just a bit strange'. It is a kind of puzzle looking for an explanation. If he had had sex with Roberts, he would remember it. Since he can't remember, he didn't have sex with Roberts and it's strange that she would make such a claim. Presumably, following this logic, if he could remember, he would 'fess up'. Further, his lack of memory is underlined because he can't remember even though he's wracked his brains, and he's been 'through it and through it and through it over and over and over again and no, nothing'. The repetition* here emphasises his point and he arrives at the logical conclusion: 'It just never happened.'

To Sum Up

In sum, since only Andrew and Roberts can be sure of what actually happened, the way they articulate their memories of events and how they account for these memories becomes a key element in the language game (the news interview) that Maitlis and Andrew are playing. Remembering and forgetting can require carefully crafted accounts. In this way, memory is not seen as a kind of archive in which one requests a particular memory and if it is there it 'just pops up' in an unaltered way. Rather, memory is brought into the game as a strategy. What can Andrew be reasonably expected to remember and how does this strengthen or undermine his version of events? As we've seen, memories can be built up, played down or made more believable through the use of several techniques such as providing details*, using reported speech, and appealing to what everyone knows. However, as elements in a game, their credibility can also be weakened and an element of doubt can be introduced if there is a lack of certainty in the memory expressed through the use of phrases such as 'I suppose', 'I think', and so on. Though, on the other hand, a certain vagueness can provide wriggle room and plausible deniability should counter evidence be provided. Also, if the memory is so mundane and normally unmemorable, the fact that someone remembers and uses it to sustain his or her version of events becomes suspect.

Further, we can see that in the particular language game being played here, that of the news interview, it is obviously the journalist who asks the questions. The interviewee is constrained to answer these questions, after which the journalist can either ask another question or evaluate the interviewee's reply (for more on this, see Chapter 6). If, as in this case, the journalist is unsatisfied with the reply, he/she can continue the questioning. In the case of the interview with Andrew, this is exactly what Maitlis does. She does not get the answers that she's looking for and so she relentlessly continues her line of questioning, casting doubt on Andrew's responses. To take a metaphor from boxing, she has Andrew on the ropes and is not letting go, she lands punch after punch, which he seeks to block as best he can. Andrew is unable to get himself out of the corner. Indeed, he could only do so by refusing to answer any more questions, or walking out. However, either of these options would have amounted to throwing in the towel and admitting 'defeat'. Perhaps, the best course of action would have been to avoid the interview. Don't take part in language games that you know you can't win, especially those where the rules of the game* (who asks and answers questions) are stacked against you.

12. TALKING HISTORY

'We didn't change history, we rectified history'

In the previous chapter we considered how Prince Andrew used his memory* to fend off accusations of sexual impropriety. Memories are not only individual, they are also collective: what we (choose to, or are allowed to) remember about our past. These memories often focus on what the French historian Pierre Nora (b. 1931) calls *lieux de memoire* (places of memory). Places of memory can, amongst other things, be statues or memorials that remind us of the past. But as we saw in the previous chapter, memories of the past are created in the language games being played in the present. Indeed history* can be seen as a 'collective memory' - what we choose to or are allowed to remember of the past. Thus history, collective memory, and 'places of memory' collide and they may become battlegrounds. What is it we choose to remember, and what is it we choose to forget of our past?

This, of course, is the essence of history, which can be seen as a grand narrative* or an over-arching story that explains what happened in the past. It also gives the past relevance to us in the present. These grand narratives are not only found in the history books, they are also talked into being, enacted and performed in and through talk in various circumstances.

The particular grand narrative that we focus on in this chapter is that of racial equality, slavery, and colonialism. Simplifying the arguments* and reducing them to their core components, on the one hand, there is a perhaps dying narrative, that empire and colonialism were good and that they brought enlightenment and civilisation to the world. On the other hand, there is an emerging narrative that re-writes the history of colonialism as one of greed, conquest, racism, exploitation, and slavery.

I stress that I'm trying to take a stance that is as neutral as possible as regards these two highly emotive grand narratives. My aim is not to take sides, but rather to analyse how these narratives are brought about by talk. It is important to note that the 'facts'* or historical reality cannot be changed – what happened, happened. The battleground is in the present as people look back on history and fight about how to interpret the past, what to remember and what to forget. In this sense the historical battle lines are drawn up in the present as people talk, and write, about history.

We can even modify the common understanding of history as being about the past. Elliot Mishler (1924-2018), an eminent American social psychologist with an interest in narrative analysis, coined the term the 'double arrow of time'. This is to say that time* doesn't only progress form the past to the present, but the present looks back on the past and 'judges' it. So, figuratively, we have a double arrow of time: one arrow pointing back from the present to the past, and the other pointing forward from the past to the present.

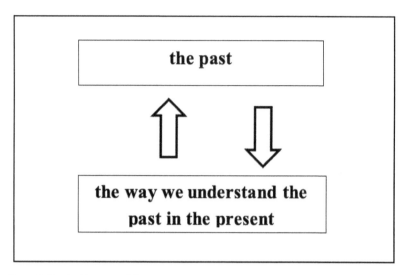

Figure 9: The double arrow of time

In this chapter we focus on the talk of Sage Willoughby, who was one of the so-called Colston Four. The others were: Rhian Graham, Milo Ponsford, and Jake Skuse. In June 2020, at a time when the Black Lives Matter movement was gaining momentum, the four were part of a crowd that pulled down, and threw into the river Avon, a statue of a 17th Century slave trader, Edward Colston. The four were arrested on charges of criminal damage, but, in January 2022, they were acquitted. We look at a short transcript taken from news coverage of their victory speech on the steps of Bristol Crown Court after their acquittal.

1.	Journalist:	Rhian what do you say to people who say you can't change history and
2.		these monuments are part of history and they should not be pulled down?
3.	SW:	We didn't change history. They were whitewashing history by calling him
4.		a fucking virtuous man. Sorry to swear. We didn't change history we
5.		rectified history.
6.	Public:	(cheers and applause)
7.	SW:	This is a victory for Bristol, this is a victory for racial equality and it's a
8.		victory for anyone who wants to be on the right side of history. Thank you
9.		everyone you're all amazing.
10.	Public:	(cheers and applause)

History as fixed

The journalist, addressing Rhian, one of the Colston Four, asks the question: 'What do you say to people who say you can't change history and these monuments are part of history and they should not be pulled down?' Giving voice* to, and putting words into the mouths of vague* 'people', the journalist retains his neutrality, but at the same time the question* suggests that history* is something fixed and immutable. The past is the past. However, such a proposition ignores the fact that history, or rather the way we consider the past, what we remember, how we remember it, and what we forget, is something we do in the present through our talk, text, and actions.

Rectifying History

In this case, Sage Willoughby immediately takes the floor and answers the question: 'We didn't change history they were whitewashing history by calling him a fucking virtuous man. Sorry to swear*. We didn't change history we rectified history.' The use of 'we' is ambiguous and slippery. Here, the pronoun* could refer to the Colston Four, for whom Sage Willoughby is acting as a spokesperson, or it could be all the supporters who form the audience*, or, more vaguely, it could be anybody who shares the same ideas as the Colston Four. It is this 'we' that didn't change history, they rectified it.

Sage Willoughby thus puts his finger on the way in which history is disputed in the present. History, or rather the way we consider the past, is mutable. According to Sage Willoughby, 'they were whitewashing history by calling him [Colston] a fucking virtuous man'. Who constitutes the 'they' is ambiguous, but their actions are clear. Sage Willoughby, knowingly or unknowingly, thus links his talk to the plaque that was on the statute's original plinth, which read: 'Erected by citizens of Bristol as a memorial of one of the most *virtuous* and wise sons of their city, AD 1895.' In a way, Willoughby's talk, therefore, stretches beyond the immediacy of the present. This in technical terms is called intertextuality*. In other words talk is sometimes built on, or refers, explicitly and implicitly, to other past texts which are weaved into the argument. Talk always comes from somewhere. It is built on what other people have said and done or are saying and doing. It is this linking of our talk with other talk and text that allows us to manage history in the present.

These words are met with applause* from the audience who clap and cheer. Willoughby then continues his victory speech: 'This is a victory for Bristol, this is a victory for racial equality and it's a victory for anyone who wants to be on the right side of history.' In this way, using the rule of three*, he identifies the victors. It is a victory for the people of Bristol on whose behalf he is speaking and on whose behalf he acted. It is a victory for the ideals of racial equality, an idea which by inference drove him to act. It is a victory for anyone who wants to be on the right side of history. Thus, when someone speaks, something above and beyond the immediacy of the talk is often evoked. Here we see solidarity with the people of Bristol and people who want to be on the right side of history, but we also see ideas, or ideologies*, of racial equality being invoked. Without such ideas being talked (and written) about, of course they would not exist. Ideas need talk (or text) to bring them to life. They animate Willoughby and drive his action, or at least he makes ideas relevant by accounting* for his actions in terms of being driven by these ideas. They justify, and exonerate, his actions.

Moreover, history is invoked as having a right, and therefore also a wrong, side. It is a moral issue. What is right and what is wrong is talked into being by Willoughby. History is also shown to be mutable: Colston shifts from being a virtuous figure, as stated on the plaque of the original statue erected in 1895, to a villainous figure in the talk of Willoughby and by extension the Colston Four and their supporters. Grand narratives - history - changes with the zeitgeist or spirit of the times. History, counterintuitively, is not really about the past. Rather, it is about the present looking back at the past as people play explicitly moral language games.

Things That Talk*

Moreover, these morally charged grand narratives congregate around, amongst other things, monuments – places of memory. While this book concentrates on talk and language games, it is perhaps worth pausing for a minute to consider that 'things' also 'talk' and are part of the rich tapestry of language games that we play. If the statue of Colston didn't 'talk' to us as a symbol, then it wouldn't have received the attention that it has. The statue of Colston, as with any other statue, tells us who or what is virtuous.

As the zeitgeist and grand narratives we live by change, so these monuments change. For example: following the 2003 US-led invasion of Iraq, Saddam Hussein's statue was toppled in Baghdad; the town of Charlottesville, Virginia, has removed the statue of the confederate general Robert E. Lee, considered to be a symbol of slavery; and since Russia's invasion of Ukraine in 2022, the Polish authorities have removed several communist-era memorials to the Soviet Red Army. Monuments 'speak' to us – if they didn't, what would be the point of having them?

At the time of writing the plinth of Colston's statue is still empty. It was briefly replaced by a statue of a Black Lives Matter supporter, which, compared with the statue of Colston, sends out a completely different version of what being virtuous means. After the statue of Colston was recovered from the river Avon, it was temporarily displayed in a Bristol museum. The statue was displayed, lying horizontally, slightly damaged, and with graffiti still on it. What the future of the statue will be is still the subject of discussion, but whatever happens to the statue it will be designed to speak to us, to give us a particular version of history. And if ever it is put in storage and forgotten, the message will be 'let's forget' this episode of the past. The statue will have been gagged. So, don't write me off as crazy if I say to you that 'things' speak to us in language games! Statues are a prime example of 'things' that are designed to speak to us, and what they say, the collective memory or history that they represent, is a potential battlefield.

To Sum Up

In sum, the key point here is be aware that any story is told in the present, whether that be a ghost story as we see in the next chapter, or a grand narrative. History is always a reconstruction of past events in the present. So, if anybody starts talking about history, it can be as much about their views of the present as it is about an actual tangible past. This is not only so for 'history', the history of England, the history of slavery, the history of warfare etc., but also the history of a project at work, or indeed any past event. That project, or past event, will be as much reconstructed in the present meeting as it will be about what actually happened in the past. The past is never fixed and factual*. It is potentially a battleground of interpretation of what happened and why, as we seek to make sense of the world in the present. History is a language game!

13. TELLING TALES OF
THE UNEXPECTED

'All I'm going to say is these are my experiences I am not going to be out there going "ah this is proof of ghosts"'

Stories and story-telling are part and parcel of the language games we play. They range from little anecdotes that are 'slipped' into conversations, to full blown stories in which we recount our lives, or parts of them. In some ways, we use stories to make sense of our lives; who we are, and why we are here. In this way, we transform a mass of raw experience into an understandable and coherent whole with an over-arching storyline.

A more general outline of the characteristics and structures of stories, and a discussion of what makes talk 'a story' can be found in the second section of the book. In this chapter, I present just one kind of story: tales of the unexpected[1]. I focus on how, on the one hand, the storyteller comes across as 'just a regular person', rather than a weirdo. And, on the other hand I consider how the

---

[1] The title of this chapter is a nod to Roald Dahl's book '*Tales of the Unexpected*' and it draws explicitly on Robin Wooffitt's analyses of accounts of paranormal activities to be found in his book '*Telling Tales of the Unexpected*'.

storyteller is able to craft a series of apparently bizarre events into something that makes sense and which comes across as believable.

Coming across as convincing and believable and as a regular guy rather than a slightly deranged bullshitter is of course not only restricted to telling ghostly tales, it is also part and parcel of any storytelling event. Telling your friends about your holidays, updating the boss about the progress of a project, explaining why a project failed, and so on may all involve telling stories about the past events that you experienced, the characters you interacted with, who said what to whom, why something was said, and what you thought about this at the time of the story, as well as at the time of the storytelling. And in these stories you've probably got a vested interest in making yourself come across as a 'good' person. Often the stakes will not be very high, as you recount your holiday adventures. However, at other times, such as in judicial proceedings, the stakes can be high as each side tells their story of the events. The credibility* of the storyteller and the believability of the story told are important factors in how the story is told.

In order to look at the way stories, or narratives*, are designed, we'll look at three levels. At one level, obviously, it's important to consider the story told: what happened, the characters involved and what they said, thought, and did. At the next level, it's important to consider the actual storytelling. Who is telling the story to whom? How do the listeners and the tellers assess the story? What is the relevance* of the story to the here and now? How is the story received by the audience*? At a third level, we'll consider the wider societal beliefs that are invoked by the story.

To exemplify how stories are designed, we look at one from a vlog[2] (i.e., a video, posted on social media) which shares the life of

---

[2] Available at: https://www.youtube.com/watch?v=CvCCYJ5oEGk

the vlogger with viewers. In this particular extract we analyse a vlog entitled 'My Paranormal Ghost Experience Storytime' in which the vlogger tells of her paranormal experiences. In fact, this is not really a single story, rather it is a series, each being one incident of several that add up to a larger story of living in a haunted house. The stakes are perhaps not that high, but nevertheless telling tales of the unexpected in the 21st Century means walking a fine line between communicating a ghostly experience and coming across as a 'normal person'.

Whilst keeping a purely neutral stance as to whether ghosts exist, or whether somebody who sees ghosts is 'strange', or not, let's have a look at how the vlogger tells the ghost story. How does she make it believable, and, as storyteller, how does she come across as being 'normal'? Because the story is really several stories rolled into one, we just look at a couple of the stories: the first in the series, and the concluding story.

The Prologue

1. So, today's video is going to be a ghost experience video and it's gonna be all about my
2. old flat I used to live in. Now before you watch this video all I'm going to say is these are
3. my experiences. I am not going to be out there going 'ah this is proof of ghosts'. What I
4. am saying can probably explain the things but I know people like to hear them anyway.
5. I just find it a little bit odd so erm yeah.

Just as in some plays, the vlogger starts off with a kind of prologue. She starts off by announcing the topic of the vlog to the listeners, i.e., the ghostly experiences in her old flat. Significantly, though, whilst announcing the story, she also works on establishing her 'normality'. She is not going to be out there going 'ah this is proof of ghosts.' What she is about to recount is just her experiences that can probably be explained. She has no particular stake in telling the stories and no point to prove. She is just telling the stories because 'people like to hear them'. Moreover, she assesses these experiences as just being 'a little bit odd'. Therefore, she downplays considerably any claim that they are 'real ghost stories'. Showing that you have no particular interest, stake*, partisan stance, or axe to grind makes your talk appear more impartial, and more believable. In this case, not seeking to make any claims about the existence of the paranormal makes her come across as a 'normal' person, rather than a 'weirdo' who believes in ghosts.

The First Story – the Moving Coat

After describing why she left her previous flat, the vlogger then begins to describe her first strange experience.

6. The first time I remember something weird happening was erm I was cleaning up and like
7. I said I didn't have much in my flat at the time. And I remember I had ... I was listening
8. to music and I had a load of washing in the living room and just as I was like going into
9. the bedroom and I literally put my coat on this chair (vlog cuts to video of her in room
10. with her coat on chair and subtitle 'even in this clip you can see my coat on the back of
11. the chair'). Went back into the living room, shut the door, continued. And I went back my
12. coat was literally at the front door so that was the first one that I was kinda like what the
13. fuck (spoken softly) that was a bit odd but anyway I just tried to ignore it.

First, it is noticeable that the events and actions surrounding the first 'weird happening' are completely mundane, something that Ms Average, a normal person, would be doing. She was cleaning up and listening to music. These are normal activities, for normal people, in a normal world. Further, these normal activities provide details of what she was doing – a more detailed* story makes a more believable story. The believability and credibility of her story is further supported by her video-clip of a vlog she did at that time, so the viewer can see the chair (see figure 10 below). To further convince the viewer of the truthfulness* of the story, a subtitle appears on the video-clip: 'Even in this clip you can see my coat on the back of the chair'. The main event of the story, that needs to be explained, is then introduced: when she goes back to her room the 'coat was literally at the front door'. As with most stories, the vlogger then provides an evaluation of the event. She was 'kinda like what the fuck that was a bit odd'. So, this inexplicable event is just 'a bit odd', it is not explained as a paranormal event and her action is just to ignore it – as any other normal person might do.

Even in this clip you can see my
coat on the back of the chair

Figure 10: The coat on the chair

The Second Story – Meeting with the Neighbour

The vlogger then tells several similar stories, and then she tells the story of meeting her neighbour.

1. So a few weeks went by and I actually met my next door neighbour for the first time erm
2. and I was putting the bins out. I was putting something in the rubbish bin outside and he
3. was going to work and he shit himself when he saw me and he was like 'Oh my fucking
4. God' and he said 'You know it's haunted in here don't you' and I was like a few weird
5. things have happened like. So anyway we just didn't really speak much after that.

In this story, embedded within the wider story of her 'paranormal ghost experience', it is significant that it is the neighbour who tells her that the house is haunted. Nobody is likely to recall the exact words used in a past dialogue, yet by reconstructing the dialogue* , word for word, the vlogger gives the story a veneer of believability and brings it alive. Through attributing the assessment that the house is haunted to the neighbour, the vlogger as storyteller avoids telling the viewer that she has this knowledge*. Through making her neighbour label the house 'a haunted house' she gives him voice* and avoids taking responsibility for the assessment. As the famous linguist Goffman (1922-1982) points out, in talk any utterance can be seen from three perspectives, notably that of: the animator (the person who speaks the words); the author (the person who formulates the utterance); the principal (the person who is ultimately responsible for the words). In this case, the animator is the neighbour. The author is the vlogger, who puts the words into the neighbour's mouth. The principal is also the vlogger. In metaphorical terms, the vlogger acts as the puppet master animating a puppet/character in the story making him do and say things at her will. The result of juggling with these identities* is that the vlogger is not the person, in the story at least, who labels the house a haunted house. In this way she changes footing* and distances herself from such an assessment and so retains a neutral stance to believing in ghosts, which of course would give her audience* cause to see her as a weirdo. She just assesses the events as 'a few weird things'. This again is designed to underline her normalness and reluctance to jump to the conclusion that a few strange experiences are anything more than just 'weird'.

She then starts another story of strange events in her flat, before coming back to a follow-up story in which a few weeks later she again meets the neighbour and they chat some more.

Third Story – Meeting the Neighbour Again

1. But he was saying that someone died in his bed. So I went to do a little bit of research on
2. the building itself and did come across, unfortunately, come across an article that did state
3. that a man in his early thirties had, we don't know if he committed suicide but yet he was
4. found dead in his bed er back in like 2010. So that wasn't a very nice though because
5. it didn't actually state the flat he was in. It just stated the building. So, I did get to know
6. my neighbour a little bit more after you know time passes and we started sharing odd
7. things that happened in our flat.

The neighbour provides the key information that a man had died in the flat and he also reveals that odd things have been happening in the flats. The vlogger, as storyteller, thus recruits her neighbour into the story. His experiences confirm her experiences. She thus is able to present an external source who provides similar accounts of 'odd' experiences. In this way, she builds up consensus* which makes her accounts more believable. It is not just her who has weird experiences; it is also others in the building.

The vlogger then tells several small anecdotal stories of other events that happened to her and others in the building. We look at the final story which closes the series of stories and rounds off her 'paranormal ghost experience storytime'.

The Final Story

1. I remember one day as well I woke up from like a deep sleep and I saw a man stood at the
2. end of my bed erm and I remember he had these piercing blue eyes. I don't know maybe
3. it was just a really deep sleep hallucinatory sort of thing but yeah that was a bit creepy.
4. At that point I was like I think it's time to go erm and then I moved to this flat which
5. is very (unclear word). There's nothing really that happens. If it was a constant thing
6. of like the same things are always happening, I'd be like yeah maybe it's me I'm a bit
7. nuts.

In this final story, the vlogger wakes up and sees a man with piercing blue eyes at the end of her bed. Again, as in the previous stories, she tries to rationalise and explain it away by stating that 'maybe it was just a really deep sleep hallucinatory sort of thing'. However, regardless of whether it was a hallucinatory sort of thing or a ghost, as implied, she assesses the happening as 'a bit creepy'. Moreover, giving voice* to her own thoughts ('I was like I think it's time to go'), she then takes action to resolve the issue of the weird happenings and she moves flat. So, the story, or rather series of stories, reaches its end with a resolution to the problem*: she moves to a flat where 'there's nothing really that happens'. This move is then assessed: if the same kind of things were happening in her new flat, she would be thinking 'I'd be like yeah maybe it's me I'm a bit nuts.' However, since nothing is happening she is not nuts, and by implication she is a sane person who had a paranormal experience in her previous flat. It's not me who's weird, it's the flat.

However, paradoxically, after making this assessment she goes on to tell a story about a weird event in her new flat and then she closes the series of stories by saying:

1. But I've really been enjoying living here I can sleep in peace there's no weirdy things
2. going on to be honest. And I have a habit of saging the flat now to keep away any
3. bad vibes. So anyway that is the end of that ghost experience.

Using 'but' to introduce a counterpoint, she concludes that she's 'really been enjoying living here I can sleep in peace'. This is because, despite just having recounted an anecdote of one weird event, 'there's no weirdy things going on' in her new flat. She then infers that this may be because she has 'a habit of saging the flat now to keep away any bad vibes'. Saging is a practice that involves burning sage, a 'sacred' herb, the smoke of which is said to cleanse

131

and purify the environment. The vlogger then concludes her story: 'so anyway that is the end of that ghost experience'. This ending is ambiguous. Throughout the storytelling she has been reluctant to assess the stories as 'ghost stories'. She has left the reader to infer that the stories are ghost stories, but she has not explicitly labelled them as such in the actual stories. This labelling comes first from giving the blog the title 'My Paranormal Ghost Experience Storytime' which frames* it in a way that encourages the viewer to understand the stories as ghost stories. This framing is then repeated at the end of the storytelling when she announces 'so anyway that is the end of that ghost experience'.

To Sum Up

So, in sum, because she tells a series of tales of the unexpected, she has to work hard to design her talk so that, on the one hand, the stories appear believable and, on the other hand, she comes across as being normal. To sum up the techniques she uses to make both the story believable and her identity* as storyteller credible and 'normal' she:

- provides details of the events
- embeds the description of the paranormal events within normal everyday activities that normal people, such as the storyteller, might do
- evaluates the events as just a bit odd. She does not explicitly say they are paranormal
- uses a character in the story to make the evaluation that the house is a haunted. She thus sidesteps taking responsibility for this label
- enlists characters in the story to corroborate her story of weird happenings by confirming that odd things happen

- uses reconstructed dialogue* to act out the event as if it were theatre, and as if the talk is an accurate reflection of what was actually said
- not only uses reconstructed dialogue, but she reports her thoughts as some kind of internal dialogue, so making the story more theatrical and believable
- demonstrates that she has no particular stake* in the story, no point to prove or axe to grind. She does this at the beginning of her storytelling, so instructing the audience how to understand the upcoming stories

Postscript: Audience* Response – Online 'Conversations'*

However, the story, in a way, does not end there. Once the story is completed, space is often left for the audience to evaluate the story, to show their appreciation of it, and perhaps even tell their own similar stories. In this case, the audience is not physically present, they are separated by time and space. But the nature of the vlog allows comments, which constitute an audience response, to be made. At the time of writing there were 18 responses. We'll just look at a couple of comments.

- **Comment one:** To be honest i think you have a bit of a gift, don't worry 'bout people thinking you crazy, Love ur Cats so cute..stay safe hun:)

Response: Thanks Eden, a few people have said that maybe i pick up on things or maybe im paranoid XD xxx

- **Comment two:** Wow spooky! There is definitely something out there xxx

Response: thanks for watching <3 xxx

We can see that in the first comment, the listener evaluates the stories by saying that the vlogger has 'a bit of a gift'. He/she advises the vlogger not to worry about people thinking she is crazy. In this space for reply, he/she thus empathises with the storyteller and supports her. This then becomes a small conversation in which the vlogger engages with the person who makes the comment by thanking him/her. The second comment follows along the same lines. The person who makes the comment empathises with the vlogger by assessing her stories as 'spooky' and agreeing with the sentiment that 'there is definitely something out there'. The vlogger replies to this by thanking the person who makes the comment. So stories are not just about the storyteller, they are also about the audience. After all, stories, as with any talk, are designed with a particular audience in mind and this audience is (usually) given the space to respond when the story, or other talk, is completed.

So, even though we don't think of social media as 'talk', in a way, it functions as conversation does. The only difference being that the speakers/writers are not physically present, and that their contributions are not necessarily synchronous (i.e., happening at the same time). Rather, contributions to conversations on social media are often asynchronous (i.e. happening at different times). Thus certain rules of conversation, or codes, such as one person speaks at a time, are looser and the lack of physical proximity and relative anonymity means that activities such as trolling - a deliberate flouting of the rules of politeness* - may be more common. But, this is not to say that there are no rules. Online conversations* sometimes have a moderator who can delete unacceptable talk. So, generally speaking, online conversations are very similar to face-to-face conversations and the tips and strategies for playing language games that we're looking at in this book - almost exclusively using face-to-face spoken data - will also be useful for you in your online interactions.

14. TELLING WAR STORIES

'It's like right we got her'

For most of us sitting at home, comfortable in our armchairs, war is a remote phenomenon. Yet, with ever increasing technological advances war is being streamed into our homes and conscience through graphic news reports, helmet camera footage of actual fighting, and so on. As with so many things, war no doubt means different things (glory, pain, suffering, national resurgence etc.) to different people (the politician, the soldier, the refugee etc.) depending on their experiences of it. Key to this, of course, is how war, the systematic organisation of mass killing, is justified. War, we are repeatedly told, is hell, but repeatedly we go to war over disputed territories, disputed resources, and disputed religions, or a combination of these and many other factors. Putin may account for the invasion of Ukraine by arguing that he wants to restore the Ukraine to its rightful place within an expanded Russia, Bush and Blair may have justified the 2003 invasions of Iraq in terms of Saddam Hussein's alleged possession of, and willingness to use, weapons of mass destruction, and Thatcher may have pursued the war in the Falklands to defend British sovereignty. Yet, regardless of the myriad of justifications, war ultimately comes down to one person taking the life of another on a battlefield. How then is this process of one human killing another human justified? In order to answer this question, an extract from an interview with an American veteran who narrates his experiences of killing during the Afghanistan war is analysed[12].

We join the analysis after the veteran has just recounted his first kill of a (male) enemy in Afghanistan. The interviewer then asks: 'Are there any other kills that stand out to you, that you remember?' This question prompts the story of killing a 'lady' in Afghanistan:

---

[1] Available at: https://www.youtube.com/watch?v=uAXCQZhtzEs

[2] This chapter, of course, draws heavily on Harvey Sacks's analysis of a navy pilot's account of bombing Vietnam, published in his *Lectures on Conversation*.

1. We were in a couple of different villages in Surobi. We gunned down these two guys
2. holding a larger machine gun a PKM and they were right next to a qalat a qalat is a house
3. a little mud hut and er a lady came out and you don't shoot women or children on the
4. battlefield. It's hard but you can differentiate between a man and a female. We were just
5. so into the moment er we watched her pick up the rifle and that was well the machine gun
6. and that was … that …was the cue. And we just opened up and there was blood up
7. against the wall. She just slumped over and it's like 'right we got her'. That was a little
8. rough only because it was a woman. You know, you kind of have a code in your mind as
9. a soldier. You don't shoot women and kids, you don't shoot you don't want to you never
10. want to because they are not the ones starting the fight. But, you know, you don't pick up
11. the weapon. They know that that country's been in a war since its inception whenever the
12. hell that country was created, ever since people started living there. In a war you have to
13. weigh someone else's life versus yours or your buddies and live with that that feeling that
14. you've killed someone because you have to go home yourself. I'm in college now. Had I
15. let them outweigh their lives versus mine you know I'd be dead. What are they doing?
16. They're still living in their little village er herding goats and that's the entire life they
17. know or they're some mercenary asshole or some Taliban dickhead from Pakistan and
18. that their life is to wage war on people. Mine is to come back, eventually raise a family,
19. maybe own a business. Who the hell knows? So is one life more precious than the other?
20. No. But in the grand scheme of things I felt like I want to go home more than they did and
21. I'm here now.

Who is 'Shootable', and Who isn't

The story takes place in a village in Surobi, which is a district in the province of Kabul. It starts with the almost banal statement that 'we gunned down these two guys'. These were not any two guys, they were holding a large machine gun which, implicitly, makes them legitimate targets in a combat situation. However, this action is complicated because a 'lady' comes out of the house next to where the men were shot. The complication is that, according to the veteran who is telling the story, 'you don't shoot women or children on the battlefield' and that even though it may be hard to differentiate men and women on the battlefield it can be done. Significant here is that the veteran uses a generic 'you' form ('you don't shoot women or children on the battlefield'). He thus shifts from a story that relates to him, to a comment about the situation that relates to the generic listener, me and you. Through such pronoun* use, we are all drawn into the story even though most of us have never been, and will never be, in such a situation.

So, in the storyworld, being able to differentiate between men and women on the battlefield, the storyteller/ex-soldier does not (initially) shoot the woman. The veteran therefore divides 'people on a battlefield' into two identities*: shootable (men) and non-shootable (women and children). Thus he applies some kind of gender and age-based moral distinction that governs who is shootable, and who is not. This moral distinction not only guides the storyteller's actions in the there-and-then of the story* but, in the here-and-now of the interview, it is also used to account* for his actions. This is later described as a code that soldiers have in their mind which dictates their action ('you kind of have a code in your mind as a soldier'). So, war is not about killing people willy-nilly, it has codes that soldiers follow. This makes the professional identity of the veteran relevant: he is one of a group - of soldiers - who follow these codes. This therefore leaves open the possibility of non-soldiers, or those that are not real soldiers, shooting women and kids. The code is: 'you don't shoot women and kids you don't shoot you don't want to you never want to because they are not the ones starting the fight'. War still has moral codes and rules that one should follow, and following them allows the killer to still be a good person (see Chapter 10). War can be waged and people shot, but there are certain (civilised) limits on this.

The Problem and the Solution

The problem is that in the storyworld, this distinction between who is killable, and who isn't, breaks down when the woman picks up the machine gun. This is the cue that, in the veteran's story, modifies the previous gendered identity and supplants it, by the more contextually relevant identity of 'person with a machine gun on a battlefield'. So, we have multiple possible identities (e.g. male, female, child, person with a machine gun, and so on) which may be more or less relevant at certain times and in certain contexts. Here, one identity rather than another being relevant has fatal consequences. It is this shift in identity from 'lady' to person holding a machine gun which is the cue that allows the veteran to shoot her. Moreover, the shooting is like 'right we got her', as if she was caught doing something she shouldn't have been doing or as a cat catches a mouse. This is reminiscent of the headline 'Gotcha' used by the *Sun* newspaper in 1982 to describe the sinking of the *Admiral Belgrano*, an Argentinian battleship, during the Falklands war. Despite its memorability, the headline was heavily criticised for its callousness towards the deaths of 323 Argentine sailors.

Accounting for and Justifying the 'Solution'

The shooting is justified because the woman picked up the weapon. Moreover, she should have known better because the country has been at war since its inception ('you know you don't pick up the weapon they know that that country's been in a war since its inception'). The woman knowingly caused her own death, it was her fault. In this way, the soldier avoids taking any moral responsibility for the killing. The veteran then offers an account* that provides further moral justification for the death. First, the context becomes explicit: 'in a war you have to weigh someone else's life versus yours or your buddies with that that feeling that you've killed someone because you have to go home yourself'. So, it's an 'either it's me, or it's you' scenario. And since you have to go home yourself, it is therefore justifiable to kill the other. The combatants are equal: facing equal risks and accepting equal consequences.

The veteran then continues his account of shooting the woman with a hypothetical story: what would have happened had he not acted on the 'it's-either-me-or-you' philosophy. The story is simple: the storyteller is in college now, but had he let the lives of his enemies outweigh his, he'd be dead. They would either still be 'living in their little village er herding goats' which is 'the entire life they they know', or they'd be 'some mercenary asshole or some Taliban dickhead from Pakistan and that their life is to wage war on people'. Consequently, using the pronoun* 'their' to differentiate the 'them' from him, the difference is that their life is to 'wage war on people'. This is what mercenary assholes and dickhead Talibans do, but it is not what soldiers, such as the veteran, do. The lives of the veteran's enemies are set up in contrast to his own life which consists of coming home, eventually raising a family, and maybe owning a business - something peaceful. This sets up a good/bad dichotomy. The 'them', those who are shootable, are the bad guys who deserve to be shot because they seek to wage war on people. They are, in this case, the asshole mercenaries and the dickhead Taliban. This technique of othering and dehumanising the enemy is a key mechanism that justifies shooting them: the 'gooks', the 'krauts', the 'ragheads', the 'slopes', and so on who are not like us. They are different and this, in certain circumstances, makes them shootable. The veteran is the good guy, who deserves to go home to a peaceful life. However, it is also noted that whilst the identity 'Taliban' and 'mercenary asshole' might point to the violent nature of the other, whom it is acceptable to kill, the village goat herder does not fit this scenario. After all, herding goats in a village is a peaceful activity. However, it does point both to a neo-colonial understanding of the relative merits of Western home and college education over the uneducated goat herder, and to the perceived higher value of a Western life over an Afghan life. Further, whilst the veteran justifies killing because he wants to go home more than those he is willing to shoot, this overlooks the fact that the Afghans are home. They cannot kill to go home, which makes the war a neo-colonial war, an invasion of someone else's home.

At the end, the veteran sums up the stories: the story of the killing of the woman and the hypothetical story of what would have happened had he not chosen to kill. To do this, he asks the rhetorical question: 'is one life more precious than the other'. He replies to his own question: 'no' and adds that 'in the grand scheme of things I felt like I want to go home more than they did'. Significantly, this doesn't really follow from previous talk in which he separated 'them' and 'me' and made a value judgement about Afghan civilisation and Afghans as living to wage war on people.

In the closing lines of the story, he sums up killing others in a war as simply about wanting to go home more than the enemy does. This therefore makes killing in a war an equal business, between similar people. The only difference between those he kills and him is his superior will to get home. This is of course somewhat contradictory to his previous categorisation of those he'd killed as future mercenary assholes or dickhead Taliban who live to wage war on people. The veteran's justification for killing is therefore fluid and contradictory. This, however, escapes detection in the rapid flow of talk; it requires that the talk is slowed down, transcribed, and analysed before this contradiction is revealed. Significantly, this points to the idea that a person's opinion, beliefs and attitudes (about, for example, war and killing) are not simply 'in there somewhere' and then reflected in talk. This changeability indicates that opinions, values and beliefs do not exist prior to talk. Rather, they are crafted in talk to fit the situation. How do we know what we think and feel until we say it? Thus, somewhat counterintuitively, it may be that all opinions, beliefs and values are generated in talk. They are not fixed, 'in there somewhere', and waiting to be transformed into words. Moreover, the veteran's account of killing is delivered so that it comes across as morally acceptable. The veteran story-teller follows a code: he doesn't want to kill women and children; he only kills dickhead Taliban and mercenary assholes; he, on equal footing with the enemy, just wants to get home and resume a peaceful life.

To Sum Up

Unlike the other chapters in this book, this chapter offers less in terms of advice about how you might play language games. Rather, I have included it so as to draw attention to the way in which perhaps the most morally reprehensible act, that of a human being killing another, can be justified. It is justified by playing language games that set up different identities, or categories of people. If language games can be so powerful that the simple setting up of differences can justify killing, then it is important that such mechanisms are understood.

Further, the reliance on interviews in the media, news reports, chat shows of the Oprah Winfrey ilk, and even for research, focus groups and so on, has even led some academics to claim that we are living an 'interview society'. If indeed, society is an interview society, it is perhaps important to realise that interview accounts, in any circumstances, may be less about asking simple questions to get honest responses that communicate feelings, beliefs, emotions, opinions and so on in a simple decontextualised manner. Rather than being simple reflections of private thoughts, feelings, opinions, and beliefs that are in-there-somewhere, interview talk may be more about language games and constructing morally acceptable identities than is widely imagined. This is, of course, not to say that the veteran, or any other interviewee/story teller, is lying. Rather, given the context*, one naturally uses an interview to account* for one's behaviours, thoughts, or feelings and this relies upon drawing on accepted tropes (i.e., ways of looking at the world), which are morally acceptable at the time of the interview and that build an identity of the 'good person' for the interviewee/storyteller (see also Chapter 10, for more about being a 'good' person).

Understanding this process is essential to understanding society.

15. PRESENTING

'Saving lives with pantyhose and paperclips'

Presentations are a language game we're often called upon to play. So, what makes a 'good' presentation? In order to answer this question, let's have a look at an academic presentation. More specifically, this is an academic presentation in which a young PhD student presents her doctoral thesis in less than three minutes. This kind of exercise is often performed in universities as a way of training speakers and of presenting the university's work to colleagues. This particular presentation was the winner of a 'present your thesis in three minutes' competition held at an Australian university. So, what we have is an extremely complex, and possibly dry, subject that has to be reduced to its bare bones and presented in a way that a non-specialist audience will be able not only to understand but also to enjoy. And this is the essence of a good presentation: making it accessible and memorable to your audience*.

Since this is a very short presentation, it is only supported by one PowerPoint slide. Slides are obvious props* for any speaker and there is an art to doing good slides. However, here, we will just focus on the talk and some of the body language*. The presentation[1] is fairly short, but even so, we're just going to have a look at the opening and the closing.

The Title

Before we start the analysis of the talk, let's first consider the title: 'Mosquito research: saving lives with pantyhose and paperclips'. The title can be an important part of engaging your audience*, of raising their expectations and orienting them to the outline of your talk. In this case, the chairperson* of the event introduces the speaker and announces the title of the presentation, which also appears on a simple PowerPoint slide. Thus, the first thing we notice, even before the presenter speaks, is the title: The title grabs our attention because it is intriguing. How do you save lives with such mundane objects as pantyhose and paperclips? Moreover, saving lives and keeping us free from danger makes the subject important to 'us'. So it engages the audience and plays on their emotions* – nobody wants to die. Consequently, the title sets up a kind of puzzle or a tease*, a question in the audience's mind: how do you save lives with paperclips and pantyhose? So, the first observation we can make is: give your talk an intriguing title that engages, puzzles and teases the audience and gives them a reason for listening. Your talk then answers this puzzling question and so satisfies the curiosity that you have aroused.

---

[1] Available at: https://www.youtube.com/watch?v=dhopJdgY6Lc

The Beginning

1. I came to Australia to study the deadliest animal in the world. Now, there may be some
2. Australian audience members thinking 'struth science has finally recognised the
3. importance of the drop bear' (slight laugh), but I am not studying drop bears around the
4. world. By transmitting diseases like malaria and dengue fever mosquitoes kill more than a
5. million people every year, making them the most deadliest animal on the planet. Now, in
6. Australia the most common mosquito-borne disease is Ross River virus and it occurs in
7. high rates in some areas, not others. My question is: why? What is it about certain areas
8. that makes them breed disease? If we can understand the environmental factors that
9. contribute to disease transmission, then we can alter the environment or target our control
10. effort to prevent human infection. But to answer that question, I had to find out where
11. the infected mosquitoes were in south Australia and traditionally testing mosquitos for
12. viruses has always been difficult.

Story Format

The presenter starts: 'I came to Australia to study the deadliest animal in the world.' Using the first person pronoun* 'I' sets up the forthcoming talk as a personal narrative*. So, the presenter gives what could be a dry academic presentation a 'human' storyline which follows the conventions of setting out a problem* (mosquitoes, the deadliest animals in the world) and finding a solution to the problem (pantyhose and paperclips). According to William Labov (b.1927), a well-known American sociolinguist, stories are often structured around a problem/solution format. So, setting up a presentation as a story makes it easy to follow because it has a simple, recognisable plotline. Here's the problem*, here's my solution and the difficulties that I overcome on the way. So, perhaps when you next do a presentation, consider how you can create human interest by presenting it as a story.

Humour*

After announcing that she will be talking about the deadliest animal in the world, the presenter adds: 'Now, there may be some Australian audience* members thinking "struth science has finally recognised the importance of the drop bear" (slight laugh*), but I am not studying drop bears around the world.' The drop bear, supposedly akin to a koala bear, is a fictitious bear in contemporary Australian folklore that is supposed to drop on humans and attack them. The idea that she is studying a fictitious deadly koala bear is funny. The humour is made more effective by the use of reported internal dialogue: the audience member who is thinking 'struth'. This has two effects: on the one hand, by second guessing what the audience are thinking it builds a rapport with the audience, and on the other hand, the expression 'struth' (coming from the expression God's truth) is a typically informal expression. By playing with register* (i.e., appropriate matching of the language with the situation) and using a slang expression in an academic presentation, the speaker causes mild surprise which in turn causes the audience to sit up and listen. So, mildly shocking the audience can be a good tactic to gain their attention.

Further, the use of humour* in a presentation, as with any other language game, can be useful to create a bond between the speaker and the audience. If the audience laugh* at your joke, then it shows that you are thinking along the same lines and you're able to connect with the audience. It also shows that you're a 'cool person', somebody who is fun and witty and this can add to your likeability* – a good, likeable person can come across as a more sincere and believable person. It can however also be high risk. If you make a joke in a context* in which seriousness is the name of the game, or if you make a joke about something that the audience doesn't find funny, you may come across as crass, ignorant and lacking in credibility*. Here, the speaker gets a laugh, so it works. But remember: humour is a strategy to use with care. It may back-fire (for more on this, see Chapter 2).

Another way of making an audience sit up and listen is surprise. The presenter announces that she is going to talk about the 'the deadliest animal in the world'. Jokingly she comments that some people may be thinking of the drop bear, but I think it would be true to say that the audience are also thinking of lions and tigers. So it's a surprise when she reveals that: 'by transmitting diseases like malaria and dengue fever mosquitoes kill more than a million people every year, making them the most deadly animal on the planet.' So, surprise the audience. This will gain their attention.

Moreover, another way of engaging the audience is to stress danger, threat, and urgency. The title has already suggested that the presentation will help save lives – what activity can be nobler than this? So, the danger of the mosquito, and how to deal with it, makes the story worth listening to. The audience will be more concerned by what threatens them and what they fear – death.

Making the Message Clear*

A speaker must be conscious of his or her message. You have to know what it is you're trying to communicate. If you are unsure of what you want to say, it's unlikely that the audience* will pick up your message (cf. Boris Johnson's Peppa Pig World speech in Chapter 17). So make it crystal clear. Here, the speaker is clear. After noting that the most common mosquito-borne disease in Australia is the Ross River virus which occurs in high rates in some areas, not others, she asks two questions: why is this so and what is it about certain areas that makes them breed disease? So, the purpose of the presentation is clear. She will answer these questions and the audience is primed to listen for the answers to these questions.

However, returning to the storied nature of the presentation, the answer is not that easy: testing mosquitoes for viruses has always been difficult. So this sets up a problem* that is in need of a solution, and it is the PhD student who sets out to investigate this problem. In the body of the talk, the presenter then outlines what she did to solve this problem and to answer the questions. Basically, she develops innovative traps made up of pantyhose and paperclips that allowed her to collect the data to answer the research questions that she set up. We skip this middle bit of the presentation and re-join it as it nears its end.

The End

1. I developed these traps on a tight budget. I used recycled milk cartons, pantyhose and
2. paper clips to make the traps. Each trap costs less than a dollar and can be reused for the
3. whole season. That was important for me because the majority of mosquito-borne disease
4. risk happens in economically impoverished countries. In India, for example, where about
5. a quarter of people live on a dollar a day, there are 33 million cases of dengue
6. infection every year. With my low budget virus surveillance and special analysis method I
7. can help any country regardless of resources to find out: where the deadliest animals
8. occur, why they are there, and how we can stop them from infecting humans? (marks off
9. the list using fingers). Thank you.

After outlining how she developed the solution to the problem, she points out the relevance* of her presentation to the audience. In technical terms this is called a coda, and it is an integral part of most stories. The chief advantage of the traps, and so their relevance, is the cost – 'each trap costs less than a dollar'. The coda is that the traps can help any country 'regardless of resources' to fight mosquito-borne diseases. The presenter underlines the coda with the comment that it was important for me. In linguistic terms, this is called meta-comment*, i.e., a comment about your own talk. Meta-comment is like framing, it serves to get the presenter's stance across to the audience and it directs the audience how to understand a stretch of talk. So, when the audience hears 'this is important' they are primed to understand the upcoming talk as important. So, pepper your talk with meta-comment. This will help you get your feelings across to the audience.

Figures

The presenter then gives an example to back up her claim. She notes that in India 'a quarter of people live on a dollar a day, there are 33 million cases of dengue infection every year'. Let's have a closer look at her use of numbers* here. Figures give a veneer of factuality* to your words. They 'prove' that you're talking about something real and concrete, but of course just like words they can be manipulated to bring about certain effects. As the saying goes there are 'lies, damned lies, and statistics'. I am not saying that this presenter is manipulating the figures, merely it is interesting to show how she mobilises figures to back up her argument*. For example, the gist of the presentation is that because the mosquito kills over a million people a year, it is the deadliest animal in the world. A million is a big number that is impressive, and the presenter gets across her point about the danger of the mosquito. But, suppose she had put this as a percentage of the total world population, let's say 8 billion. That would have given a figure of 0.0125 per cent. We're talking about exactly the same phenomenon: one looks minimal, the other looks consequential. The point is that if you're trying to gain the audience's attention, certain ways of presenting figures will do that, other ways of presenting figures will not.

Similarly, when talking of India, she says that there are 33 million cases of dengue infection every year. Taking the population of India as approximately 1.4 billion people, this gives us roughly 2.3 per cent of the population. What appears to be the most alarming: 33 million, or just over 2 per cent? Note also that we could play with the percentage here. We could say almost 2.5 per cent if we wanted to play it up, or we could say not much more than 2 per cent if we wanted to play it down. Both would be correct, they are just presented with a different spin.

Likewise, there are other ways of presenting the figure 'a quarter of the population live on a dollar a day'. The presenter could have presented this figure as just over 350 million people. Or she could have compared this with, say, the population of Australia which is currently just over 25 million. In which case, the presenter could have said something like: 'In India over 10 times the current population of Australia live on a dollar a day.' 350 million is a large number, but by making the comparison* with the population of Australia, the presenter could have made it appear even more significant. I am not saying she should have done this. I am merely pointing out a number of different ways of talking about the same figures. Each way of presenting the figures has different effects.

So, the point is numbers don't speak for themselves. They can be presented in certain ways so as to make them appear more or less important, depending on the purpose of your talk.

Concluding the Talk

The presenter closes her talk by summing up what is in it for the audience*. If you want to do an interesting presentation that captures your audience's attention, you must show some kind of advantage for the audience. Your talk has to be relevant for them. In his case, the presenter ends by detailing three advantages. As she says, 'With my low budget virus surveillance and special analysis method:

- I can help any country regardless of resources to find out where the deadliest animals occur,
- why they are there
- and how we can stop them from infecting humans.'

It is significant that, as in many other places in this book, the presenter uses the rule of three*. In order to emphasise these three points, she counts them off on her fingers (see gestures*). So, she non-verbally underlines the list as she speaks, and her body language* is coherent with her talk. The two act in synergy, so activating the audience's aural and visual senses. Enumerating the pay-off of her research in a simple list makes it clear and easy to follow. So, use lists when speaking, they will help you achieve clarity*.

To Sum Up
In sum, I think what we have here is a good presentation and even though it's fairly short, there are some good techniques that you could also use when you're next presenting. Aristotle, the ancient Greek philosopher, is said to have recommended considering three things when presenting: the message, your identity* as speaker, and the audience. In this case the speaker delivers her message clearly, setting up the question (problem) and answering it (the solution). She also manages to engage the audience, primarily, by setting up a personal narrative. Humour* and mild surprises of the 'I-didn't-know-that' kind retain their attention. Also, through

humour the speaker comes across as likeable. Likeable people are more engaging, and as we saw in Chapter 4, even more persuasive and convincing.

16. PUBLIC SPEAKING – WHEN IT GOES RIGHT

'I have a dream'

This book would not be complete without an analysis of at least part of a classic speech. This is where we would expect to see a masterclass in how to speak. Of course, there are hundreds of speeches out there which, and speakers who, would provide such a masterclass. Selecting one is not easy. I have chosen to analyse a part of one of the most iconic modern speeches, notably the famous 'I have a dream' speech of Martin Luther King. In the light of the Black Lives Matter protests that recently rocked, and are still rocking, the USA and other parts of the world, and the sheer mastery of language, this is one of the best and most relevant speeches ever delivered. But having said this, it is also worth bearing in mind that in the more everyday talk that we've looked at throughout this book we also see many of the same techniques that King uses. So, whilst most people will never speak in front of a crowd of 250,000 people, nevertheless the techniques that King uses are useable in more mundane and everyday settings. They may help you for your next PowerPoint presentation, business meeting, or even just winning that next argument with friends over a beer or a coffee.

In August 1963, Martin Luther King led a march to Washington to put pressure on the government to accede to some of the demands of the civil rights movement. He delivered his speech in front of a crowd of an estimated 250,000 people on the steps of the Lincoln Memorial, in Washington DC. In what follows, we'll just look at a few lines. The full speech is available online for those who want to hear it, and read it, in its entirety[1]. We pick up our analysis about a third of the way through his speech, after about five minutes, and we'll look at some of the rhetorical techniques he uses in this brief extract.

---

[1] Available at: https://www.americanrhetoric.com/speeches/mlkihaveadream. htm

1. In a sense we've come to our nation's capital to cash a check. When the architects of
2. our republic wrote the magnificent words of the Constitution and the Declaration of
3. Independence, they were signing a promissory note to which every American was to
4. fall heir. This note was a promise that all men, yes, black men as well as white men,
5. would be guaranteed the unalienable rights of life, liberty and the pursuit of
6. happiness. It is obvious today that America has defaulted on this promissory note,
7. insofar as her citizens of colour are concerned. Instead of honouring this sacred
8. obligation, America has given the Negro people a bad check, a check which has come
9. back marked insufficient funds. But we refuse to believe that the bank of justice is
10. bankrupt. We refuse to believe that there are insufficient funds in the great vaults of
11. opportunity of this nation. And so, we've come to cash this check, a check that will give
12. us upon demand the riches of freedom and the security of justice. We have also come to
13. this hallowed spot to remind America of the fierce urgency of Now. This is no time to
14. engage in the luxury of cooling off or to take the tranquilizing drug of gradualism. Now is
15. the time to make real the promises of democracy. Now is the time to rise from the dark
16. and desolate valley of segregation to the sunlit path of racial justice. Now is the time to
17. lift our nation from the quicksands of racial injustice to the solid rock of brotherhood.
18. Now is the time to make justice a reality for all of God's children.

Location*

Where a particular speech, or indeed any talk, takes place can have an enormous bearing on the impact of the words. Indeed, certain words only have value if they are spoken in certain locations, by certain people, playing certain roles. Thus until recently, marriage outside a church was not generally considered a proper marriage. Nor can a judge sentence a criminal outside a court, or a king be crowned outside a cathedral. In other cases, the value of place may be more symbolic. George Bush Jnr., for example, announced the end of 'major combat operations in Iraq' on the aircraft carrier *USS Abraham Lincoln*. This was not a legal obligation. Rather, it was designed to send out a message of global military power. So, location can be very much a theatrical prop in which talk is staged.

In this case, we join the speech after about five minutes, when King explicitly makes the location of the speech relevant: 'we've come to our nation's capital' (line 1). And later he says: 'we have come to this hallowed spot'. The hallowed spot that he is referring to is the Lincoln Memorial, which represents Abraham Lincoln, the president of America who emancipated the slaves in 1863. Thus, with such a monument in the background, King uses the memorial and the statue of Lincoln as giant props* that symbolically underline his message and give his words more poignancy. It is as if Lincoln himself was adding weight to King's words.

Metaphor*

The first, and most remarkable, element of the speech is the use of metaphor. At the point where we pick up the speech, King makes use of a metaphor that holds the speech together for the next few minutes. The metaphor compares honouring a cheque, with honouring the promises of the Founding Fathers of America, enshrined in the United States Constitution and the Declaration of Independence, to guarantee the people's 'inalienable rights' to 'life, liberty, and the pursuit of happiness'. Just as one has a moral duty to honour a cheque, so must America honour the constitution and the Declaration of Independence. By drawing on the audience's* everyday knowledge and experience, metaphor simplifies the situation and the comparison* makes the message more understandable and poignant.

We also see this is the comparisons between the 'the dark and desolate valley of segregation' and 'the sunlit path of racial justice' (line 16) and 'the quicksands of racial injustice' and the solid rock of brotherhood' (line 17). The juxtaposition of two contradictory images (quicksand and solid rock, and dark and light) makes the speech much more forceful and memorable. Imagery* grabs the listeners' attention and arouses their emotions. So, use strong (metaphorical) images to get your message across in an understandable and clear way. And when others use them, think carefully: are these metaphors 'true' and valid?

The Role of the Speaker

As already pointed out in Chapter 13, according to the famous linguist Erving Goffman, the speaker has up to three roles: the principal, the author and the animator. The principal is the person ultimately responsible for the words. The author is the person who originally wrote/spoke the words. The animator is the person who actually speaks the words. In this case, the 'architects of our republic'(i.e., the founding fathers of America) are the origin and source of King's words – they are the principals. They are also the authors. This is because King quotes their exact words: 'inalienable rights of life, liberty and the pursuit of happiness'. King is merely the animator or spokesperson, the person who speaks the words. Through giving voice* to the 'architects of our republic', King is claiming a legacy of the American Republic. The founding fathers of America are speaking through him. His words are not subversive, they are 'American' and as such they are difficult to dispute by anybody who is unfavourable to the ideas of the civil rights movement, yet who still claims to believe in the values of the Republic.

Empty Signifiers

An empty signifier* is a technical word used to describe words that don't point to any agreed upon 'thing' (such as a dog, cat, tree, etc.). Rather an empty signifier points to very abstract and slippery concepts, such as freedom, democracy, and happiness, that don't have a commonly agreed upon meaning. These words can mean just about anything. One person's happiness is not another's happiness; one person's idea of liberty is not another's idea of liberty; and so on. It is this plasticity of words that make them ideal for use in any (political) speech. Since everybody has an intuitive grasp of what (abstract) words mean for them, they pass without much serious thought and consideration. So, in this case, despite being enshrined in the constitution, the concepts of inalienable rights, liberty, and happiness are very vague; they can mean all things to all people. This vagueness* has the advantage that the concepts of rights, liberty, and happiness that the civil rights movement is striving for go by unnoticed and unchallenged as each member of the audience takes away what they want to hear. The same is true of the words 'justice' and 'freedom' that King also invokes in this part of the speech. So, pay attention to empty signifiers. What do the words really mean? How much 'woolly' 'fluffy' nonsense hides behind these words? Is the speaker bullshitting*? I'm not saying that empty signifiers are deliberately deployed to deceive, and I'm certainly not saying that King is bullshitting*. But I am saying that you should consider what empty signifiers actually mean, and why the speaker is using them.

The Sacred* and the Profane

A further technique that King uses to give his talk more force is to transport the talk from the profane to the sacred. For example, in line 7, King argues that honouring the debt to black Americans is a 'sacred obligation' and in line 13, he refers to the fact that they are on a 'hallowed spot'. Raising the civil rights movement from a secular to a religious quest appeals to higher authority* (God) and therefore gives his speech more strength and more resonance with American Christians, which transcends a black/white divide. Similarly, he argues that 'now is the time to make justice a reality for all of God's children'. This also gives the civil rights movement a religious, as well as secular, appeal. Transporting it from the profane to the sacred gives his talk more weight and appeal.

Factifcation*

Factification is a technical word that means making something appear to be a fact. Factifying your talk includes such techniques as 'it is obvious' (line 6). Maybe it is not obvious at all 'that America has defaulted on its promissory note'. Maybe this is just King's opinion. However, if you want your talk to appear factual and true, avoid as King does here such downgrades* or hedges as 'I think', 'perhaps', 'maybe', 'in my opinion' etc. Pepper your talk with expressions such as 'it is obvious' 'clearly', 'without doubt' and so on. This will provide a veneer of factuality that will build up to make your talk more convincing.

Collective Pronouns* – We, Us, and Our

It is significant that throughout the speech, King uses the collective pronouns* 'we' and 'our'. This, on the one hand, builds solidarity with the audience* and, on the other hand, marks King out as a leader who is able to speak on behalf of others. This is indeed something to look out for in the speeches of leaders, or would-be leaders. A leader often speaks on behalf of the group, whether that be civil rights activists, a nation, a department in a company, or whatever. The 'we', the 'us' and the 'our' are somewhat vague*, but this is a strength. It is, to some extent, the physically present audience, but, since King talks of 'our Republic' (line 2) and 'our nation' (line 17) it is also all Americans, whether black or white.

So he articulates the values of the civil rights movement: equality between all American citizens.

This inclusive message is made more noticeable by the lack of a 'them'. Difference, racial or otherwise, is often achieved in talk through a simple 'us' and 'them' dichotomy which can be used to legitimise many 'isms' (racism, classism, sexism, colonialism, socialism etc.) that rely on dichotomies between peoples, genders, social groups and so on. The 'us' and 'them' dichotomy is also a crucial element of the victim and perpetrator pair that we've seen elsewhere in this book (notably, Chapter 10). So, in this case, the victims are clearly black Americans, but the perpetrators remain hidden. If anything, the perpetrator is the vague 'America' that has defaulted on the promissory note and given 'the Negro people a bad check'. By personifying America and making America the perpetrator, King avoids being specific about the perpetrator and so he manages to send a message of justice for all 'God's children'. In doing this, he delivers a message of unity not division.

Urgency

If you want to call people to action, it is good to create a sense of urgency and high stakes. In this part of the speech, King states, using the booster* 'fierce' to give more force to his words, that there is a 'fierce urgency'. The time* to act is 'now'. To emphasise the point, he contrasts this with what the time is not. It is not the time to 'cool off' or use the 'tranquilising drug of gradualism'. Further, in order to emphasise the urgency of taking action, King uses anaphora, which is a technical term for repeating the same words at the beginning of each consecutive clause. So, in this case, we have 'Now is the time' repeated four times in succession.

To Sum Up

My main observation is that the techniques that King uses are not only for great orators on great occasions. They are also part of everyday talk. If you're switched on to language use, you'll probably be able to observe people using these techniques as they play language games around you. The way people manipulate urgency is key to sales talk (see Chapter 4), playing with pronouns* is common (see chapters 3, 21 and 22), as is playing with speaker roles (see Chapter 4). Winston Churchill was known for his avid study of great speeches. He used the knowledge that he gained from such study to hone his public speaking skills and to deliver some of the most inspiring speeches in the English language. Be like Winston Churchill, study the world's great speeches and speakers. Apply their strategies to your own talk.

17. PUBLIC SPEAKING –
WHEN IT GOES WRONG

'Peppa Pig World is very much my kind of place'

In the previous chapter, we looked at Martin Luther King's 'I have a dream' speech, which is often considered to be one of the best ever speeches in recent history. Now, let's have a look at what could perhaps be one of the worst: Boris Johnson's 'Peppa Pig' speech[1]. Through looking at what goes wrong, we may be able to get some insights on what to avoid.

The so-called 'Peppa Pig' speech was delivered, when Johnson was still prime minister, in November 2021, at the Confederation of British Industry (CBI) annual conference. The CBI is Britain's biggest business lobby group, which aims to promote an economic environment in which UK businesses can prosper. The speech was notable for its lack of cohesion, Johnson's bizarre comparison* of himself to Moses, self-indulgent mention of his previous

---

[1] Full official transcript available at: https://www.gov.uk/government/speeches/pm-speech-at-the-cbi-conference-22-november-2021

employment as a motoring correspondent, and the making of gurgling sounds representing the revving of a motor. Furthermore, amid the stuttering, pauses, and hesitations, Johnson appeared to lose his place in his notes, mumbling 'forgive me' to his audience as he sought to kick-start a flagging performance. Johnson's speech was qualified by press coverage as: bemusing, rambling, bizarre, shambolic, disrespectful, chaotic, embarrassing, and infamous. One TV journalist in a later press interview is even seen asking Johnson 'Is everything okay?'. You get the gist of just how bad this speech was.

Boris Johnson is often admired for his ability to speak, but this time his ability to charm an audience went badly wrong. Why? Let's have a look at the most widely criticised part of the speech in which, presumably, Johnson goes off-script and tries to wing it by talking about his recent visit to 'Peppa Pig World'[2]. Peppa Pig World is a theme park for children in the New Forest, in the south of England. The theme park is based on the animated TV series designed for pre-school children which follows the adventures of Peppa Pig and her family. The series was launched by a British company in 2004 and since then it has had great success, winning several prizes, and being aired in many countries around the world. In 2019 the Peppa Pig franchise was bought out by an American based multinational holding company, Hasbro, for US $3.8 billion.

Transition to Peppa Pig

As I said before the whole speech was rather shambolic, but let's pick it up as Johnson shifts topic to Peppa Pig World.

---

[2] This part of the speech is available on YouTube at: https://www.youtube.com/watch?v=dBktY__3Wls

1. And this is the most important message of all. There are limits to what governments can
2. do. And I just want to be absolutely clear about this – because this has been an
3. extraordinary period. There has been the financial crisis of 2008, where government had
4. to intervene on a massive scale. Then Covid, when government had to intervene on a
5. massive scale. But government cannot fix everything and government sometimes should
6. get out of your hair. And government should make sure there is less regulation and indeed
7. less taxation. And the true driver of growth is not government, it is the energy and
8. dynamism and originality of the private sector.

The speech at this point is reasonably coherent. Using meta-comment* Johnson orients the audience* to what is coming and frames* it as 'the most important message of all'. To sum up the gist of this this move, Johnson repeats the Tory Party mantra of less government involvement (line 5: 'government sometimes should get out of your hair. And government should make sure there is less regulation and indeed less taxation'). This, of course, is a message that might be expected to go down well at the CBI annual conference. So far, so good for this part of the speech and there are techniques such as repetition* ('massive scale') and the rule of three* ('energy and dynamism and originality of the private sector'). But it is at this point that Johnson loses the plot.

9. And Tony, yesterday, I went, as we all must, to Peppa Pig World.

10. Hands up if you've been to Peppa Pig World – not enough. I was a bit hazy

11. about what I would find at Peppa Pig World, but I loved it. Peppa Pig World is

12. very much my kind of place. It had very safe streets. Discipline in schools. Heavy

13. emphasis on new mass transit systems, I noticed. Even if they are a bit stereotypical about

14. daddy pig. But the real lesson for me about going to Peppa Pig World was about the

15. power of UK creativity. Who would have believed, Tony, that a pig that looks like a

16. hairdryer, or possibly a sort of Picasso-like hairdryer, a pig that was rejected by the

17. BBC, would now be exported to 180 countries, with theme parks both in America and in

18. China as well as in the New Forest. And a business that is worth at least £6bn to this

19. country, £6bn and counting. I think that it is pure genius, don't you? No government in

20. the world, no Whitehall civil servant in the world, could conceivably have come up with

21. Peppa. So my final message to you, as we stand on the brink of this green industrial

22. revolution as we prepare to use our new regulatory freedoms in what I believe will be a

23. very strong post-Covid rebound, we are blessed, we are blessed not just with capital

24. markets and the world's best universities and incredible pools of liquidity in London, the

25. right time zone and the right language and opportunity across the whole country. We are

26. also blessed with the amazing inventive power and range of British business. And that

27. above all is what fills me with confidence, members of the CBI, for the days ahead. Thank

28. you very much for your kind attention this morning, thank you.

Relevance* and Irrelevance

Apparently going off script, Johnson shifts topic to his recent visit to Peppa Pig World. The issue here is one of relevance*. What on earth has a visit to a children's theme park got to do with Johnson's vision of the UK and/or the message which was just revealed as the importance of lifting government intervention? So, here's the first observation: keep your talk relevant for the audience.

After initiating this surprising change of topic, Johnson then tries to engage the audience* by asking: 'Hands up if you've been to Peppa Pig World'. Now, addressing the audience directly and asking them to do something, even if it is just asking for a show of

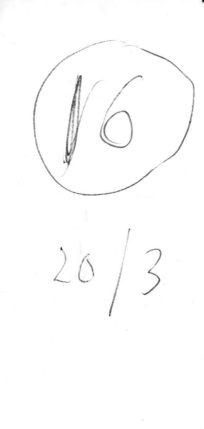

N6

20/3

hands, can be a way of engaging the audience. Unfortunately, the video, focusing on the speaker, not the audience, doesn't capture the show of hands, but Johnson in a soft voice assesses it as 'not enough'. So, we can deduce that this particular attempt to engage the audience fails: it shows a lack of connection with the audience. This is unsurprising; after all the conference took place in the north of England, over 500km (300 miles) away from Peppa Pig World and whilst parents and grandparents might take their children and grandchildren there, it is hardly on the list of must-go places for the target audience. Observation two: yes, involve the audience by asking them to react in some way and by addressing them directly, but do so in a way that anticipates a positive response.

We can add a third observation here: in formal speaking depart from a plan* with caution. When we play language games, it often difficult to plan exactly what we're going to say. This is especially so in informal conversations that may take many twists and turns. In more formal situations such as job interviews, presentations, and speeches we may have the luxury of planning what we're going to say. Of course, we don't know how these situations are going to play out exactly, but we can at least have some kind of game plan in mind which we may have to adapt as we go along. But at least we have a plan. So, my advice is: prepare. As the saying goes: prior preparation and planning prevents piss poor performance. And, through going off-script, Johnson deviates from whatever was planned. Having lost his place, Johnson, rather than digging himself out of a hole, drops himself further in the hole by making a rambling, incoherent, and irrelevant aside.

Clarity*

After having introduced the theme of Peppa Pig World, Johnson then assesses it positively: he 'loved it' and it was very much his 'kind of place'. This was because it 'had very safe streets. Discipline in schools. Heavy emphasis on new mass transit systems I noticed. Even if they are a bit stereotypical about daddy pig'. The problem is again one of relevance*: how does Johnson's assessment of a children's theme park relate to the economic situation in the UK? Why would the world of Peppa Pig, and the then prime minister's assessment of it, be of interest to the immediate audience of business people, or the extended and overhearing audience* of the British electorate? Or is this evaluation of Peppa Pig World supposed to be Johnson's vision for a future UK? Not only is the excursion into Peppa Pig World apparently irrelevant, but the meaning, if any, is obscure and ambiguous. Observation four: be crystal clear. If you don't communicate your message clearly, the audience will have to try to find a meaning, to create some kind of sense out of the disorder, and they may well come up with a meaning that you never intended.

Truthfulness*

Johnson then makes an attempt to give some kind of message, which is the lesson he learned from his visit to Peppa Pig World. As he says: 'The real lesson for me about going to Peppa Pig World was about the power of UK creativity.' So Johnson offers this as a tenuous link between his visit to Peppa Pig World and his speech to the CBI. His message is that 'the true driver of growth is not government, it is the energy and dynamism and originality of the private sector'. Whilst it's true that the originators of Peppa Pig were British and so perhaps typified the energy, dynamism, and creativity of the private sector, and it is also true that there are Peppa Pig theme parks in America, China, and the New Forest, other claims are open to question. Johnson's speech was fact checked[3] and apparently, it is not true to say that the BBC rejected Peppa Pig. Further, the figure £6 billion is apparently unsubstantiated. And, as a counter argument* to showcasing Peppa Pig World as a powerhouse of UK creativity, one could point out that the Peppa Pig franchise is now owned by an American based multinational holding company, Hasbro. So, a fifth observation is: be truthful. Now, this is not to say that Johnson is deliberately lying, but it is to say that his claims have been questioned (fact checked) and proved to be wanting. So, if you want to be taken seriously, check your facts before you speak, don't bullshit* and say the first thing that comes to mind. Prepare, and be careful about going off-script.

Comparisons*

A final point before we leave Johnson: comparisons. As Johnson comes to the end of this move, he sums up his lesson: 'No government in the world, no Whitehall civil servant in the world, could conceivably have come up with Peppa.' Well perhaps, but this is again a question of relevance*: civil servants are not generally employed to come up with TV programmes that are designed for pre-schoolers. So, in my opinion, there's a disconnect here. There's lack of logic*, an irrelevance, a comparison that doesn't work. So, a final observation: make comparisons that are valid. As we see in other places in this book, making comparisons can be a valid

---

[3] See for example the article, 'Double Check: Must We All Go to Peppa Pig World?' Available at: https://www.logically.ai/articles/ double-check-must-we-all-go-to-peppa-pig-world

strategy to make your talk more effective. But for a comparison to have effect it should not be spurious.

To Sum Up

In the previous chapter, we saw how Martin Luther King managed to deliver one of the most highly acclaimed speeches of modern history. In this chapter, Johnson delivers a real dog's dinner of a speech, but why does it fail? The main issue is one of relevance: it is quite simply irrelevant. This lack of relevance also makes the message unclear: in what way is Peppa Pig World supposed to be linked to the avowed message of the presentation which he reveals in lines 21 onwards to be about the green industrial revolution, new regulatory freedoms and post-Covid rebound. Any message has to be crystal clear. The audience have to understand the message – even if they disagree with it. If sense cannot be made out of your talk, it becomes quite literally non-sense and will just lead to ridicule. You won't come across as a 'good' person with knowledge* and goodwill. You'll come across as a bullshitter*. And, moreover, this talk does indeed contain bullshit* – (presumably) off the cuff and unfounded claims. Don't obviously bullshit* if you want to be taken seriously. It disrespects your audience and it shows that you have no real knowledge. I think the key message here is prepare – don't wing it. Maybe, you can wing it and bring it off, maybe you can't. And here, I think it's fairly clear that 'winging' it doesn't succeed. It doesn't succeed because it breaks Grice's conversational maxims*. Paul Grice (1933-1988) was a famous British linguistic philosopher who pointed out that for talk to 'work' it should be informative, clear, relevant, and truthful. He summed up these principles in his four maxims: quantity; quality; relevance; and relation.

18. DOING CHAOS

'Dear me, appalling behaviour'

As pointed out in Chapter 5, Prime Minister's Questions may appear unruly and disordered, but in fact there is an order to the apparent disorder. There are rules to the game* that the members of parliament follow. But what happens if the rules of the game are not respected? Well, quite simply, communication breaks down. By looking at a case where such a breakdown occurs, you'll see the importance of following the rules. In order to do this we'll looks at part of the Zoom meeting of Handforth Parish Council which took place in February 2021[1]. The meeting descended into chaos and farce as the authority* of the chair was challenged, a shouting match developed, and it was interrupted by one of the participants dealing with a private phone call. The meeting was posted on the web, and it went viral, receiving coverage on national news outlets and receiving literally millions of hits on YouTube.

---

[1] Available at: https://www.youtube.com/watch?v=cNVcDDWiHrs

For us, what counts is to look at 'what went wrong' and by looking at what not to do, focus on how to avoid certain pitfalls that may make your communication less effective. So, what are the rules of the game that are broken? How can you avoid breaking them?

Since there are several people on the video, it helps to have a *dramatis personae*, a list of characters, to help you orient to what is happening.

Chair = chairman of Handforth parish council

VC = vice chair of Handforth parish council

JW = Jackie Weaver, who was not the official clerk but was standing in for the clerk

C1, C2 and C3 = different councillors present at the meeting

Figure 11. Participants at the meeting

1. Chair: Right we'll start the ... we'll start the meeting and I want to repeat what I said at
2. the beginning of the last meeting that this meeting has to be called according to
3. the law, the law has been broken.
4. JW: It has been properly ...
5. Chair: Will you **please** let the chairman ...
6. VC: Mrs Weaver PLEASE!
7. JW: If you disrupt this meeting we'll have to remove you from it.
8. VC: You CAN'T.
9. Chair: It's only the chairman who can remove people from a meeting. You have no
10. authority here Jackie Weaver, no authority at all.
11. VC: She's just kicked him out, no she kicked him out.
12. Cl: Don't ...
13. VC: Just kicked him out.
14. Cl: Don't ...
15. JW: This is a meeting called by the councillors ...
16. VC ... illegally.
17. JW: They now elect a chairman.
18. VC: No they can't because the vice chair's here. I TAKE CHARGE.
19. JW: (unhearable)
20. VC: **Read the standing orders. Read** THEM AND UNDERSTND THEM
21. C2: Dear me.
22. C3: Appalling behaviour.

Opening the Meeting

We join this meeting as the chairman attempts to start it officially: 'Right we'll start the ... we'll start the meeting and I want to repeat what I said at the beginning of the last meeting that this meeting has to be called according to the law, the law has been broken.' The first, and most obvious point to make, is that this is a meeting and it is the chair* who has the right and duty to start the meeting. These are the rules of the game*, the codes that must be followed.

173

However, the meeting gets off to a false start. Jackie Weaver, the acting clerk to the meeting, begins to say something that contradicts this (line 4: 'It has been properly'), but she is not allowed to finish her utterance because the chair talks over her. The unwritten rule for any conversation is that one person speaks at a time. If you don't respect these rules, the conversation breaks down into disorder with nobody being able to get a word in edgeways. It risks becoming a shouting match. Should you ever chair a meeting, rule number one is to ensure that everybody is given the space to finish what they are saying.

Argument*

Despite not being allowed to finish her turn, Jackie Weaver's utterance has within it the seeds of argument. Of course, arguments can be more or less heated, but in essence they are nothing more than a refusal to accept the proposition of a previous speaker. In this case, the chair suggests that 'the law has been broken' and the acting clerk starts to contradict this (line 4: 'It has been properly').

The clerk's talk is unfinished because the chair orients to Weaver's talk as an interruption and calls on her to stop talking (line 5: 'Will you **please** let the chairman'). However, adding to the overall confusion, the vice chair then butts in before the chair can finish and, raising his voice, he also requests that the clerk stop talking (Mrs. Weaver PLEASE!). Even though the vice chair cuts short the chair, this can be seen as a supporting move – i.e., he mirrors the opinion of the chair and supports him. The argument is now two (the chair and vice chair), acting in tandem, against one (the clerk). In technical terms, supporting the talk of another is called a buttress* .

Roles in a Meeting: Who Can Say What to Whom, When and How

This attack provokes the indignation of the clerk who threatens to remove the chair* on the grounds that he is disrupting the meeting ('If you disrupt this meeting we'll have to remove you from it'). This threatened action is met by a counter point. The vice chair shouts: 'You CAN'T'. So, as before, we see that in linguistic terms, opposition to the talk of the prior speaker constitutes a move in an argument*. Again, acting as a team, the chair comes in to support the vice chair and again it concerns the role of the clerk. The chair claims, 'It's only the chairman who can remove people from a meeting you have no authority here Jackie Weaver no authority at all.'

So here we have a good example of the importance of the alignment of roles in conversation. If you cannot agree on conversational roles, you'll rapidly arrive at a 'you-can't-say-that-to-me', 'who-do-you-think-you're-talking-to', or 'who-do-you-think-you-are' moment. In this case, Jackie Weaver in her capacity of stand-in clerk claims that she can throw somebody out of a meeting, and the chairman of the parish council claims she cannot. Failing to agree on who has rights to do what contributes to the chaotic situation. So, if you want a conversation to run smoothly, always be aware of your identity*, the role you are playing, in relation to the other people around you. What can you say to them, and what can they say to you? Of course, in many situations, there may be unwritten, rather than written, rules governing this. Consequently, a degree of tolerance exists in most situations. But despite this flexibility, key to having a good conversation is being aware of who you are in relation to your interlocutors.

Accounting* for Actions and Words

Regardless of the rights and wrongs of the situation, the stand-in clerk kicks the chair out of the meeting. This is no doubt rendered easier by the fact that it is a Zoom meeting: one click suffices. In a face-to-face meeting we could imagine a more protracted argument. The clerk then begins to account for her actions: 'This is a meeting called by the councillors.' If we want talk to run smoothly, accounting* for actions is something we often have to do. Language games are shot through with morality – what we can and cannot do or say – and so when we do something out of the ordinary we have to be in a position to justify it.

Completing the Other's Sentence

After some talk by the vice chairman and councillor one, who are physically present together in front of a shared screen, the clerk states: 'This is a meeting called by the councillors.' However, as she is speaking, the vice chair completes what she is saying by adding 'illegally'. The full sentence is now: 'This is a meeting called by the councillors illegally.' We'll see in Chapter 22 how adding to somebody else's sentence in progress can be a move of solidarity. Here, the reverse is true. In this case, addition of 'illegally' to the sentence is an adversarial move because the original meaning of the sentence becomes distorted. Moreover, you can also use this as a way of taking over the turn. To draw an analogy with football, you tackle the opponent and take the ball off them. So, completing the talk-in-progress of somebody else can be either a supporting move as we see in Chapter 22, or, as we see here, an attacking move.

Rules of the Game*

To deal with this fairly aggressive move, the clerk simply ignores it and carries on. The full sentence now emerges as: 'This is a meeting called by the councillors, they now elect a chairman.' Argument follows: the vice chair, again raising his voice, opposes this. He says: 'No they can't because the vice chair's here I TAKE CHARGE, **read the standing orders read** THEM AND UNDERSTND THEM". The standing orders are written rules, or, if you like, the rules of the game* , which set out, amongst other things, procedural matters for meetings. By referring to them, the vice chair is trying to apply the rules of the game to limit what the clerk can, and cannot, do. As he is shouting this, he blocks out the clerk who is trying to say something. He who shouts loudest wins the argument. Well, maybe. However, in doing so, he loses his cool and two other councillors comment: 'Dear me' and 'Appalling behaviour'. So, losing it and shouting may not be the best way forward. As the saying goes: the empty vessel makes the loudest sound. There may be moments when a *display* of anger might be appropriate, but as with any player who loses their cool, that is when mistakes are made and, as in this case, maybe you'll start losing the support of others.

To Sum Up

What we've looked at here is a chaotic meeting. The underlying conflict is beyond the scope of this very short linguistic analysis, but nevertheless we can see how chaos is produced because the participants don't follow the rules. Notably, they don't respect the 'one person speaks at a time' rule. So, it's a little like a football match in which neither side respects the rules: no game is possible, or what happens is not a game, it's just a mess. Beyond the 'one person speaks at a time rule', in this meeting there is a dispute about who can say what to whom. This is basically a question of the roles we play. Let's make an analogy with a game of chess: the more powerful pieces on the board have the ability to make more powerful moves. If, when playing a game of chess, I began moving a pawn as if it were a queen, the game would soon disintegrate. If ever you have to chair a meeting be aware of these rules and enforce them.

Of course, here we've had a look at a meeting which has clear rules that should be followed – but weren't. In other more informal language games, the rules are probably more fluid. But nevertheless, unwritten rules will be there. Know them and respect them, or break them with care.

19. MAKING SMALL TALK*
– WHEN IT GOES RIGHT

'Are you a cappuccino guy in the morning or afternoon?'

Small talk* is defined by the Cambridge English dictionary as, 'conversation about things that are not important, often between people who do not know each other well'. Bronislaw Malinowski (1884–1942) a famous anthropologist writing in the 1930s, coined the technical term 'phatic communion' to describe such chitchat that is, supposedly, not concerned with communicating information. However, I don't think that talk is ever 'small'. In fact, I think that another cultural anthropologist, Edward Hall (1914-2009) writing in the 1950s, was right when he said that we cannot but communicate. In other words, in any situation, however trivial, we are still communicating who we are, what we want, and what we think. We're always playing language games and these games are the bedrock of our society. Imagine a world with no small talk? How boring that would be.

Small talk is, in my opinion, a misnomer. It is never small. Let's take an example that happened to me recently. A few weeks ago my wife and I went to a cheese and wine evening held at the old people's home where my mother-in-law is a resident. A couple and their mother/mother-in-law came and sat beside us. Now, we could have said nothing and just ignored each other, but after a greeting they revealed that they had travelled from Brussels, about an hour's drive away. Of course, my wife asked where they lived in Brussels and in a very short space of time the couple revealed that they were born in the same town as my wife and so the conversation went on. Did they know so-and-so? Did they remember such a shop? Where had they worked? And so on. True, one could say the stakes were low and we'll maybe never see these people again, but surely so-called small talk is an essential part of our humanity, or at least society. No talk, no society. We are not enclosed in separate worlds in our own minds. This is not to say that we should strike up a conversation with any stranger we come across, but maybe the world would be richer if we did!

Further, even though we use small talk all the time, for some people it can provoke unease. How to deal with total strangers? Will they like me? What can I say to appear interesting? And so on. Indeed, get it wrong and we appear socially awkward, as Rishi Sunak, at the time of writing the current UK prime minister, did when he asked a homeless person if he 'worked in business'. Obviously it would be unusual for a homeless person to be 'in business', so the comment was widely criticised for its awkwardness. So, how do we do small talk? How do we engage in so-called 'trivial' conversation with a stranger?

In order to see how this is done, I managed to find a videoclip in which American fighter jets are re-fuelling mid-air. After the jet has fixed itself to the refuelling line (the boom), the boom operator (BO in the transcript) engages the pilot (P in the transcript) of the jet in small talk[1]. By the way, it's interesting to note that in the comments that follow the video, somebody has written: 'One of my mom's friends was a boom operator on a KC-135 and she told me all kinds of cool stories. She met her husband while refuelling him over Iraq.' So, in this case mentioned in the comments, small talk did do things, or at least led to things! As I said, no small talk, no society! So, using this data, let's look at how small talk works.

1. BO: Here it goes, and there's 50, 40, 30, 20, 15, contact.
2. P: Contact.
3. BO: How you doing today, sir?
4. P   Excellent.
5. BO: You guys drink coffee down there?
6. P: All the time trying to keep warm though.
7. BO: Why you got a giant fireball beaming right down in front of you?
8. P: Yeah you know if we er put it up front by this radar it does tend to warm up a little
9.   bit. What about you guys?
10. BO: We drink some types of coffee usually it's instant coffee, but if we're lucky we
11.   can bring a Keuring (pause) fancy coffee.
12. P: I'm an espresso guy myself.
13. BP: Little shots of coffee.
14. P: Yeah little shots of coffee, something nice and dark.
15. BO: Yeah (pause), I like mine dark.
16. P: Are you a cappuccino guy in the morning or afternoon?
17. BO: Yeah, more afternoon.
18. P: Little blasphemous don't you think drinking a cappuccino after eleven.
19. BO: Say again.
20. P: It's kind of blasphemy to drink a cappuccino that late in the day.
21. BO: Why?
22. P: It's a military thing that's for the morning. You can't drink milk in the afternoon.
23. BO: Dark in the morning, light in the afternoon.
24. P: That's for tea, we're not British.
25. BO: True that.

---

[1] Available at: https://www.youtube.com/watch?v=ysrt9MSi5Lo

The Opening

We join this conversation as the business of fuelling is being conducted. The boom operator counts down the distance, I presume, between the boom and the jet (line 1: "50, 40, 30, 20, 15, contact"). Once contact is established, the complicated business is done and small talk begins as the jet is refuelling. Not unsurprisingly, we first note that the small talk between strangers begins with a greeting ('How you doing today, sir?'). There's even a joke about the phenomenon of asking how somebody is. Question: When is a question not a question? Answer: when an English person asks 'How are you?' This is because the questioner is not really concerned with how you are and, of course, it would be strange if we started to speak about our ills and ailments. The function of 'How are you' can be an invitation to talk. The reply 'excellent' is non-controversial and upbeat, thus establishing a positive identity* for the speaker and opening up the way for small talk to happen. If you want your small talk to succeed, keep it positive.

Opening Gambit

The opening gambit is in the form of a simple question '[Do] you guys drink coffee down there?' It's a polite* and safe question. So, first observation when doing small talk: keep the questions nice and simple, general, non-threatening and answerable. A question* requires a response, not to reply would be a breach of the rules of the game*. Sure enough, in this case, we get a reply: 'All the time.' But this is not just a reply. The pilot takes the ball and runs with it. He adds to his utterance: 'Trying to keep warm though.' So, small talk is a bit like players warming up before a match. The object is not, as in argument*, to win the point or come back with that witty utterance that leaves the opponent speechless. Rather, the objective is to keep the ball in play as long as possible so that the team players achieve their objective of warming up. So as with sport, small talk is a question of passing the ball to the other who runs with it and then sends it back to you. It is essentially cooperative and effort may have to be made to keep the ball in play.

Building Agreement

The boom operator finds the statement 'Trying to keep warm though' puzzling and asks why this is so, because 'You got a giant fireball (i.e., the sun) beaming right down in front of you.' Now, such an enigmatic reply, and questioning response shows a lack of understanding that could cause a problem. However, in this case the pilot agrees 'Yeah' and adds 'If we er put it up front by this radar it does tend to warm up a little bit.' I'm not too sure what he means by this, but it's clear from the second part of the utterance that he seeks to agree, at least minimally. So, out of a possibly problematic claim that it's cold despite the fact that, as the boom operator points out, it's sunny, the pilot recovers the situation to achieve agreement. Metaphorically speaking, he doesn't drop the ball. He shows that they're on the same wavelength. Observation two for small talk is therefore: build agreement.

Return the Question*

A classic way to keep the talk going is to return the question, or to continue the game metaphor: pass the ball gently back to the other player. In this case, the pilot does exactly this, he asks: 'What about you guys?' The boom operator is bound to reply and does so: 'Er we drink some types of coffee usually it's instant coffee, but if we're lucky we can bring a Keuring (pause) fancy coffee.' After Keuring, which is the make of a coffee machine, there's a pause. A pause can be awkward in this kind of talk. This is because when you finish talking, it's normally the other person's turn to talk. So, if there's no reply the conversation breaks down. The way to resolve this is to add a bit more to your talk, pursuing a response, as it were. In this case the boom operator adds an evaluation 'fancy coffee'. To continue the game metaphor, it's as if you're ready to pass the ball to the next player, but you realise they're not ready so you hold the ball a bit longer before passing it to the next player.

Evaluations and Building on Others' Talk and Agreeing

Normally an evaluation requires a second evaluation by the next speaker. So, here we have an evaluation that Keuring machines make fancy coffee. Making an evaluation is therefore one way of keeping the conversation going. Maximum agreement would be achieved here by saying something like 'Yeah sure, they make excellent coffee' (an upgrade), but here the pilot reveals that he is an expresso guy. This in fact sidesteps the comment that Kuering machines make fancy coffee and shifts topic to the pilot's identity* as an 'espresso guy'. The boom operator accepts this change in direction (see Chapter 18 for example of what happens if two interlocutors don't agree on the topic of conversation). She picks up the ball and runs with it by showing that she knows what expresso is (i.e., 'little shots of coffee'). By displaying such knowledge*, she displays similarity with the pilot, or at least that she knows what he's talking about and so they're both 'coffee people'. The pilot agrees with this definition of expresso, and adds: 'something nice and dark'. The boom operator further agrees and she adds that she likes her coffee dark (line 15: 'Yeah I like mine dark'). Observation three of small talk: work to build similarity and agreement.

Find Agreement

The pilot keeps the ball rolling by asking another question: 'Are you a cappuccino guy in the morning or afternoon?' As we've seen before, questions* require responses, and so it's an easy way to keep things going. So, the boom operator replies: 'Yeah more afternoon.' Here the pilot drops the ball: he evaluates the boom operator's evaluation negatively: 'Little blasphemous don't you think drinking a cappuccino after eleven.' In doing this, he breaks the rule of the game to agree and express similarity. After repeating the question, the boom operator questions the pilot's evaluation that drinking cappuccino after eleven in the morning is blasphemous (line 21: 'Why?'). In response to this question, the pilot persists with his evaluation that drinking milk, and I suppose milky coffee, in the afternoon is not good: 'It's a military thing that's for the morning you can't drink milk in the afternoon.' The boom operator opposes this assessment with an aphorism*: 'Dark in the morning, light in the afternoon.' Aphorisms* (i.e., sayings or pithy observations which supposedly contain some kind of general truth) can be useful because they purport to be general common sense statements about the way the world is, something everybody knows, and so they're easily agreed with. Consequently, they can be ideal for small talk, since they can be difficult to disagree with.

Yet, despite the aphorism*, an argument (action/opposition), however light hearted, is developing. The pilot's proposition that drinking cappuccino after eleven is blasphemous is opposed by the boom operator's claim that coffee should be dark in the morning and light in the afternoon. But, if the cooperative small talk is to continue, agreement must be found: the ball must not be dropped. In this case, the pilot agrees partially with the boom operator by saying that dark in the morning and light in the afternoon is right, but for tea. He then adds that we're not British. So, on the one hand he disagrees with the boom operator, but on the other hand he ends his utterance with the observation that neither of them is British. This builds sameness and offers a way out of a developing argument. This proposition is agreed with, and so the rule of finding agreement is eventually arrived at and the conversation continues.

To Sum Up

Small talk is a bit like warming up before a match. It requires gentle cooperation. Ask simple, polite, non-controversial questions ('What coffee do you like?'). Build on these questions so as to establish agreement and similarity (we're both coffee-drinkers). Add to your utterances, so that you give your interlocutor something to latch on to, to comment on, or evaluate. If disagreement builds up (whether one should drink milky coffee in the morning), side-step it and save the situation by seeking out something that can be agreed upon (we're not British). If one side appears to drop the ball by saying something ambiguous, ignore it, let it go and continue to seek agreement and similarity.

Making good small talk is an art. Here the pilot and the boom operator seem to manage okay. In the next chapter we'll look at small talk that goes disastrously wrong, mainly because the speakers don't cooperate.

20. MAKING SMALL TALK*
– WHEN IT GOES WRONG

'No, but where do you really come from, where do your people come from?'

In the previous chapter, we looked at how small talk works and how the speakers cooperate to *make* it work. Small talk doesn't 'just happen'. By way of contrast, here we're going to look at how small talk doesn't work. In order to do this we look at the tense exchange that Ngozi Fulani, chief executive of Sistah Space, a charity dealing with domestically abused black women, had with a member of the royal household (referred to as SH) during a reception about domestic violence hosted by Camilla, at that time the Queen Consort, in November 2022. Ngozi Fulani, defined by the BBC as 'a black British charity boss'[1], claims that she was violated at this event and she published her reconstruction of the offending

---

[1] https://www.bbc.com/news/uk-63865890

dialogue which she claimed was racist[2]. A spokesperson for Prince William said the courtier's comments were 'unacceptable'.

This is the first time in this book that we're working from a re-constructed dialogue that may, or may not, be close to the actual words used. Indeed, it would be an incredible feat of memory* if, after the event, Fulani could remember the exact words used. Nevertheless, regardless of its resemblance to the actual words used, the reconstructed dialogue does give us Fulani's recollection of the exchange, and so it gives us 'good enough' access to the event in order to analyse how small talk, or a meeting between strangers, went so badly wrong. In this case, Ngozi Fulani publicly claimed that the talk was a racially motivated verbal aggression. As a result of this, the member of the royal household apologised and resigned from her job.

So, without seeking to add to the political controversy surrounding the exchange, in what follows I provide a technical analysis of how small talk goes wrong and how this example of (failed) small talk differs from the previous example of (successful) small talk.

The Use of Space*

Before going on to look at the actual words, let's first take a look at what Fulani says happened before the exchange took place. According to Ngozi Fulani's Twitter account as reported in *Newsweek*, the following happened.

> *There were many guests from various organisations. I was standing with two women, including @mandureid from the @wep_uk when an*

---

[2] The reported dialogue I am working from was published in *Newsweek* and is available at: https://www.newsweek.com/palace-new-race-storm-charity-boss-describes-insulting-exchange-guest-camilla-reception-1763469

elder women (SH) approached us. She put her hand in my hair to move my locs so that she could see my name badge.

So, even before the dialogue opens we have a '*faux pas*' which Ngozi Fulani evaluated in the following way when she appeared on the BBC[3]:

When you put your hand on my hair like I'm not, I'm not even a person you can do what you want and say what you want, I don't want to be in your presence.

Ngozi Fulani's assessment of the event as an aggression is interesting because even though in this book we're focusing on language games, the space* that surrounds us when we play such games is important in the same way as in a football match; who can move where and when on the pitch is guided by the rules of the game*. Similarly, the space in which we play language games also defines what we can, and cannot, do. In this case, before the talk even starts there is, according to Ngozi Fulani, a violation of space. As the cultural anthropologist Edward Hall (1914–2009) pointed out, each individual has what he/she regards as private space surrounding them. What one considers private space may vary from one culture to another, but the point is: we don't like people invading what we consider to be our space. If we do allow people to get physically close, it is a sign of intimacy, and if we don't want people to get physically close but they do so anyway, it can be a sign of aggression. Here Ngozi Fulani considers that the moving of her 'locs' by another person is a violation of space: don't touch me. So, be aware of space and touch* and how you use it in your

---

[3] Interview with Ngozi Fulani, available at: https://www.bbc.com/news/uk-63865890

interactions. Be careful not to invade what others may consider to be their private space, and be careful of physical contact. Maybe it's appropriate, maybe it isn't. That is for you to judge depending on the context*.

The Reconstructed Dialogue*

Having made that little aside, looking at space and touch, let's have a look at the actual dialogue as Fulani reports it.

1. SH: Where are you from?
2. NF: Sistah Space.
3. SH: No where do you come from?
4. NF: We're based in Hackney.
5. SH: No, what part of Africa are YOU from?
6. NF: I don't know, they didn't leave any records.
7. SH: Well, you must know where you're from, I spent time in France. Where are you
8.   from?
9. NF: Here, UK.
10. SH: No, but what nationality are you?
11. NF: I am born here and am British.
12. SH: No, but where do you really come from, where do your people come from?
13. NF: 'My people', lady, what is this?
14. SH: Oh I can see I am going to have a challenge getting you to say where you're from.
15.   When did you first come here?
16. NF: Lady! I am a British national, my parents came here in the 50s when ...
17. SH: Oh, I knew we'd get there in the end, you're Caribbean!
18. NF: No lady, I am of African heritage, Caribbean descent and British nationality.
19. SH: Oh so you're from....

Talking Past Each Other

As we saw in the previous chapter, small talk is a cooperative game. It takes two to tango as it were, and if the speakers are not cooperating they will not have a conversation. After all, etymologically speaking, the word conversation is derived from the Latin *con*, meaning together, and *versare*, meaning to turn, so literally meaning 'turning together'. In this case, initially, the small talk fails because the interlocutors are quite simply not 'turning together'. So, how does 'not turning together' happen?

The conversation opens with 'Where are you from?' In many cases, this would be a fairly safe opening gambit, much along the lines of '[Do] you guys drink coffee' that we saw in the previous chapter. It could be understood as a search for common* ground. Your interlocutor might know the area where you're from, or have some connection with it and so we can build on this to do small talk. To pick up the metaphor that I used in the previous chapter, small talk is a cooperative game, we're not out to defeat an opponent, we're out to keep the ball in play as long as possible, just like a training session in which footballers or rugby players are practising passing the ball to each other.

Here, the problem is that the 'you' in 'where are you from' is ambiguous. It could be you the person, Ngozi Fulani, or it could be a collective 'you', the charity Sistah Space which Fulani represents. In this case, Ngozi Fulani replies that she is from Sistah Space. While this is an adequate response in the sense that it is an answer to the question, it could have been expanded into a search for common ground. For example, Fulani could have expanded her reply to something like: 'Sistah Space, we are a charity that deals with domestic abuse.' Such an extended response may have given SH more to latch onto. If Fulani had given more, SH could have perhaps used such information to ask follow-up questions such as inquiring about Sistah Space's current projects or whatever. So, to make small talk, try to give your interlocutor something concrete to build on.

Following Fulani's reply, SH returns to her previous question, slightly rephrasing it: 'No where do you come from?' This displays that she considers the previous reply to be inadequate in some way and it perhaps indicates that it is not the charity that she is interested in but the person. However, Ngozi Fulani persists in talking about the charity: 'We're based in Hackney.' The problem here is that the conversation is going on two separate tracks: SH is alking about 'you', Ngozi Fulani the person. Ngozi Fulani is talking about the collective 'you', the charity. With two people talking about obviously different things they are quite simply, as the expression would have it, talking past each other. Unless the problem is resolved, conversation is sure to break down.

SH could have resolved this issue by settling with Sistah Space Hackney as a response and running with it by asking follow-up questions, showing an interest in Hackney or Sistah Space. Ngozi Fulani could have sought to solve the issue by giving more information, trying to catch the attention and interest of her interlocutor (see Chapter 19). The problem is that neither of the interlocutors shift their position or seek to collaborate to make a conversation. In short, neither of them seeks to repair the breakdown in communication and since the problem is unresolved, SH persists in her line of questioning, asking 'What part of Africa are YOU from". The stress* on the 'you' marks out that it is you-the-person, not you-the-collective, that is the subject of her question.

Aggression and Racism

The shift to Africa opens the door to the upcoming talk that Fulani later claimed was racist. In response to the question about which part of Africa she is from, Ngozi Fulani replies that she doesn't know, because they, presumably slave traders, didn't leave any records.

Even though the speakers are now aligned on the topic, which is you-Ngozi Fulani, not you-Sistah Space, SH still apparently treats Ngozi Fulani's reply as in some way insufficient. Ngozi Fulani must know where she comes from. So, SH asks again: 'Where are you from?' Ngozi replies that she is from the UK. At this point, Ngozi could have predicted that the talk was going downhill. She, as we saw in the previous chapter, could have added more information to her reply such as 'I am from the UK, Kilburn, it's a nice place, do you know it' in an attempt to steer the conversation to safer waters.

Similarly, SH could have accepted the UK as an answer and sought to steer the conversation to safety. She could therefore have said something like: 'the UK, where exactly?' If she had taken such a path, she could have shifted to a safer topic, places in the UK, rather than where Fulani comes from. Unfortunately, SH apparently persists in treating Ngozi Fulani's replies as insufficient and asks: 'but what nationality are you?' This question suggests that somebody born in the UK might not have British nationality. This is of course possible. So asking where somebody is from might not be a face-threatening act, but in some cases it might. In this remembered dialogue (line 18) Ngozi Fulani describes herself as being of 'African heritage and Caribbean descent'. And it is this that crucially makes the difference, i.e., the implication that somebody of African heritage and Caribbean descent cannot be British. Ngozi replies: 'I am born here and am British.' This reply links place of birth with nationality – as is most often, but not always, the case. So, here we now have what is perceived by Ngozi to be an aggression which develops into an argument*, i.e., an implied proposition that somebody of African heritage and Caribbean descent cannot be British, and resistance to this proposition.

Even at this late point in the downward spiral there might have been an opportunity to abruptly change topic and seek safer ground, but SH – reportedly – continues. First, the 'no' displays that she doesn't accept the answer as sufficient, and she persists, shifting the topic slightly from Ngozi Fulani's nationality to 'where do you really come from, where do your people come from?' The action that such words perform is 'othering': you and 'your people' are different from British people. And this is the nub of the alleged aggression: your people, and therefore Ngozi Fulani as part of the collective 'your people', are not British. This could be seen as racism in its simplest terms: your people are different from mine, and your people's place is not with my people.

Opposition and Argument*

It is at this point that Ngozi Fulani stops trying to respond to SH's questions and reverses the questioner/answerer role, so taking the initiative. She says: 'My people, lady, what is this?' This makes an argument by challenging the relevance* of the collective 'your people'. SH ignores the question (what is this?) and carries on, oblivious to the suffering she is causing: 'Oh I can see I am going to have a challenge getting you to say where you're from.' Thus, at the same time as aggressing Ngozi Fulani, she also adds salt to the wound by projecting that Ngozi Fulani is being difficult by not wanting to say where she is (really) from. Once again, instead of dropping the subject and seeking to change topic, SH allegedly persists with the same line of questioning: 'When did you first come here?' This ignores, and fails to build on, the statement (line 11) that Ngozi Fulani was born in the United Kingdom and that she is British. It also projects an immigrant, non-British identity* onto Fulani, thus deepening the argument in which the parties are doing difference, rather than sameness.

Under these conditions, small talk cannot work. Argument emerges as Ngozi Fulani responds: 'Lady! I am a British national, my parents came here in the 50s when...'. The utterance 'coming here' is the trigger that SH has been apparently waiting for. Prefacing her next utterance with 'Oh'*, which is often used to signal receipt of new information, SH understands this as 'evidence' that Ngozi Fulani is not British and this is finally an 'acceptable' reply to the original question ('Where are you from?'). This assessment is corrected in the next turn by Ngozi Fulani who opposes SH's assertion with a counter claim: 'No lady, I am of African heritage, Caribbean descent and British nationality.' At this point, the reconstructed dialogue ends.

To Sum Up

Small talk is a team event, not an individual one. It won't happen by itself, as if by magic, so work with your interlocutor to make it happen. This attempt at small talk fails because of the lack of cooperation between players. First and foremost, they are talking past each other rather than to each other. If you want to make small talk, attune yourself to what the other is saying and try to align with it, and build on it. Don't give minimal replies, but add to your reply, steering the conversation to common and non-threatening topics. Adapt to the other so that you're working in harmony with them rather than disharmony, complementing and adding to their talk rather than opposing it. If you see the talk veering to potentially 'difficult' subjects, drop the subject and change topic to safer ground.

21. BEING POLITE AND IMPOLITE

'Get lost you poor idiot'

We all know what politeness* and impoliteness are when we see them. And we also know that getting the level of politeness we use 'just right' is necessary to oil the wheels of social interaction – we get it wrong at our peril. If someone is polite towards us or our friends and colleagues we can have a sense of satisfaction – we are good people who are respected by others. On the other hand, if somebody is impolite or insults us, this can, in some cases, harm our self-esteem, cause moral indignation, and otherwise upset us. As Arthur Schopenhauer (1788-1860) the German philosopher put it:

> It is a wise thing to be polite; consequently, it is a stupid thing to be rude. To make enemies by unnecessary and wilful incivility is just as insane as proceeding to set your house on fire. For politeness is like a counter - an avowedly false coin - with which it is foolish to be stingy.

But how does politeness work? How do we play language games so as to be polite or impolite? The word 'politeness' has its origins in the old medieval French word *poliss* meaning to polish or decorate. It is therefore appropriate that we cross the Channel to look at how we play the language game of being (im)polite. First, to get an idea of how politeness works, we look at a very short, but heated and impolite, exchange between ex-President Sarkozy and an unidentified member of the public at the agricultural fair in Paris in 2008. Then we look at Liz Truss's (in)famous the 'jury's out' assessment as to whether President Macron is friend or foe, and to finish, President Macron's polite reply to this impolite jibe.

Extract One – President Sarkozy

The first extract we look at relates to an incident that took place back in 2008 when Nicolas Sarkozy, the then president of France, was visiting the agricultural fair at Paris. During this incident, Sarkozy is 'pressing the flesh' of the surrounding crowd, but one man refuses to shake his hand and a brief, but heated, verbal exchange[1] takes place. The exchange, translated into English below, soon went viral on social media, and the expression 'Get lost you poor idiot' (*Casse-toi pauvre con*, in the original French) was to haunt Sarkozy for the rest of his presidency.

1. Man: No don't touch me.
2. Sarkozy: So get lost.
3. Man: You dirty me.
4. Sarkozy: So get lost you poor idiot.

We can all see that this exchange is incredibly impolite, but what makes it impolite? Politeness takes two forms: minimising any imposition (negative politeness) and maximising our display

---

[1] Available at: https://www.youtube.com/watch?v=opg9Ynj3Bw8

of respect (positive politeness). In this case, we can see that this exchange comes across as being rude, impolite, and aggressive because both positive and negative politeness strategies are missing. This was no doubt the intention of both Sarkozy and the unidentified member of the public.

Impinging on the Other's Right to Act

First, the man impinges on Sarkozy's freedom of action by telling him 'Don't touch me.' He utters this using an imperative* form with no mitigating expression such as 'I would prefer it if you didn't touch* me,' or whatever. His words, lacking politeness, are designed to insult. Moreover, he uses the '*tu*' form, rather than the more formal and respectful '*vous*' form that is usually used when speaking to others who either we don't know, or who are further up in the pecking order. Old English, like modern French and other languages, had a 'tu' and 'vous' form. 'You' singular or informal was either thou or thee, and 'you' plural and formal was either ye or you. Whilst the '*tu*' and the '*vous*' form are no longer in use in modern English, failing to address an interlocutor with respect, by using for example an honorific* such as 'sir' or 'madam', may be interpreted as impolite in some situations.

Use of an Inappropriate Register*

Sarkozy, faced with such an impolite and disrespectful utterance, responds in kind (line 2: 'So get lost'). He also uses the, in this context*, disrespectful '*tu*' from and the imperative form "get lost" which impinges on the man's freedom of action by telling him in no uncertain terms what to do. The expression 'get lost' also has a very low register and is not formal, so it adds to the impoliteness. It is not the kind of language one would expect a French president to use when addressing a citizen of the Republic who is supposedly in a free, equal, and fraternal relationship with his president.

The man replies: 'You dirty me.' This implies that Sarkozy is unclean and that if the man were to shake Sarkozy's hand, he would be sullied. This utterance is also spoken using the second person 'tu' form. The utterance, attacking Sarkozy's self-worth, is again designed to be impolite and disrespectful.

Before walking on and continuing pressing the flesh, Sarkozy gets in the last word and adds: 'So get lost you poor idiot.' This is a fairy literal translation, but it is perhaps stronger than this and was variously translated in the international press at that time as: poor jerk, bloody idiot, or stupid bastard. Thus, the register is extremely low and not what you would expect from the President of the Republic. Moreover, it is uttered both using the disrespectful 'tu' form and in an imperative form. So, taking these three elements together (register, 'tu' form, and imperative from), this exchange is a clear case of impoliteness because neither party respects the freedom of action or the self-worth of the other.

Extract Two – Liz Truss

Here we look at a less obvious case of impoliteness, notably the infamous 'the jury's out' jibe[2] made by Liz Truss, the then foreign secretary, during a husting in her successful bid for the leadership of the Conservative Party in August 2022.

---

[2] Available at: https://www.youtube.com/watch?v=fXGl5FEvcRs

1. Interviewer: President Macron friend or foe?
2. Truss: The jury's out on … (Truss smiles, turns head to audience)
3. But if I … if I … if I (applause from audience)
4. if I become prime minister I will (Truss returns gaze to interviewer)
5. judge him on his deeds not his words.

Audience* Design

In line one, the interviewer asks Truss if President Macron is friend or foe. Truss says 'The jury's out'. At this point Truss turns her head away from the interviewer to face the audience. She thus explicitly addresses the audience* – the talk is designed for them, not the interviewer. Moreover, as she does so, she smiles and so frames* her talk as funny and witty – a clever response, from a clever person.

Here, of course, one must remember that Truss is at a Tory Party husting and the audience are Tory Party members who are going to vote in the Tory leadership campaign. Truss has to convince them that she is the best candidate, and to do this she gives them what they want to hear – a witty jibe at Britain's foreign neighbours. The identity* in play is that of a Tory Party leadership candidate, not that of a serving foreign secretary, responsible for British diplomacy. As this is happening the audience begins to applaud*. They thus show their alignment with, and appreciation of, Truss's response. Truss has hit her mark in terms of aligning with her audience and moving them towards voting for her. To pick a game metaphor: she plays the nationalist card and, not unsurprisingly, wins the trick. However, her comments were widely regarded as surprisingly undiplomatic. As the audience is applauding she begins to continue her assessment ('But if I...'). When the applause* dies down, she continues, 'If I become prime minister I will judge him on his deeds not his words.'

The Overhearing Audience*

So, where's the impoliteness? The Tory audience is not insulted, nor is the interviewer. The insult is directed at a non-present third party - the over-hearing audience*. Erving Goffman (1922-1982), a famous sociologist and social psychologist, pointed out that there are different types of audience. Notably, there is the physically present audience (in this case, the Tory faithful) and an over-hearing audience, who whilst maybe not being physically present nevertheless will get to hear the talk. In this case the over-hearing audience includes Macron. Truss's comments are impolite to Macron because she attacks his 'face' – a term used by Goffman to indicate one's self-esteem. The foreign secretary of a close ally stating that she is not sure if Macron is friend or foe certainly attacks Macron's self-esteem and is therefore impolite.

In short, in ignoring the over-hearing audience, Truss curries favour with the Tory faithful, but she insults Macron. So, when you're speaking remember that you don't just have one audience – your target audience that is physically present. There are other audiences out there and they may be overhearing you. I'm thinking here particularly of comments made on social media that may be intended as a joke, but when taken out of context and presented to a wider audience can be fatal to the speaker/writer. Bear all the possible audiences in mind when you speak: whilst being respectful and polite to the present audience, you may be rude and impolite to an overhearing audience. And such rudeness may come back to bite you.

Extract Three – President Macron

President Macron is not the only member of the over-hearing audience. The press, particularly the French press, also 'overheard' what Truss is saying and, the following day, Macron is asked to comment on Truss's speech[3]. As one of the journalist in the press pack asks: 'Liz Truss says that the (unclear) cannot say if you are a friend or an enemy of Great Britain. How do you react?' Macron's reply exemplifies how to be firm, but polite. It is a diplomatic response from a world leader, not a cheap jibe from a wannabe global leader. In response to Truss's comments, Macron replies:

1. It's never good to lose your bearings too much in life. If you asked
2. me the question, because it's like that I can answer you: by inference. Regardless of who
3. is being considered for the future leadership of Great Britain, I don't doubt for a second
4. that the United Kingdom is a friend of France. And you know, we live in a complicated
5. world. You have more and more liberal authoritarian democracies, power imbalances. If
6. we are not capable between French and British to say if we're friend or **foes** (raised
7. finger, pause) the term is not neutral, we're heading for serious problems. So, yes,
8. for sure, I say that the British people, the nation which is the United Kingdom, is a friend,
9. strong, allied, regardless of its leaders and sometimes despite and beyond its leaders and
10. the small errors that they may make while campaigning.

Indirectness (Off-record)

Macron first comments that 'It's never good to lose your bearings too much in life.' Here, Macron remains polite, yet he still criticises Truss. He does this by making a general comment using a vague* and generic 'you' pronoun*. This, on the face of it, is a general statement that omits* targeting Truss directly. However, because the question is framed* as being about Truss's comment, the audience (i.e., both the physically present journalists, the audience to whom they will be reporting, and no doubt indirectly the overhearing

---

[3] Available at: https://www.youtube.com/watch?v=F9n_s-b3XZA (full text about 19 minutes)

Liz Truss) know that Macron is talking about Truss. So, Macron is polite because even though a criticism is made, the person who is the target of this criticism is not specifically named. Brown (b. 1944) and Levinson (b. 1947), the two linguists most closely associated with politeness theory, call this strategy off-record politeness i.e., a politeness strategy in which an utterance cannot be attributed a single clear and unambiguous intention. The target audience of the utterance has to decide if the utterance is impolite or not, and the speaker has a way out because he/she can claim that he/she didn't intend to be impolite.

Framing*
Macron then continues by explicitly saying that he is going to answer by inference (*répondre en creux*, in the original French). By making a comment about his own talk, he frames the talk and explicitly directs the audience to infer his meaning. This, showing some awareness of the impact of his own talk, recognises the off-record politeness strategy that he is using and he continues his reply to the journalist by stating that 'Regardless of who is being considered for the future leadership of Great Britain I don't doubt for a second that the United Kingdom is a friend of France.' Following the way he has framed his talk, we know that he is talking about Truss. So we are instructed to understand the utterance as: 'Regardless of Liz Truss I don't doubt for a second that the United Kingdom is a friend of France.' This, of course, is tantamount to saying that Truss is of little relevance, but it remains polite because it is inferred by the audience, not explicit.

Depersonalising

It is interesting to note that Macron also shifts from Truss, as a person, to the British and French people. Through doing this he depersonalises the issue. Prefacing his next utterance with 'you know'*, which claims common knowledge* and therefore agreement, Macron points out that we live in a complicated world and that if the French and the British are not able to say if they are friends or foes then 'we're heading for serious problems'. By, shifting topic away from the personal (Truss) to talking about the French and the British people, he avoids direct criticism of Truss and remains polite by not criticising her directly.

Macron then sums up the gist of his message. He again moves beyond the personal, and makes the difference between the British people and their leaders relevant. He argues that the 'British people, the nation which is the United Kingdom, is a friend' and that this is 'regardless of its leaders and sometimes despite and beyond its leaders'. It thus implies that Truss has lost her bearings and is out of touch with the British people, but because Truss is not explicitly mentioned, it remains polite.

Further, Macron notes that the British leadership, by which everyone knows that Macron is referring to Truss, may make errors while campaigning. However, this criticism is downplayed so as to minimise the threat to Truss's face. First Macron does this through the use of the modifier 'small'. Second, he uses the modal verb 'may'. The errors are not something that have happened for sure, they are something that may have occurred. Third, he contextualises the error as part of electioneering and so limits the context* in which such small errors may occur.

To Sum Up

In sum, politeness and impoliteness are something that we all intuitively know. We can see here that being impolite is achieved through: not showing due respect; impinging on the future actions of another; and by not respecting your interlocutor's face (self-worth). To avoid, or mitigate, what Brown and Levinson call a face-threatening act (i.e., an action or utterance that may threaten the self-esteem of one's interlocutor or his/her right to act freely) several strategies can be adopted. In this chapter, we see most notably the off-record strategy, which means that you imply any criticism rather than making it explicitly. Other politeness strategies are discussed in the second section of this book: language advice.

22. TEAM TALK*

'Whatever we have to tackle together or individually [it] will always be us together as a team'

Working as a team is essential to many social activities. A good football team may be made up of 11 excellent individual players, but in order to be successful they have to play well as a team. Or, to take another example: if we go to a restaurant with friends we might also work to some extent as a team or group, rather than individuals. When greeted by the waiter, one person may speak on behalf of the group. Probably after consultation with the group, one person may order the wine. One person may pay the bill on behalf of the others. And so on. In fact, sometimes the group or the team becomes so relevant to the way that we talk that it doesn't makes sense to think in terms of an individual speaking. Rather, it makes sense to think of a group of individuals speaking so as to be a team. The team is important, not the individual.

In this chapter we'll be looking at (Prince) Harry and Meghan Markle's interview given to the BBC[1] in November 2017 just after their engagement, and way before Harry's estrangement from the royal family caused such an uproar. What struck me as I watched this interview was the way in which Harry and Meghan acted as a team – future husband and wife. But, how do they do this? How do they, through their talk, show that they are a couple, a close team? Let's have a look at some of the selected extracts of their interview.

Defining Self as a Team

Perhaps one of the key elements to look for is the use of pronouns* (us, we, ours etc.) or words such as team, group, and so on, which indicate that the speakers consider themselves to be a group.

1. Harry: But I know that at the end of the day, she chooses me and I choose her. And
2. therefore you know whatever whatever we have to tackle together or
3. individually will always be us together as a team. So I think, I think she's
4. capable.

In line one, Harry states that 'at the end of the day, she chooses me and I choose her.' He then draws out the upshot of this: 'therefore ... [it] will always be *us* together as a *team*'. So here, the use of the words 'team' and the pronoun* 'us' supports Harry's claim that he and Meghan are a team. Claiming to be a team is a starting point but working as a team might require a cluster of different supporting moves in the language game. Let's have a look at some other techniques that Harry and Meghan use.

---

[1] Available at : https://www.youtube.com/watch?v=LQicq60aJaw

Agreement

5. Meg: So nicely said, isn't it? (looks at the interviewer)
6. Harry: She's capable of ... she's capable of anything

After Harry has finished, Meghan looks towards the interviewer and assesses what Harry has been saying. By shifting her gaze* to the interviewer, she marks the interviewer, and beyond that the public who are watching the interview, as the primary audience. This comment is primarily intended for them, and only secondarily for Harry. The comment ('so nicely said') is extremely positive, which shows that she agrees emphatically with Harry; she buttresses* his prior statement. As a team, they are singing from the same hymn sheet. So, in teams we may see one member of the team actively supporting the words of another member, underlining those words, agreeing with them or making them stronger. It is such supporting moves that make them a team, rather than individuals. However, one supporting move may not in itself show that you are acting as a team. In what follows we look at a cluster of techniques that Meghan and Harry use which make them a team. The whole interview is shot through with little linguistic techniques through which Meghan and Harry demonstrate that they are acting as a team – as one would expect from people who are recently engaged. I chose the next extract to look at because it showcases quite a few of these techniques.

1. Int: Starting a long distance relationship, you were working on 'Suits' you had, I
2. imagine, a packed filming schedule, you've got lots of commitments of your
3. own, how hard was it to keep things going?
4. Harry: (takes a breath) It was yeah … (H looks at M, M looks at H)
5. Meg: It was just a choice. Right? (M looks at Int) I think that very early on, when we
6. realised we were going to commit to each other, that we knew (M looks at H)
7. we had to invest in the time and the energy and whatever it took to make that
8. happen (H starts nodding). And, so yes. With the filming schedule (laughs) it
9. was not the easiest, because it of course included a lot of travel. Back and forth,
10. but … (M looks at H)
11. Harry: I don't think you had any idea what time zone you've been on for the last year
12. and a half.
13. Meg: No. (laughs)
14. Harry: Coming over here four days or a week, and then going back and then straight
15. into filming the next day. 4 a.m. wake calls on a Monday [straight (H looks at M)
16. Meg: [yeah
17. Harry: into set, you know.
18. Meg: And right off the plane and straight to set. [Just coming back into it again.
19. Harry: [yeah
20. Harry: And just trying to … just trying to stay as close as possible on two different time
21. zones. And five hours apart does have its challenges. [But … but you
22. Meg: [ehm
23. know, we made it work, and now we're here. So, we're thrilled.

Sharing Utterances*

In line 4, Harry begins his reply to the interviewer's question. He takes a breath and then starts his phrase 'It was', but he hesitates. At this point he looks at Meghan, she returns his gaze* and then she continues the utterance adding 'just a choice'. Sharing talk in this way shows that they are on the same wavelength. It's almost as if they can read each other's thoughts and anticipate what the other will say. This is a key way in which a team emerges in talk, and if you listen carefully you'll see that it is a regular occurrence.

Speaking as 'We'

As Meghan continues talking, she reports on their thought process as a team using the 'we' pronoun*: 'when *we* realised *we* were going to commit to each other, that *we* knew *we* had to invest in the time and the energy and whatever it took to make that happen'. This means that as well as speaking for herself, she is also speaking on behalf of Harry. As she is reporting on what they were thinking she gazes* at Harry who begins to nod*, thus showing his agreement with what she is saying. Nodding can therefore be a way of displaying agreement, in this case adding to the display of being a team. Such a non-verbal response has the advantage of allowing the speaker to continue without disrupting their talk – it can, therefore, be a very supportive move in any language game.

Eye Gaze*

As she arrives at the end of her utterance, she ends with 'but' which projects some further talk. However, at this point she pauses, smiles, and gazes at Harry. Eye gaze can be significant in talk. When several people are present it can mark out who the talk is directed at, and it can also be used to select the next speaker. In this case, by shifting her gaze to Harry, Meghan hands the floor over to him – just as a footballer passes the ball to another player. Harry recognises this cue to speak, and he continues with talk that aligns with Meghan's talk and supports it.

Backchannels*

Harry supports Meghan's prior talk by talking about Meghan's experience of travelling and being on film sets in many time zones. Through talking about her experiences, he shows that they are so close that he knows about her life and can comment on it.

Significantly, as he is talking, Meghan says 'yeah'. This, as with the nod, is designed to show agreement with, and support of, Harry's talk, but does not seek to interrupt him. So, if someone is nodding and saying softly 'yeah, yeah' and so on as you talk to them, it's not only showing that they agree, but it's also indicating that they are happy to let you continue talking. It's a very supportive move. These little words and gestures are called backchannels, i.e., supportive words or gestures that allow the other to continue talking and which, generally, express alignment with what is being said.

Adding To/Continuing the Other's Talk

When he has finished talking, Meghan continues. This time, she prefaces her talk with 'and'. This explicitly marks her talk as a continuation of Harry's prior talk. Further, not only does she do this, but she also, more or less, incorporates Harry's exact words. Her talk mirrors and therefore supports Harry's talk. Through uttering a sentence together they share it and so do 'being a team'. Moreover, as she is speaking, Harry encourages and supports her by softly saying 'yeah'. As she finishes speaking, it is Harry who begins his next turn with 'and', so syntactically indicating that his talk is a direct continuation of Meghan's talk and that they are 'sharing' the talk. It is 'our' talk, not just 'my' talk. Through doing 'our' talk, rather than 'my' talk and 'your' talk, they do being a team.

Laughter*

In the next extract, we'll focus on laughter*. Laughter may not be considered talk, but it is an essential element of many conversations. Surprisingly it may not even be associated with humour* and may do other things beyond responding to something that is 'funny'. Here I demonstrate how it can be important in showing that people are acting together as a team.

1. Int: Tell us about your ring.
2. Harry: The ring is ... is obviously yellow gold because that's what ... her favourite and
3.   the main stone itself I sourced from Botswana and the little diamonds either
4.   side are from my mother's jewellery collection to make sure that she's with us
5.   on this ... on this crazy journey together. And ... er
6. Meg: It's beautiful, and he designed it. It's incredible.
7. Harry: Yeah, I'll make sure it stays on my finger. (H laughs, looks at M)
8. Meg: Of course. (laughs)

In line one, the interviewer asks Harry and Meghan about the ring. Harry describes the ring and as he nears the end of his talk, he hesitates (and ... er). The 'and' projects more talk, but since he hesitates Megan steps in with a positive evaluation of the ring which complements Harry's description. To make a comparison with rugby: it's as if she sees a loose ball, so picks it up and runs with it. Harry then agrees with this ('yeah') and adds 'I'll make sure it stays on my finger.' This is a rather obvious statement that he frames* as something funny by laughing.

We rarely laugh alone. When we laugh we often invite others to laugh. In this case, Meghan also laughs, so they laugh together. Since they laugh together this shows that they appreciate the same jokes, have the same values, and so they are a team. Further, because talking at the same time, rather than taking turns to share talk, would lead to cacophony, laughing together is one of the few actions that can be done simultaneously to show we're a team. Applause* is another simultaneous activity that can show group cohesion, as would group singing or chanting. So, yes, laughter can be in response to something funny, but it can also be a key element in showing solidarity. Note here, the interviewer doesn't laugh, so the solidarity, the 'teamness', is just between Harry and Meghan – an 'in' joke.

To Sum Up

We often think of talk as an activity between, or amongst, individuals. But this is not always the case. We are often talking in teams, helping each other out and cooperating. This can be done in many ways: completing each other's sentences, supporting each other's talk by agreeing explicitly or adding further comment, laughing together, backchannelling as the other is speaking, and speaking on behalf of the other. So, look out for this; it will give you an indication of how well any teams or groups that you are involved with are functioning. And of course, if you want to act as a team with colleague, or friends, use these techniques to build the team – to talk the team into being.

23. HAVING AND SHOWING KNOWLEDGE*

'You know what I mean it ain't no easy job up there I tell you'

It's interesting to note that, with the rare exception of prominent political speeches, it is unusual that people talk about language use and analyse the performance of participants in the language game. On the other hand, performance in other kinds of games, such as sporting events, is widely commented upon – perhaps down the pub, perhaps on social media, and also by highly paid experts in the TV studio. In this chapter, we turn our gaze to the language games that are regularly played, before, during, and after sporting events in the form of 'sports commentary'. We particularly focus on the way in which 'experts' come across as being experts. This, of course, is not a skill that we only see on TV sports commentary. It is a common feature of talk, from the business meetings in which we have to be seen to know what we are talking about to the ubiquitous man in the pub mouthing off, who has to be seen to be an expert in the subject. But how do we bring off such displays of knowledge?

It is impossible to know for sure what others know. Depending on who we are, or rather the role we are playing in a particular situation, we are expected to know certain things: a history teacher is expected to have some knowledge of history; a bank manager some knowledge of finance; a professional footballer some knowledge of football; and so on. Though we all know people who we suspect are 'just winging it', and we are critical of these people: they don't have the knowledge that we expect them to have. An expert, on whatever subject, has to display to others that they indeed know their stuff – otherwise, why bother listening to them? In order to show how 'knowledge' is part and parcel of the language games we play, we'll take a look at football pundits on the TV talking about an upcoming match.

More specifically, we look at the language games played by a panel of experts prior to England's World Cup quarter finals match played against Portugal in 2006[1]. The TV programme (*Match of the Day Live*) consists of a presenter, and three 'experts' in the studio. The talk in the studio is interspersed with other interviews and commentary from outside. The presenter is Gary Lineker, a former international football player. The three 'experts' (Alan Hansen, Alan Shearer, and Ian Wright) in the studio are also all former international football players.

The first point to note is that the experts in the studio are not Mr Average down the pub spouting off about football. As the viewers probably know, they are experienced professional footballers. This is pointed out on the brief bio that appears on the screen[2] as each of

---

[1] Available at: https://www.youtube.com/watch?v=MF5dBe7jOtw&t=1355s

[2] The brief bios read: Alan Hansen 'Scotland 1979-1987'; Alan Shearer 'England 63 caps, 30 goals' and Ian Wright 'England 1991-1998'.

the experts first speaks. Consequently, their credentials as experts are made explicit to the viewer. However, this expertise brought along to the TV programme also has to be demonstrated in the programme. Without such displays of knowledge, why should we listen to these TV pundits? So it's important that the experts play the game, and convince the audience* that they know what they're talking about. So, how do they do it? Let's take a look.

Not Knowing and Politeness*

We begin this analysis with an extract of the interview outside the studio, which the studio experts then comment on. The first extract we look at is an interview with Franz Beckenbauer, organiser of the 2006 World Cup and a renowned former international player. In this interview, the interviewer asks: 'What do you think of England's chances of winning [the match against Portugal]?' At first Beckenbauer talks about the strengths and weaknesses of the Portuguese team, then he shifts topic to English team and says:

1.	FB:	It depends on the line-up of the English team er because the last time I saw the
2.		English team play you know with one striker, I don't know if it's the right it's ...
3.		I'm not... you know I'm not here to criticise anything it's the style from anybody
4.		but er to play only with the one striker, okay, but er (smiles and half laughs).

According to Beckenbauer, England's chances of winning depend on the line-up. He assesses the 'one striker' line-up by saying 'I don't know if it's ... right'. The 'I don't know' makes him appear uncertain and lacking in knowledge. Yet, as a former footballer, you might expect him to have a definite opinion on the way in which England are playing (i.e., the one-striker line-up). After claiming a lack of knowledge about the rights and wrongs of the

English line-up, a politeness* strategy then kicks in whereby he doesn't make an explicit assessment of England's strategy (see Chapter 21). First, he announces that he is 'not here to criticise'. In doing this, he frames* his upcoming comments as non-critical and then, using 'but', he shifts to project a criticism of the English tactics. However, his talk is unfinished*, and instead of completing his talk he just smiles and half laughs*. As we saw in Chapter 21, this is an off-record politeness strategy. The audience has to read between the lines to see this as a negative assessment of the English team. In this way, Beckenbauer manages to criticise, without being critical. Consequently, and importantly, as organiser of the World Cup, he maintains a neutral stance. So, though Beckenbauer does have an opinion about the English team's tactics, he plays it down.

It is his identity* as organiser, rather than experienced international footballer, that takes precedence and so despite presumably having knowledge, he chooses to mask it. Knowledge in language games is therefore less something that we have and which just comes out in talk, rather it is linked to what we are expected to know and be able to say in given circumstances. It has to be played up and played down according to the circumstances.

Contrary to the way in which Beckenbauer plays down his knowledge, in the studio talk which immediately follows Beckenbauer's comments, the studio experts play up their knowledge* as we see below.

1. GL: Well, if Beckenbauer criticizes Sven's tactics I mean …
2. IW: The Kaiser knows his stuff.
3. AH: Great player. Great man. He hates a lone striker. Doesn't like it … doesn't like it
4.   at all.
5. IW: He hasn't ever played it neither, but I tell you we know you know what I mean
6.   Al (looks at Shearer) it ain't no easy job up there I tell you. I still … I still
7.   believe, you know what I mean, of course you've got somebody like Wayne
8.   Rooney up there. He's special no doubt about that and if Frank and Steve Gerrard
9.   can get to him quickly it's not a problem you know. I think we'll cause them a lot
10.   of problems er because Carvalho, for **me**, goes to ground very quickly know what
11.   I mean.

Not Knowing and Being the Host

Despite the fact that Beckenbauer's criticism of the English team's tactics has been substantially downplayed, Lineker nevertheless recognises Beckenbauer's talk as criticism of Sven's[3] (the England manager's) tactics. However, as with Beckenbauer, the TV host/presenter is also expected to keep a relatively neutral position. Lineker's role is to orchestrate the show, rather than deliver his own opinion. So, in this case, whilst recognising Beckenbauer's criticism of England's manager ('well if Beckenbauer criticises Sven's tactics'), Lineker, through saying 'I mean', projects agreement with this criticism. However, because he doesn't finish his sentence and articulate what it is that he means, he avoids explicitly criticising the England manager and the 'lone striker' tactic. As a former international footballer and England player we would expect him to have an opinion and we can assume that if he doesn't openly express an opinion this is not because he doesn't have one, or that

---

[3] Sven-Göran Eriksson, manager of the English football team (2001-2006).

he has no knowledge of the subject. Rather, it is because his identity* as presenter doesn't require him to express an opinion openly and to take sides in a debate. Knowledge in language games is not something that we have and we just express. Rather, knowledge is something that we have to manage and which we express according to the rules of the game* and what we can, and cannot, say in certain situations.

Knowing and Being the Expert

The studio guests/experts are a totally different kettle of fish: they are paid to express their opinions. In this case, Ian Wright says: 'The Kaiser[4] knows his stuff.' He therefore aligns with Beckenbauer's and Lineker's off-record assessments. However, to come across as an expert Wright can't be seen to be just going with the flow and agreeing with prior assessments. Rather, he has to show that he has an independent opinion that he held before hearing the others. To do this he makes a clear, unambiguous statement with no 'I thinks' or 'maybes' which claims clear and independent knowledge. The 'Kaiser' knows his stuff, and I am in a position to assess the Kaiser's knowledge because I also have this knowledge. So, assessing people's talk after they have spoken and emphatically agreeing with it is a way of showing that you also have that knowledge.

First-hand and Second-hand Knowledge

Alan Hansen, one of the panel of experts, then sums up Beckenbauer's opinion: 'He hates a lone striker doesn't like it doesn't like it at all.' Ian Wright then takes the floor again. Paradoxically, after having played up Beckenbauer's knowledge in

---

4 The Kaiser: Beckenbauer's nickname.

his prior talk, Wright now plays it down: 'He hasn't ever played it (i.e., lone striker) neither.' He then plays up his, and Alan Shearer's knowledge: 'but I tell you we know you know what I mean. Al (looks at Shearer) it ain't no easy job up there I tell you.' Key here is the 'we know'. He and Al know for sure, because they were both attackers/strikers. There are two types of knowledge. First-hand knowledge, something that I know for sure, because I was there and I experienced it. And second-hand knowledge, something that I was told. First-hand knowledge generally carries more weight than second-hand knowledge. So, one way in which knowledge is communicated is by showing that you have first-hand experience. In this case, by drawing out Beckenbauer's lack of experience as a striker and his, and Shearer's knowledge, as strikers, Wright displays his right to have knowledge about the 'lone striker' tactic. This knowledge trumps Beckenbauer's, a defender's, knowledge. So, in order to be convincing, to be an expert, the source of your knowledge is important: is it first-hand or second-hand?

Consensus*

Further, by looking at Shearer and using the 'we' pronoun*, Wright creates a kind of consensus . It's not just Wright saying this; other experts will back him up. Consensus, safety in numbers, creates more believability. If others, especially other experts, have the same opinion as me, then why shouldn't I be believed?

Lack of Doubt

Wright then gives his (expert) opinion which is in favour of the tactic of the lone striker: "I still ... I still believe, you know what I mean, of course you've got somebody like Wayne Rooney up there. He's special no doubt about that and if Frank and Steve Gerrard can get to him quickly it's not a problem you know I think we'll cause them a lot of problems er because Carvalho, for **me**, goes to ground very quickly know what I mean.' On the one hand, this talk makes his opinion definite – it has little of the 'don't know' that we saw in Beckenbauer's talk. His assessments are made as simple statements of truth: 'he [Wayne Rooney] is special': 'it [the lone striker] is not a problem'; 'Carvalho, for **me**, goes to ground very quickly.' Moreover, the assessment of Rooney is boosted by the expression 'no doubt about it'. Taken together, this displays that Wright is sure of his opinion and so he presents himself as the expert who has a well-founded opinion and so who should be listened to.

My Opinion as a Politeness Strategy

However, it is also interesting to see that when Wright gives his opinion, he also presents this as just that. He presents it as what 'I believe' and what 'I think' and as he talks about Carvalho, a Portuguese defender, he stresses that he is talking for himself ('for **me**'). In doing this, Wright leaves the door open for other people to have another opinion. Giving a personal opinion becomes a kind of politeness* strategy whereby the opinions of others are respected. It avoids the 'I am right, you're wrong' stance. Failure to modify your display of knowledge in some way may give you the impression of being bigoted and opinionated. So, displaying knowledge is always a balancing act: at times you'll need to display that you know for sure. But you need to balance this with respect of other people's opinion by throwing in a dose of politeness. Wright manages to do this admirably. He comes across as knowledgeable, but polite and respectful.

To Sum Up

Knowledge is often regarded as something we have, not something we 'do'. Yes, there are things that we know, and things that we don't know but it is often the particular language games that we're involved in that allow us to display this knowledge, or not. As we see above, sometimes people don't show knowledge because it is not his/her place to show knowledge; other issues such as being polite and reserved are more important. Conversely, we've all had the experience of somebody trying to wing it, to pretend they have knowledge of the subject when they don't. Sometimes we are taken in by these performances, sometimes we're not. So, beware of how displays of knowledge are constructed, and don't be taken in by those who are winging it.

24. TALKING TWADDLE

'A backbench Tory MP said you were a Marxist with no interest in anything other than trying to tear down the government'

Twaddle is defined by Merriam-Webster's online dictionary as silly and idle talk. Or, to put it in more colloquial terms, twaddle is bullshit*. Whether one judges a particular stretch of talk as twaddle, or not, no doubt largely depends on the person: one person's twaddle is another person's common sense. However, I would like to argue that twaddle is neither silly, nor idle. All talk, whether somebody labels it as twaddle or not, is done for a reason. Common sense tells us that talk only has weight when it makes sense, but this is not the case. There is method in silliness and idleness: twaddle can be carefully designed to do things that reasonable and serious talk cannot do. Silly and idle talk can be used, for example, to confuse and obscure and, as a sleight of hand, it can be used to mask criticism, propogate false ideas, provoke and insult.

As an example of this, I take the exchange between Mike Lynch, the General Secretary of the National Union of Rail, Maritime and

Transport Workers (RMT) and the journalist Richard Madeley[1]. The exchange was broadcast live on 21st June 2022 on one of the UK's best-known breakfast TV shows (*Good Morning Britain*). Lynch classifies Madeley's questioning as twaddle, which the journalist denies. Whether the line of questioning is, or isn't, twaddle, I let the reader decide. What interests me here is not whether the journalist is, or isn't, talking twaddle, but what this talk, classified by one of the participants as twaddle, achieves.

1.	RM	Mr. Lynch, good morning to you. It's going to be a busy day for you today
2.		erm can we just get one thing nailed [to the wall before we get going here er
3.	ML	[good morning
4.		you've been accused severally in the last few weeks of being a Marxist. It
5.		happened again last night a backbench Tory MP said you were a Marxist with
6.		no interest in anything other than trying to tear down the government. Now are
7.		you not a Marxist? Because if you are a Marxist then you're into revolution and
8.		into bringing down capitalism. So are you or aren't you?
9.	ML	(slight laugh) Richard you do come up with the most remarkable twaddle
10.		sometimes. I have got to say.
11.	RM	I didn't whoa whoa whoa I am saying that you've been accused of being a Marxist
12.		that's all. That's called reporting.
13.	ML	Look, no I'm not a Marxist. I'm an elected official of the RMT. I'm a working
14.		class bloke leading a trade union dispute about jobs, pay, and conditions of service
15.		so it's got nothing to do with Marxism. It's all about this dispute. It's an industrial
16.		dispute and that what it's all about.
17.	RM	Absolutely. I emphasise I am not talking twaddle and accusing you of being a
18.		Marxist. I am merely quoting people who are, including many of the newspapers.
19.	ML	Well, that's what it sounds like to me.
20.	RM	Well, I'm sorry if it did but I don't think it was, but anyway to be absolutely
21.		clear you are not a Marxist. Fine.
22.	ML	Tell us about this letter.

---

[1] Available at : https://www.youtube.com/watch?v=QB4M4ugvaVg

The Journalist's Question*

The interview opens, as one would expect, with the journalist greeting the guest and asking a question*. This is an 'obvious' feature of news interviews – the journalist asks questions, the interviewee responds. It is so obvious and accepted that it passes without notice, but it is significant in that it allows the journalist to set their agenda and, unless the interviewee resists in some way, it makes the interviewee dance to their tune. This practice, of course, can be fairly innocent and uncontentious, or it may be more loaded and used to gain the argumentative advantage (see Chapters 2, 5, 6, & 11). In this case, Madeley presents the opening question of his interview as 'nailing' something preliminary to getting going.

Word Choice

Nailing (down) is an interesting choice of words* since, as defined by the Merriam-Webster's online dictionary, it means: to settle, establish, or represent clearly and unmistakably. The use of nail, rather than, say, 'discuss, talk about, bring up the subject of' is interesting. The word choice* implies that the upcoming topic is a subject that is opaque and needs clarity*. The subject, that needs to be nailed, is that Lynch has been accused severally (sic - presumably meaning by several people) and by an unnamed backbench Tory MP of being a Marxist. Of course, we could check Hansard (the official report of all Parliamentary debates) to see if on 20th June 2022, a Tory backbencher did accuse Lynch of being a Marxist, but this is beside the point. The issue is not what's true and what's false, but how a past event and past words are re-presented in the here-and-now of a news interview to bolster an argument* or account for a line of questioning. Thus, whilst keeping the sources of this accusation vague*, Madeley is able to suggest that this is not a one-off accusation, but a repeated occurrence. Both the apparent frequency of this accusation and the 'fact'* that various people are making it, lends it credibility*: if enough people are saying something enough, then it must be true.

Word choice* is, again, particularly important here. It is not suggested that Lynch may be a Marxist; Lynch has been 'accused' of being a Marxist. 'Accused' is a word that is used in connection with crime (one is accused of murder, rape, burglary etc.) or negative behaviours (e.g. lying, cheating, talking twaddle etc.) and character traits (e.g. hubris, arrogance, greed etc.). One is rarely accused of generosity, altruism, leadership and so on. The use of accused, therefore, frames* being a Marxist as something that is tantamount to criminality. The criminality of being a Marxist presumably consists of trying to tear down the government, which is the claim made by the unnamed Tory backbencher who is reported to have said that Lynch had 'no interest in anything other than trying to tear down the government'. Two weeks prior to this statement, the Tory party itself held a vote of no confidence in Boris Johnson, the then prime minister and leader of the Tory party. Had it succeeded, this vote would have resulted in the fall of the Johnson government. The irony of this comment is lost, and is not picked up either by the journalist or Lynch. Regardless of the irony, it is noticeable that this claim is presented as an extreme case. Lynch is presented as having *no interest in anything other* than tearing down the government. Obviously, such mono-purpose in life would be unusual, but it's the effect that this builds up, not the literal truth of the claim, that counts. Like a magician's sleight of hand in a card trick, such an exaggeration* is something that has to be slowed down and analysed otherwise it passes unnoticed. The topic is not picked up and the talk goes on, but an exaggerated* impression of a man obsessed by a single mission of bringing down the government remains.

After building up to the issue that has to be nailed, the journalist then asks the question: 'are you not a Marxist?' The consequence of this is then made clear: if Lynch is a Marxist then he is necessarily into revolution and bringing down capitalism. This is, following Madeley's logic*, what Marxists 'do'. The pseudo-logic of a simple if + then clause is used to encapsulate Lynch's alleged political logic.

The (Non)Answer

The question* makes a reply relevant, and the yes/no question format projects either acceptance or denial of the 'accusation'. Lynch, however, avoids providing the projected yes or no answer. First, he prefaces his talk with a slight laugh* which mocks the journalist. Then, he addresses the journalist by name ('Richard') which signals that the reply is primarily intended for the journalist and not the audience* of *Good Morning Britain*.Lynch tells Madeley: 'you do come up with the most remarkable twaddle sometimes'. Lynch, thus accounts* for not answering the question (initially at least) because it is twaddle. Qualifying Madeley's line of questioning as twaddle releases Lynch from the obligation of replying to it. To take a metaphor from boxing, it is a way of ducking or blocking a punch.

Changing Footing*

Footing is a technical term, coined by the linguist Erving Goffman (1922-1982), which refers to the way in which we position ourselves in relation to talk. In this case, we see that Madeley changes footing by seeking to distance himself from the comments that he previously made and which Lynch has classified as 'twaddle'. In other words, Madeley faced with this assessment of his question as twaddle is, to continue the boxing metaphor, put on the back foot. He reacts to this, somewhat defensively, by denying that he made the claim. Others, rather than him, have accused Lynch of being a Marxist and therefore if twaddle has been spoken, he is not the twaddler. This is very much a 'don't shoot the messenger' claim which Madeley classifies as reporting. Reporting is what journalists do, so he is simply doing his job. To some extent citing 'other sources' is a key strategy in any journalist's arsenal and is a well-known technique for getting opinions out into the public sphere whilst disclaiming responsibility for these claims. In this case, citing the accusations of somewhat vaguely defined others allows Madeley the opportunity to make the accusation that Lynch is a Marxist whilst not taking responsibility for these accusations. So, if Lynch is right and twaddle is being spoken, it is neither silly, nor idle: it does things. In this case, the message – intended or otherwise – that Lynch is a Marxist is communicated to the audience, but responsibility for making the accusation is denied.

The Answer – Shifting Identities*

Lynch then goes on to answer the question: 'I'm not a Marxist'. Evidently, had he said he was a Marxist, implicitly this would also, unless contested, have entailed accepting the logic that he is trying to bring down the government and the capitalist system. Having ducked the claim that he is a Marxist bent on revolution, he counter-attacks and replaces the identity* that such an accusation has projected on him with a more modest, reasonable, trade union identity. He is an 'elected official' (nothing revolutionary there), of the RMT (not Comintern) 'a working class bloke' (as many viewers of *Good Morning Britain* may classify themselves) who is leading a trade union dispute about jobs, pay, and conditions of service' (very reasonable aims, far from revolutionary, and that many people may sympathise with). This is then summed up as having 'nothing to do with Marxism'. Rather, it's an industrial dispute and so it is not aimed at bringing down the government, initiating a revolution, and tearing down the capitalist system.

Faced with this answer, Madeley accepts it and aligns with it ('absolutely'). However, rather than letting sleeping dogs lie and quietly forgetting the claim that he is talking twaddle, he still continues to account* for his question. He does this by shifting responsibility for accusing Lynch of being a Marxist to the, albeit vague*, people that he is quoting. (Don't blame me mate, blame the others: I'm 'just' doing my job reporting.) The others are now extended to 'many of the newspapers'. Lynch however, does not accept this washing of hands and, disagreeing, he argues that Madeley's talk sounded like twaddle and an accusation of being a Marxist. This, to continue the boxing metaphor, lands a punch squarely on Madeley's jaw. It elicits an apology ('I am sorry if it did'), albeit softened by the claim that Madeley didn't think it was twaddle. Madeley then sums up the answer to his initial question: 'to be absolutely clear you are not a Marxist. Fine'. Having done so, he then uses his prerogative, as presenter, to close down the talk on whether Lynch is a Marxist or not and to shift to the next topic in the interview.

To Sum Up

The key issue here is not whether one qualifies the accusation that Lynch is a Marxist as twaddle – which may depend more on your political views than the 'truth' of any such proposition. Let's assume that, as Lynch says, Madeley's talk and the accusation that he is a Marxist is twaddle, what does this twaddle achieve? It not only allows the accusation that Lynch is a Marxist to enter into people's homes and minds, and to be propagated, but it allows the journalist to avoid taking responsibility for this accusation. Moreover, even if Madeley concludes that Lynch is not a Marxist, the genie, whether intended or not, is out of the bottle. To die-hard Conservative supporters the accusation of being a Marxist might appear to be entirely reasonable, to those sympathetic to Lynch and the RMT, the accusation of being a Marxist was no doubt silly. However, what is crucial is that the silliness is not idle, it does something. It allows Madeley and *Good Morning Britain* to propagate what some would consider to be an entirely false narrative*. Refuted or not, twaddle put out into the public domain on prime-time breakfast TV once planted may take root and affect the way people perceive political reality and the society that surrounds them. This in turn affects the way people act politically: how they vote etc. Twaddle, then, can be neither silly, nor idle, in its impact.

Was Lynch right to call Madeley's line of questioning twaddle, silly and idle talk? Maybe, maybe not. It's for you to decide.

PART TWO

LANGUAGE ADVICE

THE SECRET CODES: 100 WAYS OF TALKING FOR SUCCESS

The Blarney Stone is an ancient stone that is embedded in the walls of Blarney Castle, just outside Cork, in Ireland. Legend has it that in the 15th Century, the lord of the castle was involved in a difficult court case. He appealed to Clíodhna, Queen of the Fairies, for help. She told him to kiss the first stone that he saw on his way to court. He did so, and he won the court case. He then took the stone and built it into the battlements of his castle. The legend is that if you kiss the Blarney Stone, which isn't easy because you have to lie on your back with a sheer drop below you, you'll be able to speak with force and eloquence.

That's a nice legend, but what I am outlining here are 100 ways that will allow you to crack the secret codes of talk and play language games more effectively. Language skill, the ability to play games with words and make your words 'do' things in an effective way, is not something that's innate. You're neither born with the gift of the gab, nor does kissing the Blarney Stone make you an eloquent speaker and effective language user. Effective language use is a skill that can be learned, and one way of doing this is to develop your skills by looking at the way in which other more or less skilled speakers play the game. How do they do things with words such as persuading, justifying, and apologising? Which strategies work, and which don't? What are the secret codes of conversation?

In this book we've looked in detail at some different uses of language, such as apologising, debating, making small talk, and so on – and we've looked at the strategies people have used to make their talk effective. Looking at talk, raising our awareness of how language games happen can, I believe, help us be more effective speakers. So, in this section of the book, I have pulled together 100 ways to help you crack the codes of conversation and improve your ability to play language games.

1. Accounting for Actions

As the famous sociologist Harold Garfinkel (1917-2011) pointed out, whatever actions we perform, we should always be in a position to account for them, to justify them, if demanded. If I fail to reply to a greeting and am challenged, I might account for this by saying that I didn't hear the greeting or whatever. Most of the time, we're un-challenged. People can see why we're doing a particular action, but sometimes accounting for why we do things becomes a language game. For example, in Chapter 18, the clerk of the meeting threw the chairman out of the meeting. She then accounts for this. So, be prepared to account for your actions. In court cases, as we see in Chapter 2, accounting for your actions may be the whole *raison d'être* of the language game.

Accounting for actions can also be a politeness strategy. For example, to stay polite, if you say 'no', an explanation as to why you have said 'no' attenuates any threat to face. So, if someone asks you out to dinner. You could just say 'no', but if you do say 'no' it would be politer to add something like: 'I'd love to come but I can't because....'

2. Aphorisms

Aphorisms are sayings that contain a generally accepted truth: boys will be boys; every cloud has a silver lining; don't count your chickens before they are hatched, and so on. Because they are often perceived to contain little nuggets of folk wisdom, they can be deployed like empty signifiers*. In other words, such sayings can mean all things to all people. Consequently, what such sayings really mean, and whether or not they are appropriate for a situation or whether they are 'true' is rarely contested or analysed. On the one hand, the very banality of aphorisms can allow you to sneak them into talk so that you can make your point. On the other hand, be ready to challenge your interlocutor's use of aphorisms; maybe they are being used to support loose thinking.

3. Applause

Applause is, as we all know, used to show appreciation of the other. It is often a communal activity and so it displays that those applauding are acting as a team, rather than individuals. If we're part of an audience that applauds, it gives us a sense of community, solidarity, and agreement. We are one, at least for that instant.

4. Argument

In linguistic terms, argument is nothing more than a proposition by a prior speaker that is opposed by the next speaker. I say black, you say white. From this point of view, it covers not only 'slagging matches', raised voices, and shouting kinds of argument, but also more refined debate, to small talk that begins to go off track (see Chapter 20).

The key here is to be aware of this simple mechanism (action/opposition), or structure of talk, that underlies all 'argument'. Play it up if you want to argue, play it down if you are seeking to avoid argument.

5. Audience

When playing language games, you should, of course, consider your audience and design your talk according to what you want to achieve and the expectations and knowledge of the audience. As we see in Chapter 17, there's no point in talking about your trip to a children's theme park if your audience wants to hear about the economy. Similarly, there's no point in providing technical details of malaria prevention to a non-expert audience (see Chapter 15). Indeed, what you want to say (the message) must be carefully calibrated according to what your audience wants to hear and is capable of understanding.

In public speaking, you can even address your audience directly, using 'we' or 'you' pronouns or by asking them to do something like responding to a simple question (e.g. put your hands up if). Asking the audience questions involves them, and gets them thinking. It retains their attention. However, my advice would be not to ask the audience too much. The risk is that you may get an answer that deviates too much from what you intended and you could get side-tracked. So, involve the audience, address them directly and even ask them questions, but keep these questions simple.

See also, point 58: Overhearing audience.

6. Authority

Authority, or showing that you have some kind of legitimate right to say what you are saying, is key to much talk. This authority might come from many sources, your job, your knowledge, your experience and so on, but regardless of its sources, authority has to be mobilised in talk. For example, in TV adverts it's often a dentist (or rather an actor playing the role of a dentist) who recommends a particular toothpaste and they're often dressed up in a white coat, a prop that one associates with the job. This, as Cialdini points out, is one of the six principles of persuasion and it is also a key aspect of ethos: an authority figure is more likely to persuade us to do something (see point 62: principles of persuasion).

7. Backchannels

Backchannels are those little words (yeah, sure, right, okay) or gestures (nods) or hmms. These words, gestures, or sounds are often used by speakers to show that they are listening. They are often supportive of the speaker. They show that we are in agreement with the speaker, but that we do not want to interrupt them. You could dismiss them as unimportant, but try listening to somebody without using these little words or gestures and you'll see that it will be interpreted as a lack of interest. So, use backchannels as a way of showing your interest and encouraging your interlocutor.

8. Body language

Body language relates to the way in which we use our bodies to communicate with others, through gesture, eye gaze, the use of space, and so on. In my 100 pieces of advice, I have covered these, and other non-verbal means of communicating, separately. I'm including a heading on body language in this list of tips as a word of warning. You'll see a lot of stuff out there saying something along the lines that only 7 per cent of communication happens through words, 38 per cent takes place through the tone of voice, and 55 per cent of communication comes from our body language, notably facial expression. These figures, or similar, in fact come from the research of Mehrabian, an American professor writing in the 1960s. However, his research has been totally misrepresented to such an extent that we now talk about the Mehrabian Myth. Mehrabian's original research related only to attitudes and feelings in situations in which a person was saying one thing, but meaning another. Why this generalisation of his research has passed into folk wisdom is a mystery. So, be careful of advice that over-stresses the importance of non-verbal communication – after all we can communicate perfectly well by telephone.

You'll note that the advice I've given, or the observations that I've made do not make big claims such as: crossing your arms is a defensive stance; nervousness is displayed in foot fidgeting; people who are lying look to the left. I think it is quite simply unhelpful to make such generalisations. Rather, as I've done in this book, we can look at some body language in some specific situations and see the role that it plays in the language game and assess how effective it is, but I think we should be careful about over-generalising what specific gestures and movements mean.

9. Boosters

Boosters are adjectives or adverbs (such as very, entirely, completely) that add force to the message that we wish to convey. They are quite often 'slipped' into talk to emphasise particular points. So, as we see in Chapter 3, when Johnson apologises for Partygate, he doesn't just offer his apology, he offers his *heartfelt* apology.

10. Bullshit

Bullshit baffles brains as the saying goes and it's quite surprising how much bullshit gets talked. Indeed, Harry Gordon Frankfurt (1929-2023), an American philosopher and professor from Princeton University, wrote a best-selling book, called *On Bullshit*, devoted to the analysis of bullshit. According to him, bullshit occurs when people want to convey a certain impression regardless of the truth. This contrasts with liars who recognise the importance of the truth, they just don't tell it.

Consequently, when bullshitting or being bullshitted, the rules of the game change so that whether utterances are true or false is quite simply irrelevant. Bullshit in a low stakes game can be fun. We all have friends who have the knack of spinning a story so that a mundane event in their life becomes entertaining when recounted, and we know that such stories have to be taken with a 'pinch of salt'. We like it when people shoot the breeze. But in other contexts bullshit is dangerous. If our interlocutor is speaking with scant regard to the truth, why should we trust him? Why should we be persuaded by his or her words? So be careful of bullshit and bullshitters. We know there's a lot around, but there may be more than we think.

Having said that, bullshit does have its purpose. We see in Chapter 24 how a journalist talks twaddle, but in so doing he is able to attack a union representative and make outlandish accusations. Even though the journalist then distances himself from such accusations, they are nevertheless out there in the public domain.

A recent, and famous, example of such bullshit is the former Prime Minister Boris Johnson's insinuation that Starmer, then Leader of the Opposition, was somehow involved in the decision not to prosecute the paedophile Jimmy Savile. This claim was largely condemned as twaddle, and indeed it was later retracted by Johnson. However, it did serve to distract attention from more pressing matters such as Johnson's own failure to respect Covid restrictions in the so-called Partygate scandal. This strategy is sometimes called the dead cat strategy, whereby a spurious, yet shocking, announcement (bullshit) is used to shift attention away from more pressing and troublesome issues. So, even bullshit has its uses!

11. Buttresses

A buttress is a technical term for supporting move that backs up somebody else's talk. Agreeing with a prior assessment would be a classic example. Other ways of supporting people might be adding more information or precision to a claim that somebody has made or reformulating the same claim in different words. Buttressing another person's talk can display that you're working as a team. You're colleagues, and you're working with, rather than against, each other.

12. Chairing

Chairing a meeting is something that we are likely to have to do at some time in our life. The chair's role is basically to ensure that a meeting goes smoothly. He or she usually:

- opens and closes the meeting
- opens and closes topics on the agenda
- makes sure that everybody who has a right to speak, and who wants to speak, does so
- keeps the talk on track and sanctions any deviations
- sums up what has been said so that everybody understands
- announces decisions
- ensures that one person speaks at a time

13. Clarity

Clarity is one of Grice's conversational Maxims (see point 18: conversational maxims). If you want to be an effective speaker, be clear about what it is you want to say. If you don't know what the message is, how can you communicate it clearly? Once you are clear about what it is that you want to say, say it in an appropriate manner that takes the knowledge and expectations of the audience into account.

14. Common knowledge

Be careful when you hear expressions such as: 'it is generally accepted that'; 'we all know that'; 'it is widely believed that' etc. These claims to common knowledge project the idea that the speaker is just bringing to your attention what everybody else knows. It is a way of building up a consensus. What somebody claims to be common knowledge, may be so, but it is often used to give a personal opinion, perhaps not that widely shared, that is presented as something that is more widely believed. If others believe something to be true, then so should you. If you can project that your opinion is common knowledge - something that everybody knows - it may become more persuasive. If everybody knows this, then so should your interlocutor. However, I am always sceptical when I hear such claims, my bullshit detector switches into over-drive.

15. Comparison

Comparison can be a way of getting your point across. In Chapter 5, Starmer and Sunak compare the performance of the UK with that of other countries in the OECD and G7. The UK's performance, according to Sunak, is good in comparison to others. The

UK's performance, according to Starmer, is bad in comparison to others. So, be careful of comparison. Is the speaker comparing like with like? Is the comparison valid? The comparison itself is not really the issue; the key is to consider what the speaker is trying to achieve by making a comparison.

See also Metaphor, point 50 below.

16. Consensus

Projecting consensus – whether true or imagined – is a way of making your words more persuasive. This is a tactic that is often used in argument: if many other people believe what you are saying, then so should your interlocutor. Further, if you can show that those who share your view are authoritative figures, then this adds to the persuasiveness of your argument.

17. Context

Awareness of context is very important for making your talk effective. It's getting the right words for the right occasion. This is why rather than just giving you 100 decontextualised tips for playing language games, I've presented 23 examples from real life and I have drawn the advice directly from these events. What is appropriate in one situation may be inappropriate in the next. To make your talk effective, you should consider such things as: the setting of the talk; the other participants and what they expect of you; your goals and desired outcomes; and the message you want to convey.

Dell Hymes (1927-2009), a renowned sociolinguist, devised the mnemonic S.P.E.A.K.I.N.G. This mnemonic serves as a kind of checklist that will help you assess the context of a language game and select appropriate language use.

- **S** scene or setting: where are you?
- **P** participants: who is your audience?
- **E** ends: what is it you want to achieve?
- **A** acts: the sequence of acts or moves that make up an event. So, for example, a presentation may begin with a hook to attract the audience's attention, followed by an introduction, the main points, and then a conclusion that sums it all up.
- **K** key or tone: how do you want to come across? Friendly, aggressive, kind, firm etc.
- **I** instrumentality: the channel of communication that is used. face-to-face, an email, vlog, telephone call, etc.
- **N** norms: rules of the game that are in place
- **G** genre: e.g., meeting talk, small talk, sales talk etc.

18. Conversational maxims

As Paul Grice (1913-1988), a British linguistic philosopher, pointed out, for talk to 'work' it should be informative, clear, relevant, and truthful. He summed up these principles in his conversational maxims, which are:

- **The maxim of quantity.** Provide just the right amount of information that your interlocutor requires, no more, no less.
- **The maxim of quality.** Be truthful. Don't tell deliberate lies or speak about something for which you have no supporting evidence, i.e., don't bullshit.
- **The maxim of manner.** Be clear. Be brief. Be orderly. Avoid using obscure language.
- **The maxim of relation.** Be relevant.

It is easier to see the relevance and importance of these maxims when they're breached, rather than when talk is running smoothly.

This we see in Chapter 17. Boris Johnson's 'Peppa Pig' speech fails because it's difficult to see the relevance of a British politician talking about Peppa Pig World. Perhaps Johnson is happiest in such a fantasy world, but the relevance is difficult to see. Consequently, the maxim of manner is also breached: his speech is not clear. Similarly, the maxim of quality is breached: Johnson bullshits and pulls figures out of the air to support his flagging argument.

So pay attention to these four maxims. Adhering to them should make your talk, in most instances, more effective.

19. Credibility

In order to be an effective speaker, you must be credible. This credibility is very much tied to ethos, i.e., your knowledge, your good character, and your goodwill towards others. It can be built up by for example showing that you have first-hand knowledge of what you are talking about, or that you have an identity that allows you to have such knowledge, or by displaying that you are an honest and likeable person. Whilst you may have an interest in playing up your credibility, in an adversarial situation others will surely attack your credibility. They may suggest that you lack ethos because you have a vested interest in putting forward a particular argument or that you are not qualified to talk about a subject. So for example, in Chapter 5, Sunak makes reference to Kier Starmer's union paymasters, which is an attempt to attack the credibility of the Labour leader. I wouldn't advise over-doing attacks on the credibility of others, it may make you look scornful and petty. However, be aware that undermining the credibility of an adversary is a fairly common line of attack in debate.

20. Detail

If an account is filled with detail it gives an impression of being true. This can especially be seen in stories of past events. If you want your talk to be more believable, the 'rule' is: the more detail you can add, the more believable the story becomes.

21. Downgrades

Downgrades, sometimes called qualifiers, such as slightly, almost, partially and so on have the reverse effect of boosters. They serve to play down our claims. If I say that 'I tend to agree with you', rather than simply, 'I agree', this plays down my state of agreement and may leave the door open for me to change my mind later on.

Downgrades and qualifiers are also extensively used as politeness strategies to downplay requests. 'Can I have *just a few minutes* of your time', for example, minimises the imposition and comes across as being more polite.

22. Emotions

It is often thought that emotions are something that are within us somewhere and that they somehow come to the surface and are expressed in talk. From a language games perspective, we can see them as something that we can work up or work down and display or hide when it suits us. This is not to say that any emotional display is necessarily manipulation. But it is to say that emotions can be more or less deployed and revealed at will. Moreover, a display of emotion, intentional or not, does things. It has an impact on the language game. If I display anger, maybe it'll incite an interlocutor to act.

However, don't lose it, keep your calm. *Displays* of emotion can be used to effect, but if you lose control, you'll lose the language game. To take a boxing analogy: if a boxer loses control they'll start punching wildly and they'll tire themselves out. Boxing clever means keeping your cool, managing your energy, and measuring your punches. The same is true for language games. Keep cool, be aware of what is going on. Be aware that in adversarial situations your interlocutor is maybe trying to make you lose your cool. Be aware of how their attacks are developing and wait for the moment to fight back.

Emotions are also a key aspect of rhetoric – the art of persuasion. In classical rhetoric the deployment of emotion to persuade is called *pathos*. By invoking strong emotions, such as fear, danger, death, you are more able to persuade the other. For example: much of the anti-migrant rhetoric of the (far) right relies on a fear of a nation's people being invaded and overwhelmed by foreigners; the rhetoric of the protest movement Extinction Rebellion plays on the fear of global extinction; strikers may play up the fear of disruption. So, if you want to persuade, play on people's emotions. The stronger the emotion, the stronger the persuasive effect.

23. Empty signifiers

This is a technical term, coined by the Argentine political theorist and philosopher Ernesto Laclau (1935-2014). Empty signifiers are words that can be used to mean just about anything. Happiness, freedom, democracy, liberty, equality, and so on are good examples of empty signifiers. What do these words really mean? Of course, we could find dictionary definitions, but these words are so slippery that they mean different things in different contexts and they mean different things to different people. Protesters might protest in the name of freedom, but the people who are stuck in the traffic as the result of a demonstration might have a very different concept of freedom – the freedom of movement.

These empty signifiers have their uses. They are so often used that what they actually mean is not really challenged. We all have our own intuitive understandings of these words, so they can be deployed and widely accepted by an audience. Be attentive to empty signifiers. If appropriate, challenge your interlocutor to say what they actually mean when they use these 'empty' words.

24. Ethos

According to Aristotle, *ethos* is one of the three pillars of rhetoric – the art of persuasion. *Ethos* relates to the character of the speaker. To be persuasive and credible, the speaker should come across as knowledgeable, having good character, and showing goodwill towards others. *Ethos* is therefore very much a question of creating a 'good' and likeable persona or identity.

25. Exaggeration

When people talk, they often talk with the wildest of exaggerations such as 'always', 'everybody', 'all the time', 'everywhere', and so on. These 'exaggerations' are so common that they go unnoticed, but they work at a subconscious level so that talk becomes more persuasive. This, in technical terms, is sometimes called an extreme case formulation. It can be used to give your talk more oomph. For example, in Chapter 24, the journalist presents the union leader as having no interest in anything other than tearing down the government. That somebody only has one interest in life is no doubt an exaggeration, but the use of such an extreme formulation emphasises the point and makes it harder-hitting.

26. Facts – language and truth

Language can be understood simply as a system of transmission (see figure 12 below). This theory is sometimes known as the Shannon Weaver model of communication. It was first put forward in 1948 in an article entitled 'A Mathematical Theory of Communication'. The article was written by Claude Shannon who was a mathematician, not a linguist. Since its publication, this model has come to be a fairly standard way of understanding communication.

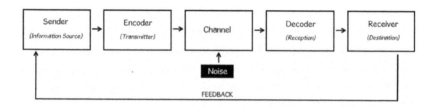

Figure 12: The transmission model of communication (source the Helpful Professor: available at: https://helpfulprofessor.com/shannon-weaver-model)

The idea behind the theory is that we perceive some kind of external real world. We encode these perceptions into language and transmit them through talk, writing, or gesture to an interlocutor. The interlocutor simply decodes the message. Metaphorically speaking language is considered to be a mirror that either reflects something 'real' that is 'out there somewhere', or it reflects some kind of psychological reality that is 'in there somewhere'. Of course, to continue the metaphor, the mirror may be tarnished so that the reflection of reality is distorted. This would be the case, if somebody were lying, bullshitting, spouting propaganda, and so on.

But, we can look at language another way, as a construction yard. Have a look at the picture below. What do you see? A rabbit or a duck?

Figure 13: Wittgenstein's duck/rabbit

Suppose you see a rabbit and I see a duck, who is right, and who is wrong? Or, moving away from an optical illusion that you probably recognised, in Chapter 5, both Sunak and Starmer give their opinions about growth in the UK: one saying that there is excellent growth, the other saying that growth is poor. Who is right, and who is wrong?

If we argue about the duck/rabbit, I have to convince you that I am right and you are wrong, or we have to agree that we're both right in different ways. If Sunak and Starmer argue about the economy, they both set out to build a version of the world that is convincing. Words will be used to construct their argument. So, perhaps it is better to see language use as a kind of construction yard in which we build our versions of what we see as true - my facts, not your facts.

If we consider that language is a construction yard, then words build our realities, what we see as true and false. So, how do we build our facts? To some extent this is the crux of rhetoric, me persuading you that I am right. There are specific techniques that are used to give the impression that my description of events is fact. In technical terms, we even have the verb to 'factify' (i.e., to make something appear as a fact) and the noun 'factification' (i.e., the making of something appear as fact). Some techniques for factifying are:

- use expressions such as obviously, clearly, in fact, and so on
- avoid expression such as I think, maybe, could be, in my opinion
- seek consensus – the more people you recruit to shore up your argument, the more credible it becomes
- use sayings to make something appear common sense, what everybody knows
- project a credible and knowledgeable identity
- use figures and numbers to back up your claims
- cite authoritative sources for your claims

A final word on fact and factifying: if we take the construction metaphor all the way, then there is no right and wrong, no good and bad, no truth and no lies. Our realities, or more to the point how we understand our realities and make sense of them (i.e., what we consider to be good or bad, true or false, right or wrong) are 'constructed in talk'. Yet in this world of 'fake news', outlandish conspiracy theories driven by social media, and the complete bullshit that some (populist) politicians feed to the electorate, is this version of language so far-fetched? I hope this book gives you food for thought, and some insight into how language is used to construct our social world.

27. Footing

Footing is a technical term coined by Erving Goffman (1922-1982), a famous sociologist and linguist. Footing refers to the way in which people position themselves in a conversation. For example, in some instances it might suit you to retain a neutral position and distance yourself from the position you are representing. Journalists, for example, almost always try to keep a neutral stance, avoiding an accusation of being biased. At other times, you may seek to have a less neutral footing, by for example playing up or down a particular identity that involves you more or less in the talk. We see this for example in the debate about the right to carry weapons where the spokesperson for the National Rifle Association positions herself as a mother. In doing so, she changes footing. She comes across as a concerned parent, rather than a 'heartless' representative of the gun lobby.

28. Formulations

A formulation is a technical term used to describe the summing up of the talk so far. So, for example, the chair of a meeting might find it useful every so often to sum up what has been said. This ensures that everybody has a common understanding. However, formulating may not always be an innocent activity. In our analysis of courtroom interaction (Chapter 2), we see one of the lawyers summing up the witness's talk so far, but she puts a spin on it that the witness didn't. So, be careful when others sum up. Listen attentively, maybe they are summing up as you would, or maybe they are either adding to, or leaving bits out of the summary. In other words, they're using a formulation to impose a particular spin on the talk so far.

29. Framing

Following the linguist Erving Goffman (1922-1982), framing is the name given to the way in which we present our talk. Just as a frame around a picture contains a picture and focuses the viewer's gaze on particular elements of the picture, so linguistic framing helps us structure the message and influence how others understand that message. Moreover, a move in the language game can be framed in many ways depending on what we want to achieve. A government U-turn can be framed as the actions of a listening government responding to the people, or it can be framed as a government out of ideas, clutching at straws, and being blown around by public opinion. Framing is thus essential to passing on our message effectively.

Framing is not only achieved through words, it can also be achieved non-verbally, through such actions as smiling or laughing, which frame the talk as humorous, unserious etc.

30. Gaze

In Western cultures, it's regarded as polite to look at people when we are talking to them. Not looking people in the eye can be perceived as a sign of dishonesty and of having something to hide. Though in other cultures not having eye contact can be seen as a sign of respect and deference. Regardless of possible culture differences in the use of eye gaze, which are beyond the scope of this book, we can note that:

- In language games in which several people may be present, speakers often use their gaze to locate the person or persons who they are primarily addressing. We see this in Chapter 21:

Liz Truss shifts eye gaze according to whether she is primarily addressing the interviewer or the public in the audience.

- A shift in gaze to another participant can also signal: 'I have finished talking, it's your turn now.'
- Removing eye gaze is a way of signalling lack of interest in, and disengagement from, a conversation.

31. Gestures

Whilst the focus of this book is on talk, body-language is also a key element of any language game. Gestures, such as raising a finger when speaking, can be used to accompany speech and perform actions such as stressing the importance of a particular word. This can be seen for example, in Chapter 15, when the presenter uses her fingers to count off the points she makes one by one. Similarly, in our analysis of President Macron's press conference (Chapter 21), we see that he raises his fingers to stress key words. So, use gestures to underline key points that you are making.

Gestures are often said to have four types:

- **beat** gestures which reflect the tempo of the speech
- **deictic** gestures which point to physically present entities, indicate directions (forward, back, up, down etc.), and point back to already discussed items.
- **iconic** gestures which are used to resemble physical objects. So making a circular movement might represent a ball, or a cyclical movement.
- **metaphoric** gestures which represent more abstract ideas. A simple and relatively common example would be making a heart shape with the hands and placing it on your chest to represent love.

32. Grammatical forms

The choice of one grammatical form rather than another can be deployed to make your talk harder-hitting. For example, we see this in Chapter 2 through the use of the emphatic do. Compare:

- I hope you'll pass your exams
- I **do** hope you'll pass your exams

Other grammatical forms that are used to provide stress and emphasise are inversions and fronting, technically called an 'anastrophe'. These techniques are perhaps best used on formal occasions. Inversion involves reversing the normal word order in English (i.e., subject, verb, object) so that we have verb, subject and object. Compare

- I have never been to Spain
- Never have I been to Spain

In this example, by placing 'Never have' at the front of the utterance, we draw attention to the negative and this gives the expression more strength. Fronting means putting the important element at the front of the utterance. This gives the key theme more weight, and more force. Compare:

- The economy sank into a deep recession
- Into a deep recession sank the economy

33. Hedges

A hedge is a technical term for words or utterances, such as maybe, I think, could be, and so on that express caution, lack of certainty, possibility, or ambiguity. They can be used to provide a way out or wriggle room that allow deniability. Conversely, a lack of hedging conveys certainty and decisiveness.

34. History

Traditionally we consider history to be about the past. However, from a language games perspective, history is as much about the past as it is about the negotiation of the meaning of the past in the present. So, as we see in Chapter 12, the debate concerns how we understand Colston. This comes down to how we reconstruct the identity of Colston in the present. Was he virtuous, as it was claimed on his statue's plinth, erected in 1895? Or, was he vile and sinful as the Colston Four, and their supporters, claimed in 2023?

So, history can be seen as a grand narrative. It is a tale, told in the present, about the past. The heroes and villains of these stories change according to the *zeitgeist* and contexts of their telling. History, as with any storytelling, is very much a language game.

35. Honorifics

Honorifics are titles such as Doctor, Sir, the right honourable gentleman, and so on. They can be deployed in language games to give your talk more weight. For example, academics presenting at a scientific conference might refer to themselves as Doctor or Professor. This therefore conveys, rightly or wrongly, the impression that they know what they are talking about. It sounds better than Mr, Mrs, or Ms.

Honorifics can also be part of politeness. It may be polite to use an honorific as a sign of respect and distance. Alternatively, not using an honorific could be a strategy employed to play down the knowledge of an adversary in a contentious debate, or to be deliberately rude.

36. Humour

Humour can be a high risk strategy. If you make a joke and others laugh, it is a sign that you are on the same wavelength and that you have the same ideas. It can even be a sign that you are working as a team. It can also add to your likeability as a person; you're cool and fun.

On the other hand, in some contexts, such as the courtroom, humour may be out of place. If your interlocutors don't respond positively to your humour it may leave a stony silence. You are not on the same wavelength, you're different. So, use humour with care.

37. 'I'm just saying'

This is one of those 'little expressions' that could be dismissed as a language tic. However, as we see in Chapter 8, Trump uses the expression to make his words appear to be honest and spoken without guile. Also the 'just' minimises and masks the projected impact of the words. They are inoffensive, meek, and mild, which may, or may not, be the case. So, beware of anybody who is 'just saying'. Maybe what they are 'just saying' is less innocuous than they seek to present.

38. Identity

As we've seen in this book, identity is closely linked with talk. In order to grasp the importance of identity to the language games we play it's necessary to move away from understanding identity in psychological terms as a true self that is in there somewhere waiting to be expressed in talk. From a language game perspective, it's better to consider identity in terms of roles that we are playing such as teacher, boxer, cyclist, mother, cat-lover, and so on.

As actors, we can shift between these roles to achieve particular effects. In short, identity is not necessarily something we have, rather it is something we do. This is not to say that we're hiding behind masks all the time, but it is to say that we could consider the world as theatre in which we are constrained to, or decide to, play certain roles.

Being a 'good' person. We always like to take the moral high ground and presenting ourselves as good people is a key objective that runs throughout many language games. This can be seen for example in Chapter 4, in which the seller plays the language game so as to be a 'good' person with the intention of giving you, the potential buyer, a good deal. In Chapter 10, being a good person is key to justifying and accounting for action: 'Yes, I may have done something bad, such as hitting a police officer, but I did it with the best intentions.'

Being a good person is not only something that we may claim for ourselves. In some cases, it is important that we cast others as good people. This is a key element of politeness whereby we may seek to build a good relationship with others by treating them with respect. In this way, we 'oil the wheels' of social interaction so that we can more easily achieve our objectives.

Being 'good' extends beyond the individual to groups, collectives, companies, and nations. We see this for example in Chapter 7 on advertising. A company, just like a person, has an interest in presenting itself as a 'good' company that seeks to fulfil the needs and wants of the customer. It is not interested in making a fast buck at the customer's expense, of course not, it has your, the consumer's, best interests at heart.

So, in the language games you play, try to present yourself as a 'good' person. As the saying goes: you catch more flies with honey than you do with vinegar.

Victim and perpetrator. These are two identities that often go together. They are not just 'out' there waiting to be used, they have to be worked up or down in talk. Creating a victim identity for yourself can be used to garner sympathy or to take the moral high ground. For example, someone who is accused of impropriety (the perp), can turn the accusation around by claiming to be the victim of a plot (see Chapter 8). This is, of course, a fairly common technique that at the time of writing is being used extensively by the likes of Donald Trump and Boris Johnson. They are the victims of witch hunts, not the perpetrators of crimes or reprehensible behaviours.

39. Ideology

Ideologies do not float around out there somewhere, above and beyond language. They have to be enacted and made relevant to the language games we play. Speakers thus draw on typical storylines and characters from these ideologies in order to construct their arguments and make sense of the world around them. For example, the French protester, in Chapter 10, draws on notions of the revolution and the people's anger against an unjust regime to justify his actions. Similarly, current conservative politicians in the United Kingdom or Republicans in the USA will often draw on a neo-liberal ideology which gives sense to what they say and accounts for what they do. Ideologies can be more or less contentious, and more or less visible. A neo-liberal ideology passes almost unnoticed in some forms of talk. A communist ideology would, in contemporary Britain, be more marked, noticeable, and less acceptable. Of course promoting certain ideologies in language games is frowned upon, taboo, or even criminal. In Western Europe, we (supposedly) have freedom of speech, but you cannot proclaim the *jihad*, nor can you deny the Holocaust without severe implications.

So, always be aware that there is an ideological element to your talk – even our analysis of ghost stories in Chapter 13 shows that the storyteller is well aware that to appear 'normal', she cannot explicitly promote an ideology of spiritualism.

40. Imagery

Imagery, creating strong mental pictures with words, can make your talk more forceful. This is because people remember the image, rather than the precise words. If you're doing a formal speech you may have the time to carefully construct the images as we see in Chapter 16 in Martin Luther King's speech. Nevertheless imagery can also be part of more mundane or spontaneous talk – you just have to think quicker to assemble the image and get it across.

41. Intertextuality

Intertextuality is the technical word used to describe prior text or talk that is incorporated into current talk or text. It covers obvious things such as quoting somebody else – a move we might use in language games to give our talk more credibility, or to shift responsibility. But it also includes the way in which we borrow from others. A theme running throughout this book is that language is part of a game we're playing – the game of living in a particular society. The expression language games draws directly on the language philosopher, Ludwig Wittgenstein (1889-1951) who made it famous. By referring to concepts that readers might be aware of, I am hoping to grab their attention and make my book more persuasive.

42. Imperative forms

The use of imperative forms can be seen as a command. What you or your interlocutors must do. For example, in Chapter 4, we see them being slipped into sales talk. The seller directs, or almost commands, the prospect to do certain things. However, because the talk goes so quickly, we don't really notice the force of the imperative, but nevertheless it's there, commanding us to do certain things.

43. Knowledge

Having knowledge is one thing, but when playing language games, knowledge can be amplified, or minimised. To some extent this depends on the particular role you're playing at a particular time. A history teacher is expected to know about history and teaching, a soldier is expected to know about weapons, and an economist is expected to know about the economy, and so on. And no doubt in many cases it's true, but sometimes talking knowledgeably is only to do with the role and not actual states of knowledge. We've recently seen chancellors of the exchequer who should have known something about economics, talking what many people regarded as complete economic nonsense. On other occasions, somebody with knowledge may not, for various reasons, wish or be able to put that knowledge on public display in their talk.

We can display knowledge, whether we actually have it or not, in various ways:

- making straightforward statements with no qualifiers such as maybe, perhaps etc. The over-use of expressions such as perhaps, maybe, not sure, and so on will down play your knowledge. Conversely, such qualifiers can be used as a politeness strategy to show that this is just your opinion. This is because such expressions leave room for others to disagree without taking an 'I am right, you're wrong' stance.
- agreeing unreservedly with a prior display of knowledge. This shows that you have the same, if not superior, knowledge. You can judge what others are saying.
- seeking to build consensus. This is an especially useful tactic if the others who you use to support your position are experts or have credibility.
- building up your expert identity. For example, in the academic world this could be done through the use of titles such as Doctor or Professor.
- claiming first-hand knowledge. I was there, so I know this for sure. This trumps second-hand knowledge which, generally speaking, is a less effective gameplay.
- using props to show that you have knowledge. For example, an academic's office may have bookshelves creaking with books.

So, don't necessarily be taken in by people displaying knowledge. This could just be show.

44. Laughter

Laughter often punctuates our talk. It can do many things. It is useful to make the distinction between 'laughing at' and 'laughing with'. At a most obvious level laughter responds to something that is funny. If I laugh at my interlocutor's jokes, it shows that we are similar and if we laugh together it shows that we share the same ideas, even that we are acting as a team. So, laughter can be very effective for social bonding. On the other hand, 'laughing at' can exclude pople from a group.

45. Likeability

According to Cialdini (see point 62: principles of persuasion), likeability is one of the principles of persuasion. If you are likeable, you'll persuade more easily. In this respect it is linked to *ethos*, one of the elements of rhetoric. Likeability, as with any aspect of our identity, can be foregrounded, or backgrounded. We see that in the sales pitch discussed in Chapter 4. At times, the seller boosts her likeability by playing the role of the helpful friend, rather than the professional seller.

46. Location

Where communication takes place can be important. Just as sports such as cricket, tennis or rugby are played in certain pitches or courts, so certain language games are only played in certain locations. So, for example, traditionally marriage takes place in a church and requires a priest or religious person to perform the ceremony. Outside of the church, the words do not have the same value. In some cases, only certain locations count: the King of England can only be crowned at Westminster Abbey, not a synagogue; important business meetings take place in the board room, not the canteen; teaching takes place in a classroom, not in a park. Of course, we can play with these conventions, but we do so at our own risk and peril.

In other cases, the rules of the game are less strict. The location can add or reduce the value or authority of your words. So, as we see in Chapter 16, the location of Martin Luther King's 'I have a dream' speech was important because this was spoken in the shadow of the Lincoln Memorial. This memorial to Lincoln, who emancipated the slaves, carries enormous symbolic value, which legitimised the civil rights movement and gave King's words more force.

So, if appropriate, think about where you speak and what this may, or may not, add to the force of your message.

47. Logic

Logic, or *logos* as it is called in classical rhetoric, is a key element of persuasion. If you want to make your talk more persuasive, it should have what appears to be a logical reasoning behind it. Logical arguments may, of course, be more or less convincing. In Chapter 24, the journalist uses the (pseudo?) logic that the union boss is a Marxist. Marxists want to bring down the government. Therefore the union boss is seeking to bring down the government. This line of 'logical' argument doesn't really convince me, but nevertheless some kind of 'logic' should underpin your argument.

48. Memory

What you can, and cannot, say in a particular language game is, as with all talk, shot through with morality. We are expected to be able to talk about certain things, and not others. The way we talk about our memories, what we can and cannot remember, is one area of our talk that is especially policed by (moral) expectations. Memories are not, as commonly thought, simply 'in there somewhere' and brought out when required in some unaltered manner. Rather, how we talk about what we remember is intrinsically tied up with (i) how we wish to (re)present events, (ii) what we are morally supposed to be able to remember, and (iii) what is commonly supposed to be forgettable. Thus we can see in Chapter 11, how Prince Andrew is at pains to remember an event that distances him from meeting Virginia Roberts, but he fails to remember events that might implicate him in alleged abuse. Thus what one can, and cannot, remember and what one is expected, and not expected, to remember can become a battleground in an argumentative situation. I recently saw an interview with Mr Bankman-Fried, the former boss of the collapsed cryptocurrency exchange FTX. It was amazing what he couldn't remember about the company which he managed.

So, like many things, memory is not something that simply reflects an internal state that is communicated in talk, rather it is something that is re-constructed in talk to give more or less credible accounts of past events. Pay attention to what people say they can and cannot remember!

49. Meta-comment

Meta-comment, or commenting on your own talk, is akin to framing (see point 29: Framing). It is a strategy used to frame the talk so that the audience understands your intent. For example, sometimes people may add something like 'just joking', which frames the talk so that it is understood as a joke. In Chapter 3, Johnson frames his talk as an apology, even though it is doubtful that he really made an apology. But by framing his own talk as an apology, he shows that the audience is intended to understand it as an apology. Commenting on your own talk is also a way of showing how you feel about what you are saying. So, use expressions such as 'I'm sorry to have to say...', 'I am pleased to say...' and so on. This will help people understand your message and your emotional stance towards it.

50. Metaphor

As George Lakoff (b. 1941), the American cognitive linguist and philosopher, famous for his work on metaphor, puts it: 'The essence of metaphor is understanding and experiencing one kind of thing in terms of another.' In technical terms, the tenor is the subject that is described, and the vehicle is the figurative language used. So, in the metaphor 'language is a loaded gun', language is the tenor and a loaded gun is the vehicle.

Metaphors are a useful strategy. They can simplify complex situations and so they can clarify your message and make it harder-hitting. However, since they rely on comparison, the comparisons can be tenuous and even misleading. In Chapter 5, Starmer describes Sunak as a second-rate football manager – but is this comparison valid? Maybe, maybe not. But, regardless of their veracity, metaphors can be extremely useful in talk since they paint a vivid and understandable image of the situation. For example, in Chapter 16, Martin Luther King uses the rich imagery of quicksand to describe racial injustice and he juxtaposes this with the solid rock of brotherhood. These clear and contrasting metaphors are vivid and easily understandable.

51. Minor points close

This is a negotiating technique used for reaching a favourable agreement. It consists of getting agreement on minor points, so that agreement on a larger point (agreeing to buy) becomes easier. However, it is not only used in sales. In Chapter 2, we see it used in a courtroom. The lawyer attempts to build up agreement on minor points so that it is harder for the witness to disagree with her formulation of events. Design your talk to get small agreement, and build up gradually to the big ask.

52. Narrative

Narratives are often used in language games to make talk more vivid and memorable. They do not have to be big stories of the 'once upon a time' variety. They may be quite short anecdotes, observations, and versions of events that are integrated into the talk that surrounds them. They are a pervasive feature of talking, and understanding how they work will help you make your talk more effective.

Three dimensions of storytelling. According to the narrative analyst, professor Michael Bamberg (b. 1960), storytelling has three dimensions. The first dimension is the most obvious. It's the actual story itself – the then-and-there of the story. But beware: these stories are not the event itself. They are inevitably biased reconstructions of past events for the benefit of the storyteller and his/her audience.

Consequently, a second dimension that we should consider is the storytelling. How is the story designed for the particular audience? What is the story designed to achieve? In the case of the ghost story which we looked at in Chapter 13, we see that it is important for the storyteller to come across as 'normal'. So, any story can be as much about the storyteller projecting a particular image of themselves as it is a 'true' reflection of past events. Further, since it is often only the storyteller who has direct access to the events, it's difficult for an outsider to say if the story itself is true and accurate. Thus stories of past events can be used for particularly persuasive effect to (literally) put forward your side of the story, to present something as a simple description of the way things were, whereas in fact the story is carefully crafted to have an effect in the present.

Third, you should think about stories in terms of ideologies which are made available in the plot, the characters in the story, and what they stand for. From this perspective ideology is not something that is abstract and floating above and beyond talk. Rather, ideology is something that is *in* the talk and that is necessary to give the talk meaning and a reason for being. Take for example, the well-known tale of George and the Dragon. Well, it enacts an ideology of male superiority, the charming prince who saves the day, and female docility. This plotline was turned on its head in Robert Munsch's book the *Paper Bag Princess* which reworks the fairy tale so that the princess saves the prince. This reversal of the role of the characters in the storyworld enacts a feminist ideology. So, be aware that any story is necessarily ideological in some sense or another.

The structure of stories. According to William Labov (b. 1927), a famous American linguist, narratives often have the following elements. First, they have an overview of the story which sets the scene. The overview also orients the reader, giving them the information they need to understand the story: who, what, why, when, and where. Stories then often have a complication, a problem that needs to be resolved and overcome. Once the problem is overcome, the storyteller often provides an evaluation of the events and a coda which gives the relevance of the story to the here-and-now. Understanding the structure of a story will help you craft your stories more effectively.

Grand narratives. We also talk about grand narratives, which refer to the stories that explain civilisation: Christianity, Marxism, fascism, and so on. So, we see in Chapter 12, two different versions of history, or grand narratives, competing with each other. Simply put, we see the grand narrative of empire's civilising mission being confronted with a grand narrative that understands empire in terms of malevolence, slavery, racism, conquest, and greed.

History, and current events can be interpreted in terms of grand narratives, and these narratives are always open to contestation. So, look for the grand narratives and how they may be conveyed and articulated in your talk or the talk of others.

53. Nodding

Nodding is a type of backchannel that is used as a way of showing agreement. It is often used while somebody else is talking, in which case not only does it display that you agree with the speaker, but it is also supportive to the extent that it does not seek to interrupt the other and stop them from talking.

54. Numbers

Quoting numbers and figures can make your talk appear a factual, scientific, and accurate representation of the world. But, as the saying goes: there are lies, damned lies, and then there are statistics. Of course, outright lies can be based on the misrepresentation of numbers. The slogan on the Brexit Bus 'We send the EU £350 million a week. Let's fund our NHS instead. Vote leave', has been characterised as a bare-faced lie based on a miscalculation. But this is an extreme case. The use of statistics is not only about lying, it is about using figures, often in good faith, to present the best possible case.

Anecdotally, a few years ago, I remember a door-to-door salesman trying to sell me a security alarm service. The price of the package was only equivalent to a packet of cigarettes a week. No doubt, but the buyer was tied into the deal for the next ten years, so at £10 a week, times 52 (£520), times 10, it cost £5,200. Yet, for obvious reasons, the salesman was not quoting me the full price. Beware of the way that numbers are presented to you.

55. Oh!

Little interjections such as 'oh' and 'ah' are often considered to have no real meaning. However, technically, 'oh' is sometimes called a change of state token. It can signal something along the lines of: 'Okay, I understand now', or 'Okay, I've received new information'. So, listen out for its use so that you can see if your interlocutor has received new knowledge.

56. Omission: what is not said

In this book we focus on what is said, but what isn't said should not be forgotten. By not saying things we avoid making them a topic of conversation. This, of course, can be used for strategic reasons and may even become akin to lying. A politician may neglect to mention that they have contacts with a company that has just received a lucrative government contract. At other times, the omission may be motivated by positive reasoning. We may choose not to bring up subjects that we know will make others angry or threaten their face. We may hate the design of a shirt that somebody is wearing but it wouldn't necessarily be diplomatic to draw attention to it, so we don't mention it. So, pay attention not only to what is said, but also to what is not said.

57. Online conversations

In this book, we've focused on face to face interaction – talk. However, don't forget that online communication, WhatsApp, emails, instant messaging, and so on can be very similar to face to face talk. The strategies that we've looked at in this book can all be used in electronic talk. The big difference is that face to face talk is synchronous, whereas electronic conversations are often, though not always, asynchronous, i.e., contributions to the conversation do not necessarily happen at the same time.

The other big difference is that most electronic conversations are recorded – they leave a trace. Conversely, most face to face conversations are not recorded in any way. So, this raises the question of deniability. A face to face conversation that is not recorded can be denied, or reworked in your favour. Similarly, an unrecorded face to face conversation cannot travel – it cannot end up in the hands of somebody else. Sure, a reported dialogue of it can travel, as we see in Chapter 20, but this can easily be denied as a biased representation of what happened.

Conversely, an electronic conversation is often there in black and white and is harder to deny. Further, it can travel. In a worst case scenario it can end up in the hands of the police and what you say in private may not look so good in court. So, be extremely careful about how you play language games in the virtual world of tweets, WhatsApp and other social media. Don't say or write anything that in another context could do you damage.

58. Overhearing audience

Talk should be designed for your audience, but don't forget that the audience is not only those who are physically present. The audience may also be other interested parties, separated by time and space, who may also hear what you have said. This audience is sometimes called the overhearing audience. For example, in a TV debate, there is perhaps a studio audience, but the audience extends beyond this to viewers at home, and beyond that to those who may read reports of the debate in the papers the next day. Therefore, you should design your talk with different audiences (plural) in mind. Failing to do so is a classic error made by some people on media posts. What is very funny when intended for your friends, might in fact be derogatory and deeply offensive when heard by another 'overhearing' audience – such as the police! Thus in Chapter 21, we can clearly see that Truss's comments were designed for the physically present audience – the Tory party faithful. Ignoring the wider (non-present) audience induced Truss into making a political *faux pas*.

A further kind of overhearing audience that you should bear in mind is the so-called ghostly audience. The ghostly audience is an audience that is difficult to define (hence the adjective 'ghostly') but it can best be summed up as referring to the *zeitgeist*. What are people of the time going to think about your words? Overt racism, anti-Semitism, and homophobia might not go down well in the UK in the early 21st Century, but 100 years ago they might not have raised any eyebrows. It is unlikely that making anti-Semitic, racist, or homophobic comments would have led to any legal repercussions. Times change, so do audiences. You should be aware of the impact of the *zeitgeist* on the acceptability of your words.

59. Passive voice

We often have the choice between passive or active constructions. Whether we use an active or passive construction can subtly change the emphasis from the 'doer' to the 'done to'. This can be used strategically to change the way in which our talk is framed. So, for example, drawing loosely from the analysis of the protester in Chapter 10, a phrase such as 'the police were hit' is a passive construction whereby the doer, the person who hit the police, is obscured. Conversely, an active construction, such as 'the demonstrator hit the police officer', emphasises the doer. The use of the passive voice can therefore be used to obscure the identity of the 'doer'. It is often used as a way of obscuring responsibility so that actions are mentioned but the doer remains vague and so responsibility for the act is side-stepped. Compare the following statements, and see how the use of the passive avoids foregrounding responsibility:

- Iraq was bombed and 50 people were killed.
- The US air force bombed Iraq and killed 50 people.
- The letter has not been sent.
- I have not sent the letter.

60. Planning

Often talk is fairly spontaneous and you won't have time to plan. However, on other occasions such as meetings, job interviews, formal presentations, and so on you'll have time to plan. So, plan. Work out what you're going to say, how you're going to deal with any curveballs that may be thrown at you. Go off script at your peril – you don't want to start talking about a visit to Peppa Pig World at a job interview or a business meeting. It will probably not look good!

61. Politeness

Politeness is something that we recognise when we see it, but we're less able to put our finger on exactly how it works. Politeness is used to minimise the threat that our talk or action might have on (1) our interlocutor's self-esteem, or face as it is sometimes called by linguists, and (2) their freedom to act. So for example, if we're on a busy train and see a free seat next to somebody we might say: 'Sorry to bother you, but is anyone sitting there?' This utterance recognises that we are impinging on their freedom to act, or to be left alone, and that we are potentially bothering them. Further, it uses a register that is respectful.

As Brown and Levinson, the two linguists most associated with politeness theory, point out, there are several ways of being polite. The first is not to do the face threatening act, i.e., the action that might either affect your interlocutor's freedom to act, or be seen as disrespectful. For example, as a teacher I might think that a student is being particularly stupid and I could say something like, 'Don't be so stupid, idiot.' But, to be polite, maybe it's best just to bite my tongue and let it pass. The second way of being polite, as we saw in Chapter 21, in our analysis of President Macron, is the so-called 'off-record' strategy. Be critical, but do it indirectly. Third, we could make the face threatening act, but we do so by wrapping up the request in politeness.

Politeness has two basic forms: negative politeness and positive politeness. Negative politeness involves showing deference and positive politeness involves being friendly and positive towards one's interlocutor. Politeness also involves minimising the imposition on the other's freedom of action, and in general the bigger the imposition, the more polite you should be. Though how much politeness you use depends on the relationship, or social distance, between you and your interlocutors. You probably would not use the same politeness strategies with a colleague at work and the CEO of the company!

So, for example, let's say we're back on the train and you are sitting next to a stranger. The stranger has their headphones on but the music is still loud and it is annoying you. Asking them to stop playing the music or to turn down the volume impinges on their freedom of action. This is therefore what politeness theorists call a face threatening act (FTA). So what do you do? You could be polite and say nothing, and suffer in silence. If you decide to act, you could do it off record by saying something like 'It's rather noisy here' and hope that the person takes the hint. This, in technical terms, is doing the face threatening act 'off record'. Or, you could be more direct and do the face threatening act 'on record'. In which case you could ask without recourse to any politeness strategies and say something like 'Turn your damned music off.' This may, or may not, work. Perhaps in some contexts being rude is an appropriate course of action to take, that's for you to judge. Or you could make a polite request, with redressive action, and say something like: 'Excuse me, sorry to bother you, but I was just wondering if you could turn the music down just a bit.' The request is made, but it remains polite because you are minimising the request ('just a bit') and maximising the padding ('I was just wondering' and 'could'). The choices that we have are set out in figure 14 below.

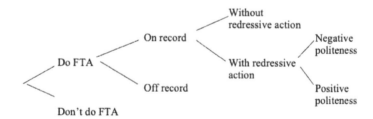

Figure 14: Politeness strategies (source: Brown, P. and Levinson. S. 1978. Politeness: Some universals in language usage. **Cambridge: Cambridge University Press.**)

Employing politeness strategies helps to oil the wheels of social interaction and makes our relationships with people run smoothly. Of course, what is polite and what is impolite can vary from situation to situation and our relationship with the person we're talking to. There are also perhaps cultural factors at work here as well:

what is polite in one culture may not be polite in another. Further, at times, we may deliberately choose to break the norms of politeness in order to do things such as expressing anger, frustration, or criticism. So, being impolite can also be part of the game, but generally speaking we try to be polite.

62. Principles of persuasion

Robert Cialdini (b. 1945) is an American psychologist and academic. His research, based on years of working in sales and marketing, was published in the bestseller *Influence: The Psychology of Persuasion*. During this period of observing the working of influence first-hand, he came upon six key principles of influencing people:

- **Reciprocity.** If I give you something, I am more likely to be persuaded to provide something in return. For example, I recently received an unsolicited request for a donation to a charity. In the pack I received, there was a little gift of some very tasteful postcards. No doubt, the idea behind this gesture was to put pressure on me to donate in return.
- **Commitment and consistency.** This relies on you getting commitment for something small first and, since people like to be consistent, building on this commitment. Cialdini shows for example that asking people to wear a lapel badge supporting cancer research made them more likely to donate to cancer research than those who hadn't been asked to wear the badge.
- **Social proof.** This is the belief that if other people do something, then it must be good and I should follow them. This is why the television is full of adverts that tell us that nine out of ten cat owners give their cats a particular brand of cat food. If

nine out of ten owners think that the cat food is good, then so should you.

- **Authority.** If somebody has authority, I am more likely to be persuaded by them. This is why actors dress up as vets to sell animal food and dentists to sell toothpaste. It also explains why celebrity sportspeople endorse sports equipment.
- **Liking.** If you're likeable you'll be more persuasive. We see this in Chapter 4: the salesperson projects the image of being 'nice'; she's doing you a favour by helping you save money. Through being likeable, she's more likely to persuade you to buy.
- **Scarcity.** If something has a scarcity value, then it will put pressure on you to act now before it's too late. This is, of course, the mechanism behind many special offers limited in time, or hotel booking sites that inform you of how few rooms remain.

Whilst Cialdini was not a linguist and he was not specifically interested in language use, I nevertheless think that it is worth looking at these principles and reminding ourselves that influence and persuasion are language games. They don't just happen, they have to be brought about, and words are a key way of bringing them about. Encoding these principles in words will make your talk more persuasive, as we see in many chapters in this book.

63. Problem, solution

Whether something is a problem or not, is really a question of how you consider events. However, in a language game presenting something as a 'problem', whether it is or not, allows you to present the solution - what you want to do. Presenting something you want to do as a solution to an existing problem, even if there is no real problem, therefore makes your argument more persuasive and convincing. We see this strategy in use in Chapter 7, an advertisement for a payday loan company. Not being easily able to get a loan is presented as a problem; the solution to this problem is provided by the loan company.

64. Pronouns

Pronouns are words that can be used strategically in language games. For example, 'we' in some cases refers to 'me and you' and can be used to stress that we are a team, a couple, a unit. In other cases, it can be incredibly slippery. How many times have we been in meetings where the boss is saying we can do this and we can do that? You nod wisely, and then the 'we' suddenly becomes 'you' and you get lumbered with the work. 'We' can also be used as a way of shifting responsibility: we the team or the company decided to do X or Y. Not 'I' the individual.

The use of 'them and us' is also an interesting use of pronouns because it creates a sense of group identity. A football supporter may talk of 'us' and 'we' when talking about his/her team. A sales-person might use collective pronouns 'us' and 'we' to create a bond with the potential buyer. Sometimes conflict and numerous 'isms' (racism, nationalism, sexism, and so on) can be reduced to no more than an 'us and them' dichotomy, which makes difference, whether real or imagined, salient and which also implies the superiority of the in-group. Migrants are not like 'us', they have no right to be here in 'our' land, as we do. Homosexuals are not like 'us', they should be imprisoned. The Taliban are not like 'us', we fight for freedom and democracy, they fight for tyranny.

The generic 'you' is also an interesting pronoun. It is used to replace 'one' which is an impersonal pronoun that is used in more formal occasions. So, for example, in a formal context, we could say 'One should not drink more than a unit of alcohol a day.' In a less formal context, we might say 'You should not drink more than a unit of alcohol a day.' Who exactly we are referring to is vague. It is everybody and nobody at the same time. This vagueness and all-inclusiveness can be used in talk, for example to make a general criticism without specifying the target. As we see in Chapter 21, Macron says 'when you lose your bearings in life'. Who the 'you' is remains vague. It is a kind of general statement of truth. Though through reading between the lines, we know he is talking about Liz Truss. In this case, the generic you is used to make an off-record criticism.

65. Props

When you talk, remember it is not only your words that carry meaning. Your words may be complemented by props - physical objects that aid the speaker. Props come in many shapes and sizes and they are often crucial elements in any language game. Some props, such as the symbolic use of crowns, gowns, heraldry, and so on that one might see in some royal (or presidential), pageants are obvious. In other instances, props are more mundane: the suit the speaker is wearing, his or her hair style, and the accessories the speaker has with them. Props can be manipulated to a greater or less extent to achieve some kind of communicative effect. We see, for example in Chapter 4, that the salesperson not only uses the image of the product as a prop, but the whole act of selling is carefully choreographed and supported by music, flashing lights, and on-screen displays.

66. Question and answers

To understand how questions and answers work in language games, it's useful to speak in terms of turns of talk. So, to draw an analogy with playing cards, each player in a game has to wait their turn and lay down their card following the previous card player. If we don't respect our turn, the rules are broken. As it is in many card games, so it is in language games, we have turns in which we can talk and then another player takes the floor. If we break these rules, we can be expelled from the game.

As you may have noted, question and answers crop up in many different language games, from small talk to political debates. The question is the first turn in a sequence, and your interlocutor is 'morally' obliged to reply in the next turn. When the reply is given, the next turn at talk often reverts back to the original questioner. This third turn in the sequence can be used to either ask another question, so setting the tune to which the answerer has to dance, or evaluate the answer to the prior question. If used to evaluate, this can allow the questioner to criticise the other without setting out their own opinion. Making the other go first can put you in a strong position.

Question and answer sequences can also be seen in courtrooms, news interviews, job interviews and even small talk, as we see in Chapters 19 and 20. Yet such patterns of talk are not innocent. We tend to think of power in 'big' terms of coercion and the ability to control the lives of others, to make laws, to levy taxes, to imprison wrongdoers, and so on. But, in a much smaller way, there is power in the way our spoken interactions are managed. In a legal setting, for example, who can speak to whom, when, and concerning which subject is meticulously controlled and failure to respect these rules, contempt of court, is a criminal offence.

Whilst the rules that govern who speaks to whom, when, and what can be said in a courtroom may be an extreme example of the exercise of power through controlling talk, power can be seen in other language games. For example, in news interviews it's fairly obvious that the interviewer/journalist asks the questions and the guest/interviewee responds. After answering a question the right to talk passes back to the interviewer. Through asking a series of questions, the journalist is thus able to make the interviewee dance to his/her tune. In this way, journalists exercise a form of power over their guests who are constrained to answer their questions. The journalist may repeatedly ask questions if he/she does not get the answer they want. As we see in Chapter 11, the journalist keeps coming back to question Prince Andrew, not letting him off the hook.

However, where there is power, there is resistance, and the interviewee has numerous possibilities that will enable him/her to avoid answering the question. One way of avoiding answering a question is to accept the question, so that minimally you have complied with the norm of providing an answer. However, once you have the floor, you use your turn to shift to a safer topic (see Chapter 5). A second way of getting yourself out of a corner that an aggressive questioner has put you in would be to ask a question in return. In this way, you shift roles. The boot is on the other foot and you start making the other person dance to your tune (see Chapter 6). A third way of dealing with difficult questions is to invoke some grounds for refusing to answer the question. For example, in Chapter 24, Mike Lynch refuses to answer the journalist's question on the grounds that it is twaddle.

67. Recipient design

Effective language use is about designing your talk for a specific audience. This, in technical terms, is called recipient design. What works for one audience, might not work for another. Therefore, it is important that you think about your audience. What is it they want to hear? What is going to persuade them? What do they know, and what do they want to know?

Always bear in mind that your audience will be thinking what's in it for me (W.I.I.F.M). If there is nothing in it for the audience, they will quite simply have no reason for listening. So, tailor your talk for the audience and draw attention to what they stand to gain from listening to you. Often, talk is less about what you have to say, than what the audience want to hear.

68. Reconstructed dialogue

Reconstructed dialogue is a term that catches the idea that whenever anybody reports a prior conversation, they are in fact making it up. Now, I'm not saying that they are deliberately seeking to obscure and misrepresent past talk, but nobody can remember the exact words they used in a prior conversation. So, when a conversation is later reported, it is inevitably reconstructed.

The original conversation is transported across time and reconstructed for a new audience, and this reconstruction is designed to 'do' something. So, in Chapter 20, we looked at how Ngozi Fulani reconstructed a dialogue to make an accusation of racist behaviour. This is not to say that Fulani's account is in some way false (how would I know that?), merely that it is reconstructed, and designed to do something. Further, since few people overheard the exchange, it is very difficult for anybody to challenge the veracity of the dialogue as reported. Consequently, reconstructed dialogue is also a way of putting words and arguments into the mouths of others, just as a ventriloquist makes a dummy speak or a playwright makes a character in a play speak. Sometimes, we may even wish to present a kind of internal dialogue which allows us to account for a thought process in particularly vivid and convincing way (see Chapter 11).

Further, reporting the actual words bring the past event to life and make it more theatrical and believable. So, there are many advantages to be had when reconstructing dialogues from the past.

69. Register

If we want to create a good impression, it's important that we get our register right. Register is the linguistic term relating to the relative formality or informality of language use. For example, pater, dad, father, and the old man may all be perfectly legitimate words that we could use to describe the relationship between a man and his children. However, the use of these words is related to the formality of the occasion. Register is not only related to words, but also phrases. For example, compare 'Give me your pen' to 'Would you mind lending me your pen?' If you get the register wrong you may at best sound weird, but at worst you may insult you interlocutor. On the other hand, using an informal register, when a formal one is expected, or vice versa, may mildly surprise your interlocutor and make them sit up and listen (see Chapter 15).

70. Relevance

This is basically a question of audience design. Your talk should be relevant to the audience. Otherwise, what is the point of talking? Judging what your audience wants and needs to hear is fundamental to recipient design and relevance is also one of Grice's conversational maxims (see point 18: Conversational maxims).

71. Repetition

Repetition of key phrases is often used to underline the message and make it stronger. This can be seen in many of the chapters in this book. There are various different types of repetition, both of sounds and of words. For example:

- **Alliteration** is the occurrence of the same or similar consonant sounds at the beginning of words that occur in proximity
  - e.g., little loans, lots of control
- **Anadiplosis:** the repetition of the last word of a preceding clause
  - e.g., 'to cash this cheque, a cheque that will give us upon demand'
- **Anaphora:** repetition of the same words at the beginning of each consecutive clause
  - e.g., 'I have a dream that my four little children will [...] I have a dream that one day on the red hills of Georgia [...] I have a dream today!'
- **Assonance:** the repetition of sounds, notably the rhyming of two or more stressed vowels
  - e.g., 'cash in a flash'
- **Negative-positive restatement.** This involves the juxtaposition of a positive statement with a negative statement
  - e.g., President J. F. Kennedy said : 'Ask not what your country can do for you, ask what you can do for your country.'
- **Palilogia.** This is the repetition of phrase or a word in succession
  - e.g., in the real estate market, it could be said that three things are important: location, location, location.

72. Rhetoric

Rhetoric, commonly defined as the art of persuasion, is obviously a key part of making your talk more effective. Unfortunately, in modern times the word rhetoric is given a negative connotation as if it were a deliberate attempt to hide the emptiness or trickery of an argument behind fine words; a distinction being drawn between rhetoric and reality. And if rhetoric is not spun as something negative, rhetorical analysis is largely limited to analysing grand speeches. But, rhetoric, as the art of persuasion, also runs throughout our everyday talk. Aristotle divided rhetoric into three aspects:

- *ethos*: good character, good will, and good knowledge
- *pathos*: emotions
- *logos*: logic

In the analyses in this book, we often find these three concepts. Use them to make your talk more powerful.

Further rhetoric can be both defensive and offensive. Defensive rhetoric involves anticipating the arguments of an adversary in debate and building up a defence. We see this, for example, in Chapter 10. The protester shows an awareness that his arguments could be used against him – he's just a violent anarchist. Consequently, he builds a defence against this anticipated attack into his talk and so pre-empts such an argument – he's Mr Normal who has been pushed too far. Conversely, offensive rhetoric is used to attack the other, so, for example, in Chapter 5, we see that Keir Starmer compares Rishi Sunak to a failed football manager in an attempt to discredit his opponent.

73. Rules of the game

Playing any language game rarely takes place on a blank canvas on which you're totally free to say what you want, when you want, how you want, to whom you want. If you want to be an effective speaker, it is necessary to know what the rules of the game are. Talk is rarely a free for all. We often follow more or less strict and more or less explicit rules when playing language games. At one end of the spectrum there are events such as (most) church services that may have a strict division of who can say what to whom and when. At the other end of the scale, conversations between friends and colleagues may be more or less freewheeling, with equal speaking rights. Business meetings might fall somewhere in between these two extremes. So, be aware of the rules of the game, what moves can you make, what moves are risky, what moves are you expected to make. What leeway is there to the rules? How can you exploit the rules to your advantage?

These rules, or codes, are also very much linked to identity. So according to who we are, or rather the role that we are playing, we have the right to say certain things and not others. In some instances, such as a marriage ceremony, this is fairly clear cut. The priest, the bride, the groom, the best man, and so on all have certain roles to play, and things to say. In informal conversation who can say what, to whom, how, and when is more fluid. So, be aware of the role that you're playing within the language game. If the rules of the game are not followed, conversation can break down completely as we see in Chapter 18, and chaos may ensue.

74. Rule of three (tricolon)

Bundling things up in threes is a fairly common feature of talk. The Romans even had the expression: *omne trium perfectum*, which means 'Everything that comes in threes is perfect.' Three seems to be some kind of magical number that is memorable. Consequently ideas, not only in speeches, are often grouped in threes, as these nationalist mottos indicate: *ein volk, ein reich, ein führer* (Nazi Germany); *liberté, égalité, fraternité* (modern France); and *le roi, la loi, la liberté* (modern Belgium). And in the Christian tradition, there is the Father, the Son, and the Holy Ghost (the Trinity).

Three is also said to be a generalisation: one does not convince, two could be seen as a coincidence, but three represents a general trend. So, group things into threes, this will make your talk more convincing. Also, it's noticeable that in speeches, the audience recognise the rule of three. Applause often coincides with the third element in a list.

75. Sacred and the profane

In some cases, raising your talk above the everyday may make it more persuasive. We see, for example, an appeal to religious authority in King's 'I have a dream' speech. But sacred doesn't necessarily mean religious. For example: Liz Truss's brief spell as prime minister was driven by a zeal to conform to the invisible hand of market laws, which was revered in almost religious terms; Putin's war in Ukraine is raised from the profane to the sacred by invoking the destiny of 'mother Russia'; the USA's invasion of Iraq was driven by a desire to spread democracy and liberty. So, if appropriate, give your talk more punch by aligning it with a worthy cause: the sacred.

76. Sarcasm

Sarcasm is a form of irony. So whilst irony can be defined as a figure of speech whereby the words say the opposite of what you actually mean, sarcasm uses irony to direct criticism at another person. For example, when somebody tells you something obvious you might say 'Really, Sherlock' (in reference to Sherlock Holmes), but you're really criticising that person for making an obvious comment. Use sarcasm sparingly, it can be seen to be aggressive. Nobody likes getting put down, and what goes around, comes around. So in the long run such impoliteness may not do you any favours. Though in more adversarial contexts, such as in Chapter 2, it may be a useful strategy.

77. Scarcity

Scarcity is one of Cialdini's principles of persuasion. It is very much part of the salesperson's repertoire. Creating a sense of scarcity, real or otherwise, puts pressure on your interlocutor to act. If a resource is scarce, you must act quickly to secure it. Thus, in Chapter 4, the salesperson projects scarcity in order to put time pressure on the potential buyer: 'There's only a limited amount left, so buy now or you'll be disappointed.'

78. Sensory channels

We have five senses: hearing, sight, touch, taste, and smell. Since all these senses can be used to communicate something, they can be deployed in the language games we play. We can send our message by different channels. It is sometimes said that we retain: 10 per cent of what we read; 30 per cent of what we hear and read; 30 per cent of what we see; 50 per cent of what we see and hear; 70 per cent of what we say and write; and 90 per cent of what we do. Well, whether this is true or not is beyond my competence to answer, but you get the drift. I think the key point here is that different senses provide different channels of communication. Multiply those channels of communication and your message will be stronger.

79. Sharing talk

Talk is often considered to be something individual. I speak to you, and you speak to me. But this is sometimes not the case, rather we work in teams and what becomes important is the team not the individual. One way of showing that you're operating as a team is to share talk. For example:

Person A: Bungee jumping is really dangerous

Person B: and it's incredibly stupid to risk your life.

In the above made-up example, we see that person B adds something to person A's talk. They construct a sentence together, using the conjunction 'and'. This shows that they are working as a team. However, sharing the turn can also be an aggressive move that alters the sense of the first part of the sentence. For example:

Person A: Bungee jumping is really dangerous

Person B: but if done professionally it's quite safe.

In this case, using the conjunction 'but', person B takes over the sentence of person A, adds to it and turns it from a negative to a positive assessment. So, completing someone else's turn can be a very aggressive and dominating action.

80. Small talk

Small talk is defined by Merriam-Webster's online dictionary as 'light or casual conversation'. But the whole point of this book is to persuade you that talk is never light and casual. Unless you're talking to yourself or a wall, whatever you say, or don't say, has social consequences. Your words 'do' something. In small talk, as in any other form of talk, your words are building a relationship. Small talk between colleagues, or strangers on a train, may have very low stakes, but when it goes wrong the consequences, as we see in Chapter 20, may be significant. It takes some kind of skill to interact with strangers effectively and make small talk happen.

We may have an intuitive grasp of how to do small talk, but here are some tips:

- ask general and non-face threating questions
- try to find non-controversial topics such as the weather, and avoid possibly contentious issues such as politics, money, religion
- look for common ground
- build on similarity of experience
- seek agreement, rather than disagreement
- drop the subject quickly if it becomes 'difficult'

81. Social pressure

Social pressure is one of Cialdini's six principles of persuasion. The idea is that if other people do something, then it must be good and I should follow them. This is why the television is full of adverts that tell us that 9 out of 10 cat owners give their cats a particular brand of cat food. This may, or may not, be true but, social pressure has to be mobilised, it doesn't just happen. Communicating social pressure is a language game. Whilst it is the bread and butter of marketeers, it nevertheless can be a useful persuasive strategy in other language games.

82. Socratic dialogue

Socratic dialogue consists of a series of questions and answers. In argument, as we see in Chapter 6, the questions are designed to push the interlocutor to examine and question the underlying assumptions of their position, and to direct attention to any underlying inconsistencies in their argument. Socratic dialogue is also used in teaching situations. In this case, it is used not so much to reveal inconsistencies in thinking, but to promote critical thinking by forcing the students to reconsider their position, either rejecting it, or strengthening it by counter argument.

In teaching situations, rather than argumentative situations, the question and answer pattern often has a third move - evaluation. So teaching often uses an initiation-response-feedback sequence. In other words, the teacher asks a question, to which he/she already knows the answer, the student replies and then the teacher evaluates this response in an attempt to force the student to think through their argument.

So, to take a simple imagined exchange as an example:

- teacher (initiation): What is the capital of England?
- student (response): London.
- teacher (evaluation): Very good.

If the student response is considered insufficient, the teacher has the right to continue asking until an acceptable response is given. For example:

- teacher (initiation): What is the capital of England?
- student (response): Birmingham.
- teacher (second question): Why do you say Birmingham?

83. Space/proxemics

Proxemics is a technical term which relates to the use of space in social interaction. It was coined by Edward T. Hall (1914 – 2009), a highly acclaimed social anthropologist. His work was primarily in the field of cross-cultural communication, which is not our particular concern in this book. However, his notion of proxemics is interesting for us. He pointed out that we have different comfort zones surrounding us: intimate distance for touching, embracing, or whispering; personal distance for friends and family; social distance for interaction with colleagues and acquaintances; and public distance for interaction with strangers (see figure 15 below).

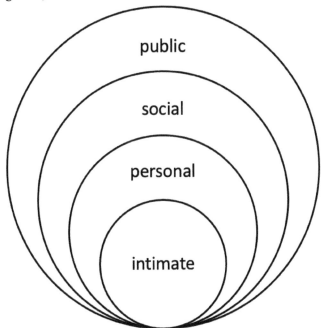

Figure 15: Proxemics

In talk, we police these distances. So, if you want to be an effective speaker, don't encroach on the private space of others, or do so with care. We see in Chapter 20 that an invasion of private space is a cause for the failure of small talk. Though, at other times, such as showing sympathy, movement into someone's private space may be a 'good' strategy.

The use of space can also be an essential part of other language games. Teachers for example stand in front of the class, the boss might be at the top of the meeting room table, the judge is on a raised podium above others, and so on. Space is therefore something that, on some occasions, can be manipulated to your advantage. One example that comes to mind is Putin meeting President Macron before the war in Ukraine sitting at one end of an extremely long table, and Macron at the other. The message was clear: 'You are not close to me', 'We are not friends and allies'.

So, be aware of your, and others', use of space. Use it to your advantage.

84. Spin and spin doctors

Spin is the art of providing a biased presentation of 'the facts'. The word 'spin' often has negative connotations. It is seen as a modern form of propaganda and way of deceiving. There is no doubt that political and commercial communication is shot through with interest, but I think that's true of just about any form of communication. We're always trying to do something when we speak: words are actions.

Let's be generous and see spin merely as presenting your augment in the best possible light so that you get your message across effectively. So, in Chapter 6, Wonga.com says pay back early and you'll pay less – this is true. Pay back later and you'll pay more is also true. But, of course, the former sounds better than the latter.

So spin is not always about masking lies, it is more about presenting your argument in the best possible way.

So, my advice is: don't be shy of spinning, but steer clear of lying. There's a spin doctor in everyone!

85. Stake

The way we spin our talk is often a question of our interest or stake in the language game in progress. In an adversarial situation, if you want to be aggressive, you can attack your interlocutor on the grounds that they have a vested interest in what they are saying. This is a kind of 'You would say that wouldn't you' argument.

However, whilst you may wish to attack the other's vested interest, you may also be attacked for your own vested interest. So, in adversarial situations, it may be prudent to build up your defence against a claim that you are acting out of self-interest. This in technical terms is called stake inoculation. We even see stake inoculation in the analysis of the ghost story (Chapter 13). The teller of the ghost stories explicitly states that the story is not designed to convince others that ghosts exist. She is therefore not partisan, and she has no particular point to prove. Not having a particular axe to grind, or stake in the story, makes her talk more impartial, neutral, and thus believable.

86. Strawman argument

A strawman argument can be effective. It consists of attributing an argument to your interlocutor, putting words into their mouth as a ventriloquist makes a dummy speak. However, the argument is a weak argument and after putting words into the mouth of the interlocutor, the speaker goes on to defeat the argument just as one can easily knock down a strawman. In linguistic terms, the person setting up the strawman argument is the author and the animator. The adversary is the principal. This strategy can be useful in debate. We can see this technique in action in Chapter 5. Starmer puts a weak argument into Sunak's mouth, and then goes on to knock down this strawman.

87. Stress - pronunciation

There is a natural rhythm to talk and we stress certain words as we speak. Changing the stress pattern can change the meaning of the utterance. If I say, 'I am **driv**ing to the shops' (stress on the first syllable of driving) this emphasises the method of transport. I am taking the car rather than my bike. If I say 'I am driving to the **shops**' (stress on shops), I draw attention to where I am going: the shops not the pub, or work, or whatever.

This is a fairly unconscious element of our talk, but it can also be used more strategically in language games to draw attention to particular elements of talk. Macron for example draws attention to the word 'foe' by stressing it, the protester in Chapter 10 stresses the word 'saw' so as to put emphasis on his eye-witness status, and in Chapter 20, SH differentiates between 'you' the person and 'you' the organisation through her use of stress.

Shifting stress patterns can therefore change the meaning of your talk, and can be used to foreground and background certain elements of your talk.

88. Swearing

Swearing can boost what you're saying and make it stronger. We see this for example in Chapter 12, when one of the Colston Four says that Colston was not a 'fucking virtuous man'. This undoubtedly adds force to his words, displays strong feeling and emotions, and makes the audience sit up and listen. The force of swearing lies in the fact that it breaks social taboos. This speaker recognises that he breaks the rules of the game, and he apologises for swearing. Paradoxically, it is in breaking the rules of the game that he adds force to his words. So, even though swearing can be appropriate and can add force to your words, use it with care. Often it will be inappropriate and might damage your image as a 'good' person. Certainly, it will often be seen as impolite.

89. Team-talk

Sometimes when you talk the group identity is more relevant than your identity as an individual. So, at times, you or somebody else may use 'we' or 'us' to speak on behalf of the group and become the spokesperson of the group. This can be clearly seen in politics, for example, where a politician may speak on behalf of his or her constituents, or the people of the country, and so on. But it is also fairly common in less obvious ways: such as phoning up a restuarant to book a table. I might do this on behalf on my fellow diners, in which case we became a group rather than a collection of individuals. So, you may be part of many teams or groups, but pay particular attention to how you and others construct this group identity in talk. If group cohesion isn't constructed in talk, maybe there are problems.

We see Meghan and Harry being a team in Chapter 22. They:

- use pronouns such as 'we' and 'us'
- speak on behalf of each other, showing that they are on the same wavelength
- complete each other's utterances

- buttress and support the other's talk by following it up with statements that confirm, agree with, or develop each other's talk.
- nod, and otherwise display that they align with the other while the other is speaking
- refer to themselves as a team

90. Teasing

Here, rather than using the word in the sense of gently mocking, we use it in the sense of arousing interest. This kind of teasing can be a way of attracting people's attention. This strategy is often used in advertising to build up the tension and expectations before full details of the product launch are revealed. For example, a company might simply say 'Check your inbox this weekend for some exiciting news'. The lack of precise information encourages sepculation and creates a buzz.

The same teasing technique used in marketing can be a strategy to increase audience expectations and involvement in everyday talk. Thus we see in Chapter 15 that the title of a presentation 'saving lives with pantyhose and paperclips' is something unusual that puzzles the audience. It engages them with the talk, creating a kind of curiosity that needs to be satisfied. And, of course, the presentation reveals the link between these three different things.

So, tease the audience if you can, it will build up tension and engage them in your talk.

91. Things that talk

Of course, only humans have the capacity to talk. But artefacts, statues, buildings, clothes, and so on communicate things to us. We particularly see this in Chapter 12 when we look at the statue of

Colston. The statue symbolises and communicates certain values. So be aware that it is not only humans that take part in language games, it is also things and what they symbolise. What these things symbolise may be in dispute. The statue of Colston, as it was, symbolised acceptance of Bristol's part in the slave trade. As it is now, disfigured and horizontal, it symbolises a rejection of this past.

So, don't underestimate the role of 'things' in language games – they 'speak to us'. The architecture of a building can speak of power and riches, the books on a shelf can speak of the owner's erudition, the cars people drive are deliberately designed to speak of the driver's character and wealth, and so on.

92. Time

Time is often considered to be something neutral, something that is beyond our control. The seconds and hours tick by, regulated by the hands on our watch. But, we're also aware that in some instances time flies (when we're having fun) and in other instances it drags. How we present time in talk, therefore, can be a way of making our talk more effective. For example, in sales, or otherwise persuasive talk, time pressure can be put on your interlocutor. There is a limited window of time in which action must be taken. Therefore, action must be taken quickly.

Time is also something the can be emphasised or de-emphasised to rhetorical effect. In Chapter 3, Johnson says that he wasn't at the 'work gathering' in Downing Street for long. He thus attempts to minimise any possible breach of moral codes and the law. On the other hand, Amber Heard's lawyer plays up the amount of time that the expert witness spent at Johnny Depp's house (Chapter 2). Time is thus not something that is neutral and is 'just there', rather it is something that can be crafted and employed to make your talk more effective.

Time can also be a way of reframing arguments. The 'We tried it in the past and it didn't work' argument makes a comparison, whether valid or not, between a past failure and a current attempt to do something. The way round this is to acknowledge this, but to deny the validity of the comparison. 'Sure, it failed in the past, but times are different now.' So, time can be a tool to be deployed when you play your language games.

93. Touch

The use of touch, or haptics to give it a technical name, can be an important part of body language. It's akin to proxemics – the use of space. We only allow certain people to touch us in certain ways, in certain circumstances, at certain times. These rules are often unspoken, but break these rules at your peril. As we see in Chapter 20, unwanted touching landed the 'toucher' in hot water. In other instances, touch would be expected: a handshake, a hug, a kiss on the cheek. So touch can be deployed to 'do' various things such as expressing sympathy, respect, solidarity, and so on.

94. Truthfulness

Be truthful, don't bullshit or lie. People who are winging it are soon found out, as are liars. You may lie or bullshit once and get away with it, but you will never be respected if you do so. Being truthful is one of Grice's conversational maxims. Without truth communication loses its moral compass and we end up in the fantasy world of bullshitters – the post-truth era of fake news, outlandish conspiracy theories, and totalitarian governments.

Truthfulness is also one of the key elements of rhetoric, the art of persuasion. To be persuasive you should have good knowledge of what you are saying and be of 'good' character, displaying good-will to your interlocutors.

95. Unfinished phrases

We tend to think that people talk in a nicely structured way, with complete sentences as we might see in written text. However, because of the spontaneous and unplanned nature of most talk, it is often messy, with incomplete phrases, false starts, ums and ers, and grammatical errors. Of course, sometimes a sentence is unfinished because we are literally lost for words. But, at other times unfinished utterances can be strategically deployed in the language game. They can project a sense, a meaning, a request, a criticism or whatever without actually making it explicit. Projecting something, but not making it specific can be a way of doing something off-record as a politeness strategy. We see, for example in Chapter 23, that utterances are left unfinished. In this way criticism is implied but not made explicit. It is left to the audience or your interlocutor to read between the lines.

96. Vagueness

You would imagine that talk should be clear and concise – this is what the communication manuals tell us at least. However, vagueness has many uses and can be strategically employed during the language games you play. Vagueness can be used to obscure the true import of your words. It therefore can act as a kind of euphemism. In Chapter 8, Trump uses the vague word 'thing' as a way of obscuring that he actually wants Raffensperger to commit electoral fraud.

Pronouns (such as 'you', 'we' and 'they') can also be deployed in a vague manner so that who we are talking about remains obscure. For example in Chapter 21, Macron avoids direct criticism of Liz Truss by talking vaguely about when 'you lose your bearings'. He's clearly talking about Truss, but the use of a generic 'you' allows him to be vague (who is the you?) and to imply that Truss has lost her bearings without making a direct criticism.

However, vagueness should be used in moderation. Too much vagueness can, in some circumstances, be seen as evasive and therefore less convincing. In Chapter 24, we see how the journalist is vague about his sources, and this could lead the listener to begin to question if the sources are purely fictitious.

97. Voice and making others speak

Surprisingly, when you speak, it may not be just you who is speaking. What I mean by that is that we may be speaking on behalf of other people. We give other people voice in much the same way as a ventriloquist makes a dummy speak. You may speak on behalf of your family, your team, your colleagues, your business, or whatever. This can be quite powerful, since the people on whose behalf we speak may lend us their 'clout'. A president may shore up her position by speaking on behalf of the country, a journalist may give his words credibility by citing sources, and believers may draw on their god to justify their actions or add weight to their talk.

The linguist Erving Goffman (1922-1982) talked about three possible roles for the speaker/writer: the principal, the author, and the animator. The principal is the person who is ultimately responsible for the sense of the words. The author is the speaker/writer who is responsible for the content or form of the language used. The animator is the person who actually writes or says the words. Mystics might for example claim that God (the principal) is speaking through them (the author and animator of God's words). Politicians (the animators) might cite the exact words of the US constitution as written by the 'founding fathers' (the authors and principals).

Shifting between roles, and giving others voice, is a common strategy in language games. It can serve many purposes. In Chapter 24 we see how the journalist cites (vague) sources so that he can 'accuse' the interviewee of wanting to bring down the government, yet he is able to deny responsibility for these words. The journalist is the animator, but he sidesteps being the author and the principal. This is a common technique used by journalists so that they can get what they want to say 'out there', but they can still remain (officially, at least) neutral by making others speak through them. Consequently, they can avoid any legal or moral repercussions: they're 'just' repeating what others have said, they are not making these claims themselves. Often, the sources, the principal and the author, are obscured, for example: 'Sources close to the prime minister say that...'.

But it's not only journalists who use this technique: it is part of everyday talk. In Chapter 22, we see that Meghan and Harry put words into each other's mouths. They speak for each other as a way of showing that they know each other so well that they know what's on the other's mind.

98. Word choice

We often have the impression that words are fairly neutral things, they represent certain phenomena in the world. But the words we use and the way in which we employ them are a powerful resource for making our talk more effective. When playing language games

301

choose your words with care. For example, even though we are talking essentially about the same thing, calling somebody a hack, or a journalist, a foreign fighter, or a mercenary, a remoaner or a remainer will have totally different effects.

Words are said to have denotations and connotations. Denotations refer to the literal sense of the word as found in a dictionary. Connotations refer to what the word implies, which, of course, may vary according to the circumstances of its use. Through using one word rather than another, different meanings are conveyed. The choice of words can therefore change the message completely. As we saw in Chapter 10, the protester says that he 'advanced on the police', but he does not say that he hit, attacked, or assaulted the police. The choice of words thus is strategic to present a particular version of events. Have a look at the following and see how the choice of words conveys different meanings.

special military operation	war
the Troubles (in Northern Ireland)	civil war
doctor	quack
customer	punter
being economical with the truth	lying

Figure 16: Word choice

99. Wriggle room

At times, it might be a good tactic to give yourself some wriggle room. So, in an adversarial situation it could be advisable not to be too sure, to use expressions such as 'to the best of my knowledge', 'I think', 'as far as I am aware' and so on. That way if you are later proved to be wrong, you have room to backtrack – 'I never said I was sure, it was just to the best of my knowledge.' Though of course, the danger is that if you build in too much 'wriggle room', your argument may appear unreliable.

100. 'You know'

'You know' could just be seen as a language tic, but I think that it does more than this. 'You know' can be used to project agreement on the other. If somebody peppers their talk with 'you knows', it's important to resist this and say that you don't know. Otherwise, it will be taken as read that not only do you know what the other person knows, but also that you accept what they are saying. We see this, for example, in Chapter 8, in which Trump uses 'you know' to project that his interlocutor agrees with him, even though this is not the case.

ACKNOWLEDGEMENTS

I thank my colleagues and students who have inspired and enthused me throughout my academic career. Without them, this book would not have seen the light of day.

Nor would this book have been written without the insights of linguists, philosophers, sociologists, and psychologists, past and present, on whose work I have drawn.

JONATHAN CLIFTON

Dr Jonathan Clifton is a conversation analyst. He is an associate professor at the Université Polytechnic Hauts-de-France, Valenciennes, France, and an associate editor of the International Journal of Business Communication. For more than 20 years, he has taught business communication at various European universities. He is the author of over 50 academic articles on communication, has edited numerous collections, and has co-authored three books. He has a doctorate in applied linguistics. This is his first work for a popular market, in which he explains the codes of language.

Publish with Us

We give writers the opportunity to see their work in print

We specialise in memoir, biography, autobiography and history,
but will consider other factual genres.

haythorp.co.uk

contact@haythorp.co.uk

Milton Keynes UK
Ingram Content Group UK Ltd.
UKHW020117160224
437879UK00004B/72